TOUCHSTONE

Also by PHILIP BERRIGAN

No More Strangers
Punishment for Peace
Blood Brothers: Prison Journals of a Priest
  Revolutionary (*Vincent McGee, ed.*)

WIDEN THE PRISON GATES

WRITING FROM JAILS
APRIL 1970–DECEMBER 1972

PHILIP BERRIGAN

A TOUCHSTONE BOOK
PUBLISHED BY SIMON AND SCHUSTER

SBN 671–21637–6 Casebound edition
SBN 671–21638–4 Touchstone Paperback edition
Library of Congress Catalog Card Number: 73–13118
Designed by Eve Metz
Manufactured in the United States of America

1 2 3 4 5 6 7 8 9 10

The journal entry from Danbury dated May 1972 first appeared in the March 1973 issue of *Win* magazine and is reprinted with the editors' permission.

My gratitude to the Vietnamese people, whose resistance made this book possible; to the Harrisburg defendants and lawyers, whose love and strength drew light out of dark days; to resisters in jail and out, whose solidarity was always palpable; to Carol and Jerry, whose services knew no limit; to Jeremy Cott and Dan for giving sense to outrage; to Alice Mayhew, without whom these reflections would not have reached the reader.

To Frida,
my mother,
who has fought the good fight,
by no means over

We must widen the prison gates, and we must enter them as a bridegroom enters the bride's chamber. Freedom is to be wooed only inside prison walls and sometimes on gallows, never in the council chambers, courts, or the schoolroom.

Gandhi

PSALM FOR TWO VOICES

(For Elizabeth McAlister)

Dry stones we bruise we are bruised
    as we fall to the well bottom
Cast me not down forever
    Many jails many horrors the betrayal of many minds
    to instant cruelty
Could not undo
    The exactions of worse times the breaking of the bones of
    friendship
    connivance
      betrayal
    worse even could not undo
    could not no
    We stand like stones scarce warmed by the cup
      it is consummated
    who we are what we dare hope for
      Out of the depths
You have saved us from grotesquerie from self-mockery from
    the souring of good things
    from the enforced cruelties
    that rend the gentle
    Therefore I shall exalt Your name
You have traced our fate an X in the dust: Stand there
    until I return.   Therefore exalt
You have snatched our world from us our friends the paths
    we walked in joy
      out of the depths
    Yes, and affection apprehension
    our open and unspecked eye
    the exalted the sensuous the free
      out of the depths

You have taken ecstasy and left the dark
        joy and left a promise
        past and present
    and set our feet without recourse
        toward the unknown
 I will bless Your name
You have tried us and found us wanting tried us again and been
        silent
    whether in scorn or approbation we cannot tell
        Nevertheless I will bless You
You have plunged us from furnace to ice from evil to good report
    as if uncaring as if without heart as if by chance
            as if You were not
        as if You were not
            You Who are
        We will bless Your name.

                                        Daniel Berrigan

New York City
    St. Gregory's Church
West Street

APRIL–MAY 1970

April 21

The FBI busted us with alacrity, ruthlessness and relish. Interesting to witness at first hand the violation of Church-State "concordats."

Obviously the Bureau was out for blood. My brother Daniel had evaded their nets at Cornell some few days before, wounding and deriding its professionalism. Now he was reported on a program at St. Gregory's Church in New York.* Too much!

Dan had the intuition not to overtax the scene—too many intangibles. As for us, we had to go ahead. Either one trusts a community of work and risk, or one settles for nothing. And so we trusted Father Harry Browne—what other clergyman in the New York area would consent to such a caper? We trusted our friends, who were no strangers to conviction, risk, hard work.

It was nonetheless a doleful scene. The Church's service to the State—very nearly total—had won us a variety of immunities, one of them the inviolability of a Catholic rectory. "To hell with the concordat—it's unofficial anyway!" The agents seeped in in impressive numbers, observing all the courtesies, until they proved unavailing.

Father Browne abruptly lost his confidence in Mr. Thomas Walsh, an old seminary friend in charge of the FBI's operation. It became terribly apparent that Mr. Walsh had no intention of allowing us at the rally in exchange for our surrender. And Browne had no place to put us but a closet. It was like trying to run in oversize pants with no belt.

The agents raised the quotient of pain, as our leaders would say. First, raps on the apartment door, and "Father Browne?" No answer. Retirement for consultation. Next, knocks become

---

* On May 17, 1968, Philip Berrigan, S.S.J., and Daniel Berrigan, S.J., with seven others, invaded the draft board in Catonsville, Maryland. They rifled the files, dumped three hundred in trash baskets, and burned them with homemade napalm. They then prayed and awaited arrest. (Philip Berrigan had previously been convicted for pouring blood on draft files in another action, in Baltimore.) Philip Berrigan refused to give himself up on April 9, 1970, the day he was to start a six-year sentence, and was arrested in New York's St. Gregory's Church on April 21.

thumps, the "Father Browne?"s more urgent. Retreat again. Then battering at the door in earnest. It finally gives, and ten agents burst in to scrutinize and to reclaim us. Knock and enter, as they say.

In that half hour I learned some sympathy for animals in traps as the dogs approach. A young agent brought out the handcuffs. I objected, he insisted. "Listen, big boy, you're in our power now!" True, but not entirely.

We learned later that one hundred agents had been deployed on the block and a good share returned for the rally, which stirred our people, from all reports. The agents' presence and our absence seems to have accomplished at least that.

We were booked at FBI headquarters (Sixty-ninth Street) and chatted amicably with the agents. Their triumph complete, the agents were perfectly anxious to discuss themselves, politics and the rising cost of sending their kids to Catholic schools. When we got to politics, the nuclear arms race and the war in Indochina, an agent commented, "We're out to defuse both sides, far right and far left. And we'll do it."

April 24

West Street. They lock us up in maximum security —one hour's exercise a day, bring us our meals, etc. The building, within spitting distance of the West Side Drive and Hudson River, resembles a converted warehouse and serves as a federal detention center for the metropolitan area. It is a prison for transients—men just arrested, men on trial, or men waiting for sentence or for transport to permanent prisons, etc.

West Street is old, dirty, hot, and pulsing with life. Mice and cockroaches are tame and confident, savoring the food much more than the convicts do. As for the population, its variety is striking— drug people, bank robbers, check men, counterfeiters, gunrunners, espionage agents, tax evaders, car thieves, resisters and revolutionaries. Here, as in other prisons, I notice one striking absence—the rich do not contribute to the cross section. Not the established rich at least, not the plutocrats who skim the cream from the milk jar. Only once in a while a moneybags comes through, stunned by the unlikely reality facing him. But this is more to lend credibility to the myth of equal justice than it is to enforce equal justice.

At any rate, I like West Street. It possesses an element of diversity and casualness quite absent from other maximum-security institutions. The people here are not dull, and they are not finished. Before we arrived, nine men had attempted a hazardous escape.

But West Street fascinates me, mostly because of the people. They preoccupy David [Eberhardt] also. He often wanders around between head counts, drawing cons into conversation and returns looking stunned. "Incredible richness!" he remarks, over and over.

There is Lyle, busted for hash—his beard, hair and seriousness like some young John the Baptist, a knotted and frayed blanket about his waist or sometimes pulled over his shoulders. Lyle went to India, gave away everything he had, and walked the roads as a poor man. "Needed some wisdom," he explains diffidently.

There is Tony, the "Mad Gunner," charming, ebullient, the best con man and jailhouse hustler I've met. Tony not only knows where the action is, he has it—steaks at midnight, contraband booze, gambling—any stakes, pot or hash, hard dope. Tony hasn't gotten women in yet, but then he hasn't been at West Street that long. He doesn't like the "Mad Gunner" nickname. "Moment of weakness," he explains. "I was lifting this bank with a Thompson sub [Thompson sub-machinegun], and this doll, one of the tellers, stalled when I asked for cash. So I sprayed the wall and shot a clock off. They needed convincing." Apparently the judge thought the same. He got thirty years.

Chico, a Cuban, has just flown in from the West Coast with some of his buddies. Chico is warm, soft-spoken, with the instinctive Latin reverence for a padre. Yet he is an incorrigible rightist, Batista admirer, Bay of Pigs veteran, anti-Castro propagandist. I asked him where he had trained for the Bay of Pigs. "Guatemala." "Who trained you?" "Your CIA."

Tom was a war hero, ambassador extraordinary, soldier of fortune, gunrunner, international shyster. He is a little wisp of a man, prematurely gray, with bright, quizzical eyes, buck teeth, and a way of summing up everything at a glance. A mangled right leg from the Second World War and a few scrapes since. Tom is a suicidal schizophrenic. One side of him is brilliant—linguist, scholar, Buddhist monk, Christian philosopher, litterateur, engineer, pilot; the other side is brutal and incredibly fragile— alcoholic, gun- and dope-runner, undercover agent, several times divorced, several suicide attempts.

He clung to me because Catholicism had once attracted him and because I listened. He had flown guns to the Pathet Lao, V.C., Israelis, Greek Cypriots; had smuggled pure heroin from Thailand to Hong Kong; had served two years in a British jail; had fought in the Congo as a mercenary; had trained fighter pilots for an impressive number of nations and brush wars; all while pursuing some wisdom to keep himself from going mad. What he fought day by day, he told me, was the next suicide attempt.

One day he went to court and did not return. Unexpectedly the judge freed him. The night before, he had written that same judge, and showed me the letter. It was a mishmash of florid vocabulary and runaway self-pity. I had told him to tear it up and get a grip on himself. He confessed a temptation to suicide again, and was already relishing the judge's face paling.

"Go to bed and hang on," I said. "You've got more friends than you need."

He hadn't thought of that—it was an interesting concept. And enough to combat his demon. He got through the night, and the judge let him out. I hope he's found a few of those friends.

May 1

We leave West Street by bus in mid-afternoon for the Federal Penitentiary at Lewisburg. Departure causes mixed feelings. I love New York City despite its grime and noise. But we sorely need some sun and fresh air.

My brother Jerry comes in for the last visit at West Street. He assures me Dan is well and safe. People are inclined to marvel, I suppose, at the bond between Jerry, Dan and myself. It has a deep rationality as well as deep fervor. The fact is, we have grown up together in the last ten years—first theologically, then experientially and politically.

We eat sandwiches on the way, and make the trip in six hours via one of the Bureau of Prison's new buses. A good investment, these buses, not only for transport of prisoners but also for taking guards and marshals to troublesome urban areas. If policy calls for mobility, motivation has to do with overtime for the guards. The combination serves to keep the peace when peaceniks get strident.

There is no want of color aboard. Two Frenchmen sit behind us, shackled hand and foot, proud bearers of a forty-year sentence for smuggling heroin. A chargé d'affaires from the French Embassy tells them they'll be out in eight years.

There is a black from Baltimore who had been badly hurt two months ago in an escape attempt from West Street. Among the last to go down the blanket rope from the roof, he fell three stories when the lifeline snapped. With internal injuries and compound fractures of the legs, he dragged himself into a truck, where police discovered him, half dead, in the morning.

There is Hank on his way to serve a three-year sentence for threatening to assassinate the President. It seems that Hank, an alcoholic, tried to escalate the chances of therapy one night by calling Bellevue and telling them if he didn't get quick treatment he would shoot the President. Hank got quick treatment.

Lewisburg Federal Penitentiary (Pennsylvania)

MAY–AUGUST 1970

May 4

Capitalism is notorious for breeding self-interest, evidenced by competitiveness, rugged individualism, and entrepreneurship. Collective interest as well; give a community steady wages, plus a few benefits on the fringe, and it will do— or make—pretty much anything for you.

At least, some of the more lethal aspects of community interest are missing from Lewisburg. It is not Bel Air, Maryland, supported by Edgewood Arsenal (chemical warfare); or Frederick, Maryland, sustained by F. U. Detrick (biological warfare). It merely has Lewisburg Federal Penitentiary (including Lewisburg Farm Camp and Allenwood—minimum security) and Bucknell University.

The penitentiary is federal, and operationally more military than civilian. So much for its politics. In somewhat sterile contrast, Bucknell has liberal aspirations, with a lot of irreverently bright kids who have started giving the raspberry to affluent parents. The two serve to neutralize each other and to make this community freedom-loving, flag-waving, God-fearing.

It is simple to foresee conflict with the bureaucrats. Their regulations make little provision for people with our feeling of responsibility and style of life. I suppose we'll be in trouble within two months.

May 6

I begin to feel like a football in a sandlot game— too many people playing with me. First the FBI, and now my new masters here.

Having left West Street with an Allenwood classification, I blandly suppose I will return there routinely, remembering my experience with its space, boredom and cow manure in 1968. Unfortunately my masters fail to share my vision and desire.

I encounter hemming and hawing while official fingertips tap one against the other. "You did abscond, you know. How do we know you won't run again?"

"Absconding is the FBI's business; my conduct here is yours. And you have had no evidence, before or now, that I can't be trusted."

"Yeah? Well, we think that your conduct outside and here are linked. We wanna see, anyway."

"This your decision or Washington's?" Dan is still underground.

"It's all one family. I'll admit we'd like to see you all together again." He smiles broadly at his cleverness. "You just wait a while, and we'll see how it works."

I'm beginning to grab their battle map. I can't run from here—no escapes since 1952; I can't organize—they've heard of this capacity, or divined it; and I might get stupid enough, or careless enough, to leak something about Dan. (They're convinced I know where he is and what he's doing.)

Just like the little FBI agent at St. Gregory's, they are saying to me, "You're under our control now, big boy!"

May 8

Came across a sterling piece by the brother in the latest *Village Voice*. Peace people need a vast amount of shaking up, and no one matches his capability for doing that. Also, a friend from Baltimore dropped off a recent *Sun* containing an article on his NBC appearance. Strange how the big networks, despite their institutional allegiances, will do something great from time to time.

May 9

I get another whistle from Control. It's like a summons from the White House—one does not ignore it lightly.

The associate warden has a strike manifesto in his hand. Have I seen it?

"Yes. I read it two days ago."

"Did you write it, or do you know who wrote it?"

"No. It has been passed around—several hundred prisoners have read it by now."

He breaks the dialogue to refer to the manifesto's language (educated), its demands (very demanding), its tone (nonviolent).

I disagree somewhat—its language is affected, its spelling bad. But the demands are good.

One thing becomes clear. The administration abhors strikes and has decided not to have them.

"How can we be sure you have nothing to do with this?"

I laugh at him, a gesture that is, in warden-prisoner relationships, tactically unsound and even dangerous. Wardens do not forget being laughed at by inmates.

I tell him, with smug good humor, that if I were to organize a strike I'd take six months to do it. And it would be done right. But, say I reassuringly, "Penal issues are not my bag. It's the scene outside that occupies me."

He seems satisfied, and we part cordially. I leave complacent —always a bad position.

May 13

(Letter to Dan)

In the eleven days I've been here, have had at least three conversations with head hacks of varying hierarchy. I have told them that I'll refuse to work, go into isolation and begin a fast if I'm not out of this place by June 1. They got very upset at that, accused me of threatening them, and then, à la carrot, got me out to a good cell with David Eberhardt, and gave me a job that leaves me free all day long. They also promise to get us to Allenwood as soon as possible.

25

The administration has asked me to meet with two noncoopera-
tors who are in solitary. These kids have them frantic—one has
attempted suicide to gain redress, they have both fasted, and
have been beaten and maced repeatedly. And their opposition
hardens. One will not even accept a visit from his parents, if that
requires that he shower, shave and dress in clean clothes.
Totalitarianism of conscience, I call it. In any event, I don't expect
miracles—I will hardly draw them from their chosen path.

Eberhardt has been fine—he has a job in personnel. The kid
had more than a few cares about the homosexual thing here, but
that seems to have evened off by now.

Liz wrote a little outline of your intentions and plans. They
struck a chord immediately. If Nixon appears at Notre Dame,
I hope you can make it. Your ideas about having others share
your jeopardy are eminently solid—let alone the possibility of our
hearing your words in contrast to those of the Head Hack.

You must write me when you get the opportunity. Send a note
of explanation to Richard Drinnon, Department of History, Bucknell
University, Lewisburg, Pa., and he will get it to one of his students, an inmate* here who is very devoted to us. Drinnon expects to be writing in R.I. this summer—he is a good scholar, and
a good enough human being to consider one of our rhubarbs. But
he'll be out of it for our purposes here.

The inmate will probably get a research grant for the summer,
and will therefore remain the intermediary. If we are sent to Allenwood, the problem will be getting things to him here. But we can
manage that.

If in writing me you are sensitive about postmarks, then you
can get the stuff [letters] to Liz [Sister Elizabeth McAlister] and
she will handle it.

You have them apeshit, Bru. I think your agile mind will
discover new ways of tormenting them and building the Movement
in the process. More people asking for you than you can imagine.
And I tell them, "I haven't heard, but I know Dan's in charge."

* Boyd Douglas was to betray this confidence, inform on Berrigan, and testify
against him at his trial.

May 20

The powers seemingly desire to get me to Allen-wood, or Lewisburg Farm, both meccas of minimum security. They reclassify me to medium security, trusting me enough to work outside the Wall doing carpentry maintenance.

Most medium-security maintenance ends up in what the inmates call Hacktown. Hacktown is a presuburban suburban community for the penitentiary staff, built in the middle thirties by the first prisoners to fill the newly finished WPA penitentiary. The cons rushed Hacktown to completion for tactical necessities—transportation then wasn't what it is today, and if trouble broke out, there was your tactical force. Occasionally the emergency muscle in Hacktown was routed out by riot, proving the wisdom of those early planners.

My first trip to Hacktown reawakened the nausea I feel with most suburbia. It is a flabby disaster; its somnolence, primness and order disguise the stagnation and violence of middle America. And more. It is the patronage system exposed—all paths lead to the federal pork barrel. Inmates clip the grounds, paint the houses, repair the plumbing, electricity and heating. Rent is low, and the larders are supplemented from prison kitchens.

No one gets excited. Stealing is a traditional heritage, a cultural given. Nearly everyone, high and low, steals. From time to time some impudent muckraker unearths a particularly stinking case of larceny and a plutocrat loses a reputation he never deserved and goes sulkily to jail. And people settle back into stealing, a little more canny and adroit. The case is proudly cited as another proof of checks and balances inherent in our "democratic" system.

June 11

Got a haircut, and discovered that the life here made it an event—actually found myself planning for it and feeling grateful that it helped to break the tedium of the day. The most content here are those who are inventive in creating distractions.

Letter from my "main man," as inmates would say, vastly cheering. Spoke of teamwork, working both sides of the street —here and there. Don't know about that, since I don't know about this side—we haven't solved that little puzzle yet. About the first time recently that I've been caught without leverage, so tactically it's impossible to walk waters at all.

June 12

Just down attempting to offer the Eucharist for the first time. The officer at Control sent me back after checking the memorandum, which permits me to begin next week—on Monday, Tuesday and Friday.

Am beginning to cope a little better with the crushing boredom. They expect us to remain around Education some eight hours daily—four classes. The teachers, most of them ex-high school men, are tepidly conscientious, exhibiting bureaucratic energy and sacrifice.

As for the men, they know from long experience that their main function in school is to give the bureaucracy a program for public relations. This takes bodies, books, classrooms—all the surface show of supposed effort.

Apart from the insipidity of the staff here, the men contribute personal factors to daily boredom and failure of the program. One does time by doing it painlessly—that is a *grand* aim. One does not introduce needless pain (effort); the unnatural cost of the life is painful enough. Second, grown men who must learn ABC's and multiplication tables are generally more prone to discouragement. Too much lost ground to recapture. To be bored, I suppose, means seeing little hope in doing what one does, or little hope of doing something better.

June 13

I read my brother's first notes on the underground. "No one issue remains truly human unless it is organically connected with all others." He slowly emerges as singular spokesman for freedom. Who can match his credentials—that sensitive, disciplined mind, his mastery of language and position of risk? He fast becomes the Trotsky of the Movement. Maybe it's not too much to hope that a foundation of sorts has been laid for him upon which to put up a building.

June 15

Discreetly called aside by Mr. Mish [George Mische, one of the Catonsville Nine] to learn that Dan has been picked up. Moreover, rumor has it that another friend has been taken with him. May the Lord give him peace of mind and hardihood of will that he may endure the local jails well until he comes here to some of his people.

Had a morning cup of coffee with the Catholic chaplain's assistant, one of the most popular and trusted men here. He spoke of nearly losing his life by getting a knife in his back ten times. An inmate did it—a friend—and John refused to prefer charges. "Against the code," he said simply. They kept him in the hospital four months, after much surgery and many transfusions. He just now is getting back on his feet.

"Three times before, I should have died," he said. "Once as a kid when a car hit me, twice in Korea." When I inquired about the latter, he remarked, "I guess the worst time there was getting hit seven times, having a broken leg and shoulder, bleeding a lot, and holing up in a swamp for two days, hiding. I was sixteen and pretty strong."

I told him he either had a cat's lives or the Lord had big work for him. Neither possibility struck him as strange. He said with a little smile, "Both, maybe!"

June 16

No further revelation on Dan's status. Pretty content now that it was bad information. If the Feds had grabbed him Saturday we would surely know it by now.

Christ called Satan "Father of Lies," and I take that to mean "Father of Violence" also. For violence rests upon a lie—the perception of reality is unreal, and the action flowing from that perception is unreal also. So racism is violent, because a black is simply not what we choose to think him. And this place is violent, because life here is what the country has decided these men are. And they aren't that. And little things like breakfast food are violent, because claims are extravagant for low-nutrient junk.

Great readings in today's Eucharist. Hebrews 12:4, "In your struggle against sin, you have not yet resisted to the point of shedding your blood." Indeed, I have not, either for my own sins or for the sins of others. The Sinless One continues to haunt me, "Who submitted to such opposition from sinners" (12:3). The yardstick against which I must measure myself is not, supposedly, weaker people but the innocent who die needlessly everywhere, and the Innocent One Himself.

What becomes more clear as insanity mounts and we tick off our last hours? Not that many men must die, for they are dying now in increasingly impressive numbers. But that some will have to die voluntarily—to restage the crucifixion. God alone knows how many. It is an inexorable divine and human law—no life without death, no resurrection without Calvary. We had better believe it.

June 1970

I am beginning to understand where life comes from—not just from parents or from the table or from the bulk of human knowledge kicking around, so much of it distracting

LEWISBURG FEDERAL PENITENTIARY, 1970

and useless. It comes from God's word, which brings a man to fullness, as sun and rain bring a plant to harvest. "The Spirit alone gives life; the flesh is of no avail; the words that I have spoken to you are both spirit and life."

And so, quite against inclination, I invest time in the Gospel daily. It's not just that I hope thereby to get the Book into my guts, or to derive from it an intelligence of the heart. It is to drive back some of the darkness within, to shackle some personal devils, to put under higher control those mysterious deadly forces so incomprehensible to me, so resistant to *my* control. "Lord, that I might see!" Lord, I believe—help me with my unbelief! "When your eyes are sound, you have light for your whole body; but when the eyes are bad, you are in darkness."

From time to time a passage rivets my attention, such as Luke 9:59 et seq. "And He said to another man, Follow me! But the man said, Lord allow me first to go and bury my father. Jesus said to him, Let the dead bury their dead, but you go and preach the Kingdom of God. And another man also said, Lord, I will follow you, but first let me go and bid them farewell, who are at my house. And Jesus said to him, No man, having put his hand to the plough, and looking back, is fit for the Kingdom of God."

Hard, unequivocal, demanding words—but so what? Either the properties of the Kingdom of God—truth, justice, freedom, peace, love—are values demanding allegiance, or they are not. If they are not, why pretend that they are? And if they are, why not preach them as they are, in the hope that people will meet honesty with honesty, and live them?

The disaffection of concerned people with institutional religion lies in the fact that the Christian Church claims privilege by the Gospel without preaching it or living it. If the Church were true to the Gospel, privilege would be its last desire. It would fear property, condemn war, and oppose power with its life and blood.

As it stands, however, the Gospel the Church preaches is a precise statement of the life it leads—a degenerate stew of behavioral psychology, affluent ethics, and cultural mythology, seasoned by nationalist politics. It distorts the Gospel, as the State distorts the Declaration of Independence. In fact, both rely heavily

31

on rhetoric and propaganda to anesthetize their followers and guarantee their support.

The cryptic, peremptory "Follow me!" implies: (1) You ought to know me by now. (2) You ought to know I'm worth following. (3) You ought to know there's some hope for you, otherwise I wouldn't call you. "Let the dead bury the dead, but you preach the Kingdom of God."

There's no discussion of such minor problems as family, or possessions, or fears, or politics, or racial or religious credentials. Just the one critical "Follow me!" Minor difficulties fall under the justice of the Kingdom: "All these things will be provided. Your Father knows that you need these things." But He knows that people need the Kingdom more, and that man will not accept the Kingdom, or strive to build it, without accepting the Lord's cross.

In the next chapter the Lord excoriates those towns to which the Gospel has brought no life. "Alas for you, Chorazin! Alas for you, Bethsaida! If the mighty works had been done in Tyre and Sedon, which have been done in you, they would have repented long ago, sitting in sackcloth and ashes. But it will be more bearable for Tyre and Sedon at the judgment than for you. And you, Capernaum, will you be exalted to the skies? No, brought down to the depths!"

He reserves similar, pungent language for Pharisees, lawyers, rich men. "You Pharisees! You clean the outside of the cup and plate; but inside, there is nothing but greed and wickedness. . . . You lawyers, it is no better with you! For you load men with intolerable burdens, and will not put a single finger to the load." "But God said to him, 'You fool, this night you must surrender your life; you have made your money—who will get it now?' "

To make such language contemporary and meaningful is not easy, but this much remains certain: the Church rarely, if ever, even tries. It is too muddled, ambiguous, emasculated, and nationalist to single out nations, classes, professions, or individuals as untruthful, rapacious, brutal, or warlike. It has no stomach for it, because it has rejected the price of prophecy, because its patronage comes precisely from those nations and classes who war against life, from those whom it should condemn and withstand.

One is forced literally to rely on oneself, and upon a minuscule number among humanity, to reach the conclusion that Christ's morality was so intensely human that it could be both nonviolent and revolutionary. He was the political man par excellence. The values He taught and lived were revolutionary ones: faith in the Father rather than in human power, and integrity, justice, freedom, love. Sooner or later the ruling elite had to notice Him, had to react to His threat by executing Him. Some local theocrats unwittingly testified to the seriousness of His menace to raw power by conspiring with pitiable Pilate and the Roman Empire to kill Him. "If you let this man go, you are no friend of Caesar; any man who claims to be king is defying Caesar."

The Christian West—except the Central and South American "colonies" of the United States—has earned the same condemnation as Capernaum. The West condemns and perhaps destroys itself by its obsession with war in a world where peace amounts to survival, by its racism in a world two-thirds colored, by its extravagance in a world burdened by terrible want and verging on starvation. Its crimes are monumental. Can one hope that its dissolution will not bring down the rest of the world with it?

Yesterday's Pharisees are today's hierarchs who brush elbows with the mighty as court chamberlains, who neuroticize the middle class by sanctifying its moral insipidity, and who neutralize the poor with false promises, both spiritual and material. In dull abjection to their superiors, they think, or pretend to, that preaching at the White House brings morality to high places, that such issues as abortion and state aid for education declare independence from Caesar, or that heading a civil rights commission can influence Nixon's role as chief spokesman for American racism. (Even such moderate liberals as Father Theodore Hesburgh are indigestible to Nixon.) Only a handful of murdered or jailed Latin American priests and a few Christians in the United States, jailed or underground, rescue the Church from total and willing manipulation by the respectable murderers.

The lawyers of Christ's era are the professors of our own. "Alas for you lawyers. You have taken away the key of knowledge. You did not go in yourselves, and those who were on their way in, you stopped." Most academics assume that the way to keep truth intact is to keep it hermetically sealed from life; that politics is what the government practices rather than that politics is about upright life and just relationships; that their students may be emulated on occasion (if it is safe); and that truth and knowledge cost no more than financing a degree. They claim academic freedom without paying for it, and instruct their students how to enter war-related industry while they make big money researching the empire's weapons systems. They are passive before the reality that campuses are Big Government/Big Business/Big Military turf.

As for the rich, the Lord accords them harsh treatment, not so much because they possess more than they need and desire more still, but because they personify a perverted image of man which is yet attractive enough to build society around (literally). Which is to say that the rich are social pimps, exemplifying in extravagance, ruthlessness and false authority a prostituted version of life, and in the process, creating a public temptation of horrifying proportions.

More basically, what effect have riches on a man's soul? Is there something about his affluence that keeps him ignorant of the poverty of others, or contemptuous of it? This much can be said: Wealth creates a caricature of humanity that leads a rich man to assume that his supposed superiority is a personal right, his dominance a political necessity.

The seductive power of wealth in the West (which contains nearly all the billionaire and millionaire clubs) is graphically displayed by the manner in which the rich have eaten whole, and digested, institutions such as government, military, church, and university. (Some will dispute this, saying that the Corporate State, or technocracy, runs itself and everything else, including the rich. But for whose profit does it run everything?)

Government endows the rich with legitimacy; it supports them with propaganda and legalisms. "The Parliaments of the State are only highly ritualized capitalist marketplaces" (Kenneth Rexroth). The military lends them coercive authority ("the battlefield is only the most advanced form of trade"). The Church intones on the rich the benisons of the Almighty; it blesses them in blessing the rubrics of the nation-state. The university sacrifices its brains to them as the ancients gave to Moloch (the god of the Phoenicians and Ammonites to whom children were sacrificed)—"You're channeled man, wherever you go, draft or G.E."

The consciousness of the West is the consciousness of the rich—inhuman, antisocial, immoral. It makes this country, to take a leading example, one vast collective that is unhappy, frantic, helpless, insane, a human ant heap as thoroughly immunized to its own delusions as it is to the misery of others.

The rich must be told the truth, and they must be treated as public enemies. There will be no justice, no peace, until the commodity wars that start with them (and infect us all) are rigorously opposed and terminated, until love and compassion replace greed and exploitation as matters of public policy.

"Next a word to you who have great possessions. Weep and wail over the miserable fate descending on you. Your riches have rotted; your fine clothes are moth-eaten; your silver and gold have rusted away, and their very rust will be evidence against you. . . . The wages you never paid to the men who mowed your fields are loud against you, and the outcry of the reapers has reached the Lord of Hosts. You have lived on earth in wanton luxury, fattening yourselves like cattle, and the day for slaughter has come. . . . You have condemned the innocent and murdered him; he offers no resistance" (James 5:1–6).

June 22

A certain guy teaches with me in the Education Department. What commended him to me initially was his reticence—he didn't do handstands when I first came, didn't

35

try to discover what made me tick, didn't try to con me. He kept a natural and dignified distance and watched me carefully for the same consideration.

In time I discovered that he is Jewish, thirty years old, vegetarian, busted for grass and sentenced to ten years. Before jail he watched over a rich New Yorker's Catskill estate, close to the earth's pulse (as he put it), enraptured by trees, animals, and sunsets. He was searching for God, he said—and himself.

This morning in the yard he began to talk for the first time of his struggle behind walls. I listened, astonished. "There are dark powers controlling this place," he said. "They use institutions, you know—they are active wherever men fail to treat one another as men. But especially here, in the government, corporations, military and church. And people don't even believe in them."

I told him that it was the first time I had heard people speak of the Powers and Dominations in years—the world rulers of darkness, as Paul called them.

"You know how they hit me in prison?" he inquired. "The 'bring-down.' Everything around here wears you out, empties you, brings you down. The hacks can't say anything to me that refreshes or lifts me up. Neither can the wardens or social workers. And the cons sure as hell can't, they're walking 'bring-downs.'

"It's a conspiracy," he continued, "in a very evil sense. And that's where my struggle comes in. For if I succumb, the disease spreads, and they have their way easier somewhere else. And that means more insane people, and more dead."

I looked at him—his strong frame, dark animation, patrician, almost Roman features. Another searcher, or as Saul Bellow would say, another Be-comer wanting to be a Be-er. I remember the lawyer who asked the Lord for the first commandment, and that Christ showed pleasure with his honesty: "You are not far from the Kingdom of God."

So with our friend.

June 27

One of the brothers dropped off week-old Philadelphia and Wilmington papers. Friends, identity unknown, have trashed draft boards in Wilmington and attacked a National Guard armory. I feel gratitude and new hope. Nothing like knowing there are people outside who recognize the executioner before their turn comes, nothing like seeing our "freedom" institutions embattled and with their filthy linen torn out of the closet—Du Pont, Selective Service, and the National Guard.

I showed the clippings to a young resister, here for similar "crimes." He read the account and looked at me impassively, as though I had referred him to Frank Robinson's batting average. "You don't build a revolution that way," he said.

Sweet Lord, here we go again, I thought, into the Paris communes and dictatorship of the proletariat, Mao versus Stalin, and maybe even the Strawberry Statement. And then, for icing on the cake, a long wrangle on violence versus nonviolence.

A prolonged and fruitless rationalization, usually a distraction from the work at hand, which is simply to be serious with one's revolution. How can one be serious unless one pits his life against the military, for example, which controls world and national policy?

Behind Mars and his mailed fist is Croesus and the coffers of the rich. Elementary, one might say. Wallow in luxury while millions starve, and you're going to need bombs, jets, cannon, mercenaries, merely to keep the fillets on the table and the Scotch on the sideboard.

June 30

The hacks change shift every three months, so we must adjust to a new regiment of "cage and key" men, as some fondly call them.

A new shift tends to be self-conscious and insecure, so they strive hard for the impression that they're the toughest jocks around. (Actually most are fat, out of shape, and disinclined to mix it. They have a tendency to find a closet and lock themselves in at the first sign of serious rumbling.)

The busts begin. A man goes to the Hole for having two pieces of cake, one given him by mistake; another for running in the yard; another for running after the buzzer closed the yard. Tonight another man went to the Hole from mess line for taking an extra slice of bacon.

I had my own little brush. This morning on the track a hack calls me over suddenly: "Berrigan, shakedown!" He acted shamefaced about it, mumbling something like "the word is out" as he patted me down, and "You don't have anything on you, do you?" Astounded, I submitted, wondering if he expected me to be carrying a shank [knife].

Last night a lieutenant—one of the more enthusiastic Nazis in the place—and a troop of hacks shook down the sacristy of the chapel. (I vest there for Mass, and suspicions have it that I'm hiding contraband.) They retired frustrated and empty-handed. I have nothing to hide except a few notes like these. Were I inclined to hide them, it would not be there.

July 6

Sunday morning Eberhardt and I had walked down with Tom Melville after Mass before he returned to the farm. "Out of bounds," a lieutenant tells us. Then we arrive early for dinner—again out of bounds. We explain, but he is adamant, writing us up on report. That means court on Monday.

Court is a burlesque, like many of the courts outside. It's a defendant's word against an officer's, with other officers constituting the jury. The captain reads the charges, we give our version, and then step outside to await the verdict. The verdict comes—a week's restriction to quarters. We are already restricted unjustly behind a twenty-four-foot wall. Two-thirds of our day is spent behind locks and bars, and the few hours remaining are subject to arbitrary limitations, criticisms, persecutions.

Apart from the contextual injustice of restriction to quarters, David and I have been taking it up the rear exit since arrival. I can bring readily to mind a dozen painful injustices, and with a little pondering, perhaps a dozen more. Obviously a line has to be drawn—we have to destroy the illusion that we are both likely and easy targets.

We tell the captain that we are rejecting punishment. He orders us to return to quarters and to work. We tell him we won't work, and he says, "You want segregation, huh?" We say no, we just won't take his punishment.

My cell in segregation is larger—six feet by twelve feet—than the one I share with David back in quarters. I have a sink, commode, pallet on the floor, and western exposure—the sun sets directly into my window. I have a Bible to nourish me—if no food. And I have more peace and freedom than I've had since coming here. It's good to smell a little battle smoke again.

July 7

The Catholic chaplain comes to see me. He is a nice guy. (The number of nice guys around sometimes frightens me.) I should not be too hard with our friend—he wants to help. He tells me how hurt he is to see me "here"—in solitary. (I begin to understand that he and officials and inmates look upon solitary with the same loathing that outsiders look upon jail. Which alone makes it effective as a punishment.) "But others are hurt as well." My ears perk up. He says the captain wants us out tomorrow, with all punishments dismissed. I reflect cynically that the captain's sensors have picked up a little incoming heat, and he sees that we're stoking the fire right in our little solitary cells. The thing to do is to get us back to population, where we can be handled.

The chaplain leaves to talk with David. Twenty minutes later the captain appears, ignores me—he's lost a dogfight or two previously to me—and talks to David. Cleverly he whets our friend's indignation, who grandiloquently lays out the whole battle —our intentions, plans, demands, etc. The captain listens, stunned, his jaw drops, and he leaves without a word, his little mind busy with strategies of his own.

I feel an intolerable longing for mayhem as Eberhardt shouts all this down the corridor. Helpless before their muscle, with only our wits, fasting, and pain to use against them, and we tell them, "We don't like you, and here's how we're gonna show it." It's like calling the air force to say, "We're hijacking a bomber or two. Would you please have them ready?"

July 8

The euphoria wears off a little, with an increase of hard reality. Much hunger, but little weakness yet. David has constipation and feels the weakness severely. He is fasting for the first time.

We had hoped to go to court so as to bargain with the captain. But he merely sends word, through a train of messengers, that we can return to quarters anytime, all punishments lifted. Since there's little to choose between their freedom back in quarters—with harassments calculated to keep one just short of rage—and our freedom in a solitary cell, we stay here. Nothing to lose.

An ironic note: My mail begins to appear again, after I have seen none for ten days. People in solitary have no right to mail. Yet here the guards come with letters and the *Times,* their faces screwed up with solicitude. They are about as subtle as the juggernaut we send to Indochina, lumbering around the jungle shooting itself up—and a lot of peasants, of course.

One of the letters is from my mother, who broke her hip in a fall six weeks ago. With no word for two weeks, my anxiety has mounted. Her letter takes nine days to reach me, which means people here have sniffed at it for six. My gratitude is hard to restrain.

We gamble on support from outside—from the press, from those who will make noise in Washington, etc. But it may come to nothing; Americans are scattered for vacation, the local campus is drowsing through summer school, the men here are handily controlled. We might not make our objectives, might not pinch anyone but ourselves. What the hell! In this game you lose four to win one. And if you don't like the odds, get out of the kitchen.

July 9

I fight to keep strength, doing twenty push-ups, a quarter mile running in place, arm and neck calisthenics. It might be push and shove for a good deal longer.

I notice that the associate wardens, the captain and caseworkers will not talk to me. They talk only to David. They appear casually, just happen to notice him, and stop for a chat. But they avoid me.

George [Mische] has a visit from his wife, brother and sister-in-law. They will leave well briefed. He gets word to us that things are moving and to hang on.

July 10

The guards begin acting strangely, hiding in the corridors and coming by unexpectedly in the hope of catching us eating.

A hole in the dike appears. One of the docs shows up, with an eye to our health. He has a serious, paunchy man with him—somebody from the Bureau of Prisons.

Why are most prison officials and guards paunchy? A young

41

Muslim referred caustically to their dewlaps and short breath one day. "I don't eat the swine [he refuses pork in the mess line]," he said, "because if you eat swine, you think like a swine, act like a swine, become a swine. I'm a man"—he dismissed the subject with this—"and I ain't got no time acting like a pig!"

This may do my paunchy friend from the Bureau an injustice, but the point sticks on—he was paunchy, and as contented as a well-grained porker. The job says something about the man, no doubt about it. "What kind of man can make his living from locking people up? What kind of a man can live off so damn much misery?" I heard an old con ask those questions one day, a man shrewd, hard-bitten and balanced.

In any event, the questions about my health evaporate in favor of more real ones: "What are you guys up here for?" and "What do you think you're accomplishing?" I lay it on them, and the Bureau man's eyes begin to bug like a kid's at a snake show. The doc promises to come back Saturday and Sunday.

Before this little fracas is through, I vow, they'll crawl. Or I will. And I don't hope to. Vindictive? Hell, no! One has to test out the truth on oneself and on others. We're looking for living principles—principles worth living.

July 12

I have been furiously writing some of the doves in Congress, some twenty of them, as many as I can remember. I ask them to look into the situation of political prisoners, into the gripes that put me fasting in this solitary cell, and into the reasons why we're still not at Allenwood or Lewisburg Farm.

I don't hold much truck for those in politics, whether doves or hawks. Politics is about the organization of profits, and usually at the real expense of people. From the same party, young Frank Church of Idaho can take on the war in Indochina, because his constituency's interests are mainly cattle grazing and tourist trade, with a little mining thrown in. But John Stennis, who chairs the Senate's Armed Services Committee, needs Litton Industries at Gulfport, Mississippi, because his state is nearly impoverished. Neither asks what's wrong with an economy that now requires permanent war for its viability. What a monstrous obscenity that this society—maybe the Soviets too—needs permanent war to keep power where it is and to keep the masses stuffed and somnolent.

So I use the politicos when I can—call it unethical or ambiguous if you will. Many of them, like Phil Hart or George Brown, are fine, decent men, who, like Caesar's augurers, look for living signs in a dead carcass.

The young docs come around peering at us, shy and slightly frightened. They strut about in military uniform, having chosen conscription here rather than in the army. This doesn't make them antiwar—the point with many of them is merely this: "The military is so damned inconvenient. Who wants to screw around down South in the sand, sun and chiggers, and then go to Vietnam? You gotta be kiddin'!" So I see little in the young eyes but shyness and a little fright. "Yeh, doc, I'm all right!"

He'll have another bizarre story for his young wife tonight. "Jesus, Laurie, that place is full of weirdos. They got this priest up there. . . ."

July 13

As of this moment I'm high on Saint John. Don't know whether it's my empty gut or the shining floor—I've just wiped it up—or the Holy Spirit. But the Lord makes powerful good sense.

John threw me with some big questions. In Chapter 7 some of the brethren berate Christ because He will not go up with them to the feast "to manifest" Himself. He turns on them with something resembling fierceness: "My time hasn't come yet. But your time is always here, and the world cannot hate you. But it hates me, because I testify of it that its works are evil." By the "world" He meant the wealth, interlockings, contracts, secret deals, police and armies by which men in power insulate themselves from the wrath of the masses and a fall from power. This world "hates" Him because He uncovers its lies, postures, viciousness, death. Later the world kills Him, representing in His death all men, insofar as they desire to dominate others rather than to serve and love Him.

Why doesn't the "world" of today, mostly embodied in the Superstate as its politician, "hate" more Christians?

July 14

The captain calls us, and we go to his courtroom-office, escorted by four huge guards, like two sailboats brought to haven by battleships.

We went nose to nose. It was inmate to cop all the way. The captain sneered about "playing games" by fasting in solitary. Then he charged that harassment was legitimate in light of my attempts to get contraband information in and out of this prison. I told him the attempts were in his mind—where was the evidence of moving contraband? He then accused me of wanting to make a deal. I said yes—either they let political prisoners alone or I hung on indefinitely. And I got up to return to solitary.

Back in the cell, I am nicely settled into some work when the guards squadron us again, this time to see the lieutenant. The warden has ordered us moved to the hospital, where we can be under "exact medical supervision." The fasting is getting to them, I reflect, especially in a bucko of my age and notoriety.

July 15

The associate warden comes in, a day back from his vacation, tanned, cocksure, brimming energy and goodwill. He wants to be filled in, pretending he's had no time yet for details. This is a put-on, I perceive; he knows more of our recent history than we do.

He decries my "nit-picking"—tactics, requests. He gives me a limpid, paternal look and says, "You know, you should have waited till I got back, and we could have worked this out. Man to man! Yessir!" He gives my knee a Rotarian slap.

I am weak and pretty fuzzy. It's been ten days with nothing but liquids, and no great quantity of them. I tell him we'll think about what he said and ask to discuss everything with David. He says, "Sure. We'll send David right up, and you two talk!" I never see David.

At suppertime he sends in a message: "Pursuant to our conversation, I'll expect you to eat!" He's very confident. Unlike our military, he's never lost one.

I don't eat—and it's a long night. I am weak, sleepless, not too flashy in my thinking. To give up is unthinkable, with a demonstration coming up, and with the main heat against them still to rise. We hope! There is nothing to do but stand pat and trust. Trust, and don't panic. Every moment is one for faith, but especially now.

July 17

The demonstration was yesterday, though it was shooed away from the prison and down to the front entrance by the barons.

My con friends, who get information to me in my hospital cell, number the demonstrators from three hundred to two thousand, and locate them just outside the wall or near Route 15. Their information lacks accuracy, but their enthusiasm lacks nothing. And I rejoice at that, because I know we're getting to the men.

The guard shoves my clothes at me, and I go to court. The associate warden faces me, a lawyer from the Bureau of Prisons, the head of the Education Department, and somebody from the

Protestant chaplain's office. The tone is conciliatory, a far different line from that we've been used to.

The warden brings me greetings from the demonstrators, mentioning a little flak from them, but mostly goodwill and common sense. He remembered two spokesmen, Father Paul Mayer and Sister Elizabeth McAlister.

Now, this warden is a tremendously facile guy—I appreciate him more and more as a formidable ombudsman (reverse). He can take the most dolorous incident or circumstance here and sell it to critics as penal philanthropy, as "long-range compassion," as "significant rehabilitative process." It's not astonishing at all that he can soothe a pack of demonstrators, assuring them that all is sweetness and light, despite "minor misunderstandings."

Nonetheless he's honest enough to admit getting "bent" by us. The media have done their work, so have letters, phone calls, questions form the Federal Bureau of Prisons and the U.S. Senate. He "wants us out," and eating. The indirection and vibrations become almost plaintive.

I say to them, "Give me something I can get a grip on!" Translate: "What are you offering?" They give me a lotta blah about their helplessness to offer anything. "We can't just ship you guys to Allenwood."

They can if they get motivation enough. I make them no promises and they make me none. I go back upstairs to the cell and fasting.

July 21

Yesterday David and I ate a bite at noon, then whistled for the guards, who gladly led us out of isolation and back to population. Our friends greet us joyously, and strangers stop us to inquire about our health.

The experience confirms me in nonviolent tactics even more

profoundly. We had mounted an attack on the administration, caused it to be scrutinized by higher authority, ridiculed by the press, and resented by the inmates. It welcomes us back with genuine relief. In the process we have made no enemies—and many friends.

The associate warden, looking understandably harried, has a guest for us, a psychiatrist from Harvard, Dr. Robert Coles. I have heard of Coles, who has done exemplary work in the South serving civil rights workers. More recently he has researched rural poverty, mostly in the Deep South, and has written passionately about it. Representing a group of young Boston physicians, Coles obtained permission from the Bureau of Prisons to see us.

Nevertheless officialdom sat in through the associate warden. We could not help feeling inhibited. Coles protested this vigorously, claiming that the Bureau had guaranteed him a private interview. A painful compromise finally emerged: Coles could speak to us in the company of the head medical officer.

Is it inherent in bureaucracies, this resistance to free speech and well-argued criticism? Judging from performance, one would tend to think so. The apprehension in that room was heavy enough to be palpable, and one could feel the menace flowing from it.

We talked to Coles about the oppression of the federal mentality and the reactionary nature of local politics. Given time and a certain logic, our masters could as well convert this seat of misery into an extermination camp, and stoke the furnaces, convinced that they were serving God and man.

The head psychiatrist of the Bureau of Prisons appears today, anxious to appraise our mental health. Before seeing him I labor under the notion that he comes as a friend of the defense rather than the prosecution. But it quickly becomes clear that he intends to report on our hypersensitivity, and perhaps neuroticism.

Perhaps David, who talks with him first, softens him up. Or perhaps I strike a lucky chord with him. But I try to explain simply what the radical Christian Left is about—poverty, non-violence, risk. His questions improve, and I catch his eyes glowing.

"Why come to jail," he inquires, "if you think that survival is the main moral question facing mankind? Why not leave, or resist underground?"

"Because we will survive only if people pay the price of survival. At this stage I may help them more to change through an extravagant sentence than by doing what you suggest. Furthermore, we need to learn much about the role of prison in non-violent revolution."

We went on and on, and I left reflecting on his cordiality as we said goodbye. Maybe he suspected, I thought, that he wasn't free, or that survival was as much his business as mine. Or maybe, even, that *his* mental health wasn't together, and that the sanity of his private and professional life had serious aspects of public lunacy about it.

August 1

This afternoon I follow the Catholic chaplain to the hospital (familiar turf) to see Joe Ramirez, a draft resister from Allenwood. Last Monday Joe refused work in solidarity with David and myself, and once brought here, began a fast in segregation. Since then he has taken only water, and not a great deal of that.

The guards and medical men welcome us. They express a dumb uneasiness over a fasting man, as they would over a pup with a broken leg. Never having suffered for a principle, a man like Ramirez dumbfounds them, and makes them feel guilty.

They let us into the hospital cell, and there he lies, smiling bravely at us. Joe is Puerto Rican, black, twenty-one, and emaciated from his fast. Sporting a week-old beard, he is all eyes and strong teeth, but his mind is clear, his voice strong, and his language salty. He is an utter stranger to me.

48

"Hoped you'd come," he says. "I wanted to know if you were okay."

I gape at him like an idiot. "You wanted to see that *I* was okay?"

"Yeh! I heard they were screwin' with you. The guys and me talked about it. But talk gets bullshit after a while. So I pressed the no-work button. You know, they got boxes in the back of their heads, and you get to know the no-work channel. So they grab me and bring me here. When I get to segregation I begin to fast."

I tell Joe that we had quit fasting and come out of segregation nearly two weeks ago, that we had "bent" them a little more than plenty, and that now they were immobilized, if not converted. Different ball game, I said.

"That's awright," he answered. "Communications haven't been that good. But the point is, we gotta stick together."

I ask Joe what he's taking, and he says, "A little water." Then, how he felt, and he says, "A little weak." Then I say, "Joe, we're worried about you. When you gonna eat?"

"Don't be worried," he answers. "I've fasted before, and it gets to be a habit. I'll eat anytime. I just wanted to know first that you're okay."

I gape again. All alone, he had refused work, had gone to segregation and undertaken a week's rigorous fast for a stranger. Then he had waited patiently for me to show up and release him from his commitment, as though it were the most natural thing in the world. Which it was, certainly—just natural enough and human enough to be singular.

I manage an emotional thanks for myself and for David, George Mische and Bob Malecki. He shrugs me off, as best he can from flat on his back. "Don't thank me. I've got my head together again. It's been a real vacation."

He's in control, and there's nothing more to say. So I leave with the chaplain, silent and slightly overcome. We might not win the revolution, I think, but we'll win a lot of people. An ancient Christian concept.

August 3

Today I am the butt of restless rumors that buzz about here like pigeons that nest in the gutters. First, Dan has audaciously spoken in a Germantown [Pennsylvania] church last night and slipped away afterward. (Inmates relate this with relish at the sport Dan plays with the Feds outside.)

Then doleful looks and solemn news. "They grabbed your brother after that talk," says one reliable source. "I got it on the noon news." Others come up to tell me substantially the same. My fugitive brother is free no longer.

I offer my solitary Eucharist, making it a *Te Deum* for his safety, and resign myself. He's been fox to their hounds for four months now, and in the course has made brilliant assaults on the general myopia and apprehensions. He knows that the only way to make revolution is to dice up one's brain and heart and scatter them about.

Counterrumors after supper. "No, they didn't get him. He made tracks in water and turned to laugh at the hounds." So says a literary friend.

Relief and rejoicing; my faith returns. He will embarrass and harass the Dominations as long as that outweighs in good his presence in jail. When it doesn't any longer, he will surrender creatively or be captured. There are too many waves yet to walk (for both of us) to think of drowning in adolescence. For as we approach fifty, we grapple with the revolution's infancy, and therefore our own adolescence.

August 11

The news has just come in—no chance of rumor this time—that the FBI captured Dan this morning at Block Island, right off the coast of Rhode Island. They have taken him to Providence for arraignment, to be followed by quick transport here. Relief mingles with the shock and disappointment I feel.

Quite spontaneously, I think of something from Scripture—"It is an awful thing to fall into the hands of the living God." Indeed it is; a man is a fool to ignore either His mercy or His judgment. But it is not necessarily an awful thing to fall into the hands of Caesar. One has normal human apprehensions about it, certainly. To risk Caesar's justice, or to experience it firsthand, is an enterprise that tests one's humanity, one's obedience to God and to man. A fear-full enterprise, from which most of us shrink. But to be Caesar's friend might mean, in these dolorous times, being God's enemy. Given America's crimes, keeping the law is rejecting Christianity.

Dan's faith told him this and immediately he made the point clear. The issue was not fugitive status versus going to prison but resistance to Caesar, in whatever context resistance could provide.

Almost to the day, he has endured four months of danger, uncertainty, tension, new and inexperienced friends to whom he trusted his safety and to a great extent his effectiveness. To have an eye cocked over one's shoulder, to wonder when a careless friend or a malicious enemy would betray him, to prepare nonviolently for possible police violence—this more than matches the anguish and uncertainty of prison.

To be a fugitive is burden enough for an ordinary man. The temptation is to drop out, to burden others with one's security, to seek an insulation in which identity and duty are lost. This side of the underground he rejected from the start, meeting constantly with Movement and press, speaking publicly, traveling thousands of miles, often one leap ahead of the hounds. The object was neither skin nor reputation but people, and what the path to justice and peace might entail.

The mystery of Providence strikes me, but also its astonishing certainty. For I knew—with a knowledge beyond description or semantics—that he would remain unharmed in the underground, that he would lose his freedom at a time propitious for others, and that his service as a prisoner would eclipse his service as a fugitive.

August 13

Give the Bureau of Prisons credit—they know how to survive. And they know the route is expediency.

While pressure builds to win me release into minimum custody, Dan gets caught in Rhode Island. Big Brother wants no more of me here, or at any of the prison farms. But even less does he want Dan and me together in this locale. Solution? A humanitarian gesture indicating that Big Brother can sorrow as deeply as a war widow. "Berrigans to Be United in Connecticut Prison"—so the headlines hail his decision. And so justice is fulfilled.

Senator [Charles] Goodell called last night from Washington to tell me. It is easy to like him since he's helping me. But more to the point, he is helping me with obvious cost. This fall he fights for his Congressional life against the Ottinger millions. And he needs a case like ours like a hole in the head.

The question of whether I am confined in minimum or maximum security, Allenwood versus Lewisburg, has suffered preposterous exaggeration. One can understand the lies of officialdom—that follows habit. But one expected something slightly better from two "head" men in the case, Coles, the Harvard psychologist, and Dr. Norman Barr, head psychiatrist of the Bureau of Prisons. Alas!

Neither man, I'm convinced, is fit to deal with Movement people. They know too little of the politics, too little of the principles, too little of the psychological and emotional strength that flows from nonviolence. Coles, who represents a group of M.D.s from Boston, sins by being too much for us. His zeal to win us more livable conditions has become too personal. The several articles I've read strike me as emotive, strident, and in some points simply untrue. According to him, David had verged on a "psychotic breakdown" when we left segregation, while I was "frightened, anxious and depressed." I regard such assertions as incompetent, frantic and close to falsehood. Coles has goodwill, but goodwill does not justify distortion.

Closer to the truth, the greatest problem David and I had was not segregation, fasting, psychotic breakdown, fright, anxiety or depression, but how best to use the administration's lies and brutality against itself, how much nonviolent rope to give them.

Barr, a career bureaucrat whose over-all credentials are narrower than Coles's, opposed us because the Bureau did. His quote in *Newsweek* attains an astounding peak of unintelligibility: "It would not be in Father Berrigan's best interest to allow him to work near CO's. . . . The behavior he would exhibit would be self-destructive." So God speaks through his new oracle, a government shrink. What does Barr suppose I've been doing for the last several years?

Propaganda out of the scientific community assures us that the new saviors of mankind are the behavioral and natural scientists— recently physicists, now chemical biologists. Together, the claim goes, they will form the new Adam—technological man.

Not quite. If they are prototypes of the new Adam, then advisedly one ought to drop out. Neither the head scientists nor the lab scientists—excepting men like Oppenheimer and Szilard— have insisted that man must live in order to live as a man. They haven't been where we have; they know nothing of civil disobedience or jail. Who exempts them from those duties?

Man—me included—needs the Coles, Barrs, and the developers of MIRV and Safeguard like an extra rectum. Impending doom comes—not a little—from their head-tapping and their arrogant manipulation of matter. What builds a healthy head and a sane society? I would rather go to a draft resister for answers than to them.

August 17

Inmates dislike prison guards roundly, and in not a few cases hate them. There is a certain inevitability about this, flowing from the relationship between officers and prisoners. Society punishes inmates through their guards, expecting the guards to administer its disgust and rejection. Inmates, in turn, hold guards accountable for society's abhorrence. The result is an existential conflict, a quiet and sometimes not so quiet war.

As guards go, Smith is a startling exception to rule and practice, a deviant in his own right. On his job he will elaborate the motions of correctional rigidity with rote theatrics convincing enough to satisfy superiors. Meanwhile he does his thing, which is fraternizing with the cons. He lives a dual existence—performing for the brass but enjoying the inmates, who obviously are the only real people he knows.

The tales about Smith are legion—and affectionate. Seldom has he written a "shot" (violation), and only when it was grievous enough or notorious enough so that it could not be overlooked. Late suppers of contraband food will find him snacking with the rest, playing cards and dice, an enthusiastic and astute gambler. A quasi socialist, Smith believes fervently in just distribution. Without displeasing affluent cons, he can skim off their cigarettes and literature to restore a balance of justice. "If they were all like Smith," says one con, "there'd be no need for this place." Heads nod vigorously, agreeing with his fervor if not his logic. With some justification, Smith looks on service and risk as two-way traffic. He expects inmates to protect him, even as he protects them. Recently he had no choice.

The Wall is justifiably famous. Since the early fifties it has not been scaled, pierced or tunneled. A massive, ugly rectangle of reinforced concrete, it encircles the entire compound, jutting twenty-five feet above ground level (sinking the same distance below), surmounted by sensors, which, ironically, were designed by an inmate.

Above loom the guard towers—eight of them—where the guards' sole occupation is to see that no prisoner gets even near the Wall, much less through or over it. The Wall lives in minds as well as in itself, serving not only to keep us restricted but, more noxiously, to convince us that life is essentially different on the other side. Big Wall is a paradigm of Big Lie.

Smith had tower duty. Now, tower guards, as Smith well knows, are the outer shell of the prison, the last rampart between deadly men and an innocent public. Guards have the sacred duty to "watch" and preserve the Wall's mythology. As training theories go, no one can make it over, under, or through the Wall if guards "watch."

Like his colleagues, Smith "watches." But unlike them, he "watches" only when he has nothing better to do. In his opinion, forty hours a week of "watching" for a three-month tour is stupid and goddamn boring. In his opinion, "watching" that much might encourage hallucinations, leading one to conclude on cloudy or foggy nights that shadows are inmates massing for assault upon the Wall. Or worse still, that at one's back people are actually trying to get *in!* In either case, Smith feels, a guard might do bizarre things with a rifle—things that wardens, home in their warm beds, might frown upon. GIs did bizarre things in Indochina—like turning rifles on their officers, or joining the NLF and turning them against America. If something similar happens here, too much "watching" could be to blame.

Smith "watches" when his eyes are tired of reading or doing crossword puzzles, as a diversion from two-hand checkers or gabbing on the intercom with the next tower. Or when he gets bored with the preposterous flesh in the girlie magazines left by the previous shift. But regulations require periodic inspections by teams to insure the fidelity and vigilance needed for keeping sweeping towers clear of "nonwatchable" materials and, if need be, "nonwatching" guards. They are unscheduled. One afternoon an inspection team approached implacably, with Smith trapped in his tower. He couldn't hide his distractions, couldn't burn them in the tower, and couldn't get caught. The cons below on recreation were the last hope and resort. Now we'll see how philanthropy pays off, he thought desperately.

Within hailing distance was a young con named Ragan, whose humor and stamina he had often admired. "Hey, Ragan, c'mere!"

Ragan sauntered over. He was bright and cynical, quick to grasp the irony.

"Ragan, the lieutenant's coming on inspection. He just left the next tower. I gotta get rid of some of this stuff up here. Understand?"

Ragan grinned. With efficient haste, Smith lowered his bag of distractions. Ragan hid bag and cord under his jacket and non-chalantly strolled away.

Smith watched him uneasily. Ragan now had power over him, a slice of his life was under that jacket. "Listen," he shouted, "I want them books back tonight! Hear?" Ragan ignored him.

Inspection came and went. That night, as recreation filled the yard, Smith frantically looked for Ragan. Desperate, he sent a runner, then another. Still no Ragan. An hour passed, with Smith in near despair. Finally Ragan wandered under the tower, eyes on the ground, like a lad after four-leaf clovers. "Ragan, for Chrissakes! Where ya been? Where's them books? Send 'em up!"

Ragan looked up. "What books?"

Smith got his books back, but not before a broadening of education. Ragan could blackmail him—perfectly, ruthlessly, hilariously. And he could do nothing to save image or job.

But why blackmail Smith? Make him sweat a bit, so that he'll better understand he's on the right track. And that cons accept him as "people" despite his bad taste in jobs.

August 19

Four friends arrive to hassle the new warden—two priests and two nuns. They see themselves as ombudsmen between the front office and me, as surveillance against the maltreatment of political prisoners.

I await them anxiously, not having seen them in four months. Hard to describe our manifold and rich relationship—they are simply my working family. Apart from them, I tend to feel like an amputated limb, brutalized by accident and mindless surgery.

My hunger for company stems from resistance against the powers, which react punitively, reducing visits to a bare minimum. In four months I've had four visits, which might have satisfied me socially, but could only whet my appetite further for contact with my revolutionary friends.

The chaplain tells me of their arrival, and I wait two hours —no call. In my cell I try to master my fury, telling myself that waiting and disappointment are integral to resistance. How often the Gospel refers to waiting (readiness) as a prelude to manifestation (action). It is a lesson inescapable from life; revolutionaries of every age have consumed time in waiting—so that others might have time.

Finally a call comes: report to the warden's office. Once there I break in on animated conversation, in which forbearance and disagreement struggle. The associate warden, for one, appears unhappily apoplectic.

It could only happen in this awesome paradox we call the United States. Four Christian revolutionaries sit there, calmy but totally at loggerheads with two State functionaries, who find the encounter incomprehensible and disturbing. During World War II one of six federal prisoners was a resister, but they had no advocates like these. History is knocking even at wardens' doors.

The dialogue gives me secret amusement. On a human level our hosts are hopeless. Swallowed alive by an ambiguous and power-mad bureaucracy, they can neither define life nor hope in it. Society has given criminals into their charge for one reason —to exact punishment to the last ounce.

Politically the dialogue had more significance. For perhaps the first time these wardens are encountering serious public scrutiny. They can no longer do just as they please, no longer force men to *accept* depersonalization for punishment, as *they* have accepted it for privilege. The values they have adopted as standards for parole and release are being publicly dissected, and discarded as pompous, illusory, vicious and simply obsolescent. The Wall outside, symbolizing the impenetrability of their preserve (out or in), possesses swiftly widening cracks. Prisoners talk about lying awake at night and hearing it break up like ice floes softened by spring.

They politely agree to talk about moving me to Danbury, and ask how it strikes me. I reply that it's a clever public-relations stunt, designed to mollify the public with ersatz humanitarianism

—"See, we have even put the brothers together!"—thereby keeping me out of Allenwood, where I would most certainly agitate the resisters.

Their expansiveness is dampened somewhat until I agree to go. I agree to go for my own reasons—a need to see Dan and to study a different prison population. But if it shows no promise I will return to Allenwood in three or four months.

The Tombs in New York City has erupted, and strikes have swept the federal system—at Leavenworth, Atlanta, Petersburg, Alderson, here at Lewisburg. We must yet reckon with "convicts" as an essential part of resistance. In God's plan, and in our day, the wretched of the earth will have their hearing.

Danbury Federal Correctional Institute

(Connecticut)

AUGUST 1970–AUGUST 1971

DANBURY FEDERAL CORRECTIONAL INSTITUTE, 1970

September 1970

I transferred here by bus on August 25. We stopped for an hour in New York City—at West Street—to pick up 8 or 10 men, and then continued on. The New Yorkers pleaded with the driver to remain in the city rather than take an express highway. He obliged by following Eighth Avenue, allowing us sight of the few people on the street. At this time of year it is mostly the poor who remain in the city.

I developed a miserable headache, caused, apparently, by a combination of New York City smog and menthol cigarettes, government issue. If I am any proof, they are a deadly combination.

After initial processing, I discovered Dan in A & O [Admittance and Orientation]. Impossible to describe my anticipation, or the meeting itself. We had not seen each other for four months— perhaps the toughest four months that either of us has lived.*

I notice no startling changes—deeper etchings in the face, perhaps—new lines of experience as well as pain. Otherwise the expense of underground does not show itself—he is still limber and wiry, still full of wit and luminous smiles.

He and the young people had planned a celebration. One had composed a song honoring our arrest at Catonsville and the underground, another had concocted huge quantities of punch. It was a spontaneous, human, affectionate evening, precisely what we needed. It was in welcome contrast to the grim paranoia practiced at Lewisburg, where such a celebration would never be allowed.

I compared what I saw with what I'd heard about Danbury. "Heads" [narcotics offenders], protective-custody men (rats, in the vernacular, held here for personal safekeeping), and elderly embezzlers of varying stripe compose the population. Plus only one or two draft resisters. I puzzled over what I could mean to such

* Daniel Berrigan was ordered to prison on April 9, 1970, for his part in the Catonsville draft-file burning. Instead of surrendering, he had gone underground, escaped from a Cornell University rally inside a puppet, eluded the FBI for four months. He was finally captured at the summer home of William Stringfellow and Anthony Towne on Block Island, R.I., on August 11.

61

men, or they to me. Today's welcome by a few flower children, obviously nonpolitical, will be scant answer on the morrow.

I will try to learn and see. At first glance the potential of these men seems incredibly low. For the vast majority the only variation from standard behavior involved their crimes, which almost without exception were performed for personal benefit. Resistance is a long leap and perhaps impossible at this time.

September 1970

A month here and only slight accomplishment to point to. I have not even gotten the high points on paper—a very annoying failure.

Of course I can offer excuses. For one, dormitory existence—I refuse to call it living—conflicts with prayer, reflection, writing. I have still not found a tactful way to tell the men I live with that I'm *not* a listening machine, not a counseling automaton, not an indefatigable physician for all needs, spiritual and material. And so the young, especially, tailor me to their convenience. They have no interest in my vocation, but they refuse to let me forget it.

Yet apart from the sheer strain of survival in a warren like this—pets get better treatment in America—we talk to people seriously and methodically about life, society, identity, meaning. Slowly the amorphous takes form, and a tiny community begins to stir, leaf out and bud. I can imagine no greater joy or satisfaction than witnessing people slowly gaining control of themselves, breaking the slaveries that afflict them. It's like being a spectator at creation.

Issues abound, as they do in any prison. Our prison industry contributes to war by manufacturing cables and missile components for the nuclear subs built at Groton Connecticut. Education is boring and teachers are condescending. Recreation can handle only a third of the swollen population. Our quarters provide no room for privacy or quiet; the personnel is paternalistic, sluggish and mediocre; the bureaucracy is punitive and insensitive.

Despite the official propaganda, we inmates get the message immediately: this is a jail, and we are here for punishment.

Nonetheless our priority is not prison reform. Like welfare centers and lobby offices in Washington, the federal penal system is a child of the capitalist State. To confront it as a diseased organ without remembering that it exists in a diseased organism is to invite both failure and further punishment. Any small cure immediately gets reinfected by the pus in Big Brother's veins.

Dan and I try to insist on one point. One does not merely get ready for a strike here; rather, one uses a strike to ready oneself for the Movement. One has to learn to relate to people, to remain calm under pressure, to master organization and tactics—in a word, to be a man. To expose prison industry as slave labor, or overcrowded quarters as penal tenements, is merely to offer oneself an occasion for discipline, tactical flexibility, community. It is not to presume naively that inmates can humanize this jail or the penal system. Both jail and penal system are too much a part of the Great-New-Fair-Frontier Society.

September 1970

The social introversion here creates a human fishbowl, leaving people fragmented, lonely, antisocial. It breaks down the violence of the old life with a new and subtle pattern of violence, one that is nonetheless (and this is critical to the penal bureaucrat) socially controllable.

That might smack of overstatement, but the fact is that the penal system—and this dump is no exception—is not intended to "rehabilitate," or to reduce "crime." It is intended to control, to prevent a shift in power. It protects the men of property, and it punishes those who consciously or unconsciously challenge their sanctimonious greed.

Reasonably enough, therefore, when the men here gather together to inquire about their lives and who runs them, it is a cardinal crime. Let there be no confusion about this—the desired control is total. The administration wants not only your body but your head. They want your body available for count, and your mind and tongue with it. When mind and tongue disobey, control has slipped. And stenuous methods might be necessary to reestablish order.

In spite of this, Dan and I start to talk out without knowing where it will lead. (Knowing only that doing nothing with people leads nowhere.) A few youngsters transported for strikes in other joints, a few Zen and/or Yoga people, a few fringe enthusiasts whose politics consist of knowing that something is wrong. A modest beginning, but every beginning is modest.

We start gently and tentatively with a book and a report on it. The grapevine catches it, and thirty people gather. One lad gives his interpretation, and several others plunge in. Appalling. Heat grows and light diminishes, a five- or six-sided argument replaces what began harmlessly and hopefully. One would think that it was a bunch of Catholics arguing about abortion, or Arabs about Jerusalem.

I check the outer circles of those squatting on the grass. Some are frankly bored, others disgusted. They have tried to talk with one another before, and have failed traumatically. And as the scene proved, having Dan and me, two new "magic men" around, wasn't going to change that.

"Not to share the general insanity": I know good people whose total energies are devoted to that, with less than total success. They are as fully convinced as these young people that this society is mad, bent upon destruction like some berserk elephant. But fine abstractions like that are fine excuses for not dealing strenuously with the madness in oneself.

So one answer to the infantile and violent talk of the evening is not to talk, or to register boredom and disgust. Which is to say that the problem of facing ourselves and one another is as monumental as facing society. One decides unilaterally that madness is *his* and not mine, *society's* and not mine.

We part somberly, convinced that book reports are not the best route to reality. We'll have to try a different one, and ride a different horse. And if necessary, another and another. In revolution, reality and stamina are "convertibles," to use an old scholastic term. And both equal love, which experience insists is the chief weapon of the revolutionary.

September 1970

Our plot simmers and thickens. We have long, tense conferences on security and back-up people, on publicity and behavior under heat. A few more join, swelling the group to eleven or twelve "stand-up" men.

Blacks have been sniffing the wind, curious about our constant huddling and furtive stares. We know a few leaders by now. "You plannin' a hassle for the Man? Write me down! But we gotta have them outside people!"

Everyone knows the compound needs change, but the blacks point to "industry" (the plants). "We gotta work there, man! Buildin' all that war shit. You know what they pay us?" They promise to sound out their people and get a reaction. And see how the Spanish-speaking feel.

Spirit runs high, a very heady contagion. The blacks, as in most jails, tend to hang together under the old, honored, institutionalized oppression. They know, with varying insight, that Whitey still regards them as his burden, still degrades them with his culture, boxes them in with his laws, sends them to his jails. They know that Whitey expects prison to dilute them into antiseptic Toms who will help him with his thing, or failing that, keep them out of sight and out of mind for a dollar a day. "We together, man! You'd better believe it." I had no reason to doubt it.

One could say something similar of the Spanish-speaking, mostly Puerto Ricans, with a few Cubans and South Americans. Their alienation from the Man is quite as total, but for different reasons. They have seen what Yanqui acquisitiveness has done in the Islands and on the South American continent; they have seen too many lies, too many promises broken back home and in the barrios of the Northeast. The WASP culture, they have seen, is interested only in bigness and acquisition, like a giant octopus terrorizing the sea floor. And so they cling fiercely to one another, their families, language, religion. The whites on the compound discreetly let them alone. "Don't fight with them Spics, man. You fight one and you'll hafta fight 'em all!"

We meet with the black and Spanish-speaking leaders. They want only one assurance, and it's about a divsion of labor. "You got the outside down, man? You gotta have publicity, demonstrations, lawyers bangin' on the gate, people on the phone! Unnerstand what we're sayin'? You get us these things, man, and we'll shut down industry. But if you don't, we go first, unnerstand? The Man'll make goulash outa us. He'll shove us in the Hole, slap charges on us, ship us out. He don't treat us like you, unnerstand?"

We promise that outside friends will help, and satisfy them on that score. Now the real, intensive headwork begins, multiplying questions faster than our little band of neophytes can possibly answer them. Should we strike just industry or the whole institution? Would a strike be a good occasion for a fast by some, or would a partial food strike by many be better? Should services for the men, such as laundry, hospital, dental clinic, recreation, be struck also? How do we keep the strike nonviolent under almost certain provocation from the guards? How do we get wider support from the marginals without endangering security? "Fifty percent of the people here belong to us," remarked the captain (the head correctional officer) one day. How do we keep up morale, with people hungry? When the inevitable bust comes down, who goes to the Hole first? (The administration will try to pick off the leaders.) What about contingency plans?

We keep reminding ourselves, Dan and I, sometimes with a hint of desperation, that these men are critically important to the new order. If Christ would attach sanction and life to the visitation of prisoners—"For I was in prison and you came and visited me"—he must have use for us.

October 1970

A bus comes in from New York City (West Street) and points west, notably Lewisburg, Pennsylvania. It brings us a noteworthy addition, transferred for agitating at Allenwood. I know him personally and know his reputation—one of the most formidable young revolutionaries in prison today—bright, tough, creative, nonviolent. If I had any reservations about him at all, they would have to do with his addiction to the kind of sterile, ideological arguments so common in the Movement. Despite that, however, he remains a lovable and disciplined guy whom we welcome gladly.

Newcomers process through A & O. There one attends lectures, takes a physical, submits to photographing and fingerprinting, gets assigned to a caseworker, etc. In a loose, almost casual process, one is slipped into a slot and program which is only revised slightly for the unusual or idiosyncratic. "You get slotted, man, or you find a slot. There ain't no difference!" You keep your name, but they add a number, and your number tells more about identity (or lack of it) than your name.

Our friend goes from the bus to A & O, his reputation and record preceding him—political prisoner, nonconformist, troublemaker. "Corrections" have a difficult and ticklish job with him: How to program him so that their enlightenment may prevail over his?

"Corrections" lose from the start, but so does he. A & O complains that he misses orientation, breaks appointments, is always somewhere other than where they want him. For his part, he stretches the umbilical cord taut, gleefully waiting for it to snap. For him it's a little guerrilla theater on the inside, a little Yippie scenario.

Meanwhile we approach zero hour for the strike—some ten days away. Our skittish young colts, strange to the racetrack, are jumpy and irritable. "Corrections" notice this and eagerly exploits it. A lieutenant, dubbed "Strychnine" for his lovableness, comes on night shift to sniff our tracks like a blue-ribbon bloodhound. Strychnine knows we plan a strike, but doesn't know when—which is our sole protection. So he dogs us and sweats us, waiting for the one mistake that will allow him to break us up. If we meet, he'll listen, or stare us down, or write us up; if we walk, he'll follow us; if we separate, he'll warn the other hacks. Wherever we are, he is there, paunch out, eyes beady behind glasses, cigar, like a malevolent old owl watching for field mice.

The next morning the newcomer misses another A & O lecture, and the officer warns him that one more absence will mean lockup. He relates this to us, inspiring more pleas to keep his nose clean and avoid carrying incriminating evidence.

That afternoon the A & O officer notices he is missing, discovers him in the yard, shakes him down, finds a strike manifesto on him, and locks him up. We hear the news and stand around wordlessly, like country bumpkins caught trying to overturn the outhouse on Halloween.

Quid dices? What does one say? One can fulminate or one can try to understand. The former is pointless, but maybe one can use the experience as an object lesson on reaction to violence. Sensitive and responsible men often react mindlessly to mindless treatment. Too frequently we have small capacity to absorb the garbage that passes for life here, to internalize, transform and express it as something better. Instead we absorb the garbage and transform it into more garbage—childish games destructive to serious work. In a matter of moments our friend ruined six weeks' work. Consciously he would rather die than do this; subconsciously he could do nothing else.

October 1970

With that single bust, two months' work dissipates like smoke at a pot party. First it's there, then suddenly it ain't— as useless as tomorrow's dust on furniture. Our headstrong young friend languishes in the Hole, and that prompts our sympathy. But it does not prompt our gratitude.

Rumors come flying out from the front office, exploding in the compound like tiny bombs in a fishbowl. They narrow down to this: (1) The FBI will investigate the imminent strike. (2) Our young friend will face charges for incitement to riot. (3) He will be transported back to maximum security (Lewisburg).

Most in our gallant band take the bait like hungry trout, heads swimming, jaws snapping. In their small-boy arrogance, they dismiss the Man as stupid and cowardly. But when he makes a confident show of teeth and muscle they scatter in ragtag flight.

More than that, our friends invite rumors and threats, and add a real quality to their unreal groundlessness, as though they needed the Man's blustering to rescue them from their plans, from all precipitous steps and consequent dangers. Their credulity and bewilderment are in fact a cry for help: "Save us from this strike! We don't want to go to the Hole, don't want to lose good time, don't want extra charges or shipment to Lewisburg. Help us to submit with dignity!" The rumors of course are merely trial balloons to test our mettle, like growls of a dog over his bone, warning other dogs off. To take them seriously is absurd. Why would the FBI investigate a strike that never happened, or prosecute a man for merely talking about one? But in this case, trial balloons are eminently successful; in fact, successful enough to provide a formula: "Watch the leaders and bust one at the first pretext. Then release rumors about what you intend to do to him. The rest will cool it."

The experience has been nonetheless providential, proving at minimal cost to us that one does not begin to understand others except under stress, where qualities of heart are paramount. A lifetime of reading or rapping does little to educate the heart, as we discovered again. We have with us curious, well-intentioned, pseudoradicals—not men. They may be men later, or they may never be men. More certainly, they are not men now.

The focus shifts from dealing with the sheer injustice of this unhinged, vacuous dump—industrial slavery, overpopulation, poor food, etc.—to our young man in the Hole. Knowing that threats of investigation and prosecution are cheap bombast, we try to protect him against reshipment to maximum security, helping with lawyers, and so on. Beyond that we can presently do little except ward off the worst fears, or offer people painful explanations. There is, for the moment, no one left to work with.

October 1970

Initially we overestimated some of our friends here, accepting enthusiasm as a substitute for preparation. For their part, they fool us with rhetoric and devotion, tempting us to forget the derangements of family and society they have endured. Culture shock, one might call it; and its remedy includes far more than dropping drugs or dabbling with communes. Or, for that matter, contact with a couple of Movement gurus like Dan and me.

Making mistakes in prison resistance is stupid and dangerous. Our friends, almost without exception, have already been deeply hurt, and are under punishment as well, with solitary, loss of good time, refusal of parole. On the other hand, who knows where to wade between the shallows and the rough water? The need for organization has its own urgency, simply because the times demand it. So the question stands as insoluble: Is one more harmed by taking public risks while unprepared or by immobility while, as the kids would say, getting one's thing together?

October 1970

(From a letter to Sister Jogues Egan)

As usual, consistent gratitude for your most recent letter, which I duly passed on to the brother.

Let me share with you a few observations about which there is virtual consensus. Trying to grab an issue here is like trying to catch a greased pig in a muddy barnyard. The temptation is to give up the attempt as hopeless.

Part of this arises from the nature of a jail like this. The inmates call it "a freak show," designed especially for the "head." An expensive and pitifully ineffective narcotics program dominates the place—its regulations, securities, values—and promises to enlarge shortly, until seventy percent of the population will be "grass" or drug offenders of some sort.

Obviously, drug people, hippies, freaks, do not fit the common categories of criminality. They are, for the most part, gentle folk—antiestablishment, individualistic, and highly exclusive. To a sobering measure, the epitome of the good life is "a rap while high," which critics—with more than a little truth—interpret as "cheap fellowship under cheap stimuli." Nonetheless they neither think nor act like the common lawbreaker, and administration reflects awareness of this.

As for the staff, they are of the soft variety, if one compares them with colleagues at the "hard joints"—Leavenworth, Atlanta, Lewisburg. Relations with the inmates seem tolerant, even permissive. Mind you, personnel quality is neither better nor worse than at other federal penal institutions—mediocrity appears to be the main qualification. (One inmate had his own appraisal of staff excellence: "You can travel through the whole damn system and not meet a man among them.") But the point is, when mediocre permissiveness becomes policy, it tends to obscure, even eliminate, more critical concerns, whether here or outside.

Nearly half the men here work in industry—defense-related and shamelessly profitable because of the slave labor. Quarters are one hundred percent overcrowded, and the cable factory builds an expensive new expansion. Education is aimed at mere literacy or high-school equivalency; for the hundreds here with higher desires or attainments, there is virtually nothing to hope for. Recreation is severely limited by lack of space and facility even though the whole property includes some several hundred acres. While outside, the national society suffers a heedless and violent sundering, helpless to understand or to remedy—the Indochina war, rising unemployment, Middle East tensions, ABM and MIRV, etc., etc. The quality of life here implies that such questions are somebody else's business, certainly not an inmate's.

I should not allow such a statement to hang—it might be misleading. The fact is that the permissiveness is for appearance and propaganda. An unpenallike freedom is allowed in all areas except critical ones. But when one goes "political," even in a tiny thing like criticizing the food, or when one emphasizes a given such as freedom of worship—four Jewish lads are now in the Hole for insisting that Jews already there be released for the New Year— or when one attempts to identify freely with human-rights militants outside, the velvet comes off the mailed fist, and one quickly learns about power from its seat.

All the inmates know this or quickly learn it. And so the joint remains depressed, stagnant, joyless, purposeless. There is nothing left but to do time, do one's thing. And as on the outside, that goes nowhere.

We'll look to Monday, and with great anticipation. Stay the best thing around—for the sake of us all.

Love, peace, the Lord's blessing.

October 1970

A birthday tomorrow, my forty-seventh, and the second I've spent in jail. It's probably not presumptuous to conclude that it won't be my last.

I don't feel forty-seven, or at least the way a forty-seven-year-old American usually feels. For many reasons. I possess superb health for one thing, mostly attributable to a simple formula— body and spirit must be worked in conjunction, at roughly the same tempo. I believe in what I've done and what I'm doing, which has a great deal to do with vitality. My relationship with both Mother Church and Mother State is bound to deepen—and that's a prospect I invite with great relish, though neither may welcome my ministrations. But that's a dilemma that I'm as unwilling to remove as they are helpless to remove it.

This is a strange compound, almost unnatural. Set in a spacious five hundred acres—the prison once had its own hog and dairy farm—it resembles outside a quasi-modern, technical factory of the kind you find around large cities. Inside, one gets a better view—buildings forming a rectangle, with warehouses and factories stuck on the far end, indicating development from agrarian to industrial economies.

Most prisons have a semblance of a compound for exercise, recreation and socializing. But most prisons, particularly federal ones, have other facilities to take burdens off the compound—education, library, inside gymnasia, more numerous cellblocks, etc. Here there is almost nothing. We are squeezed into a tiny yard, some 75 by 150 yards, to fare as best we can with time and one another.

To use Jung's term, introversion results. A few play sports, like seeks out like to talk and walk. But before many months all the faces have been learned, all the experiences heard, all the cliques established, and all the interest is gone. An eroding boredom sets in, because there is no life and nothing happens.

One might have struggled with the Man in the past, but one's presence here indicates defeat as one's lethargy marks defeat's acceptance. Almost without question one deadly illusion is accepted as fact—one cannot *live* in prison, one has to *wait* for release.

Example: A young prisoner comes across a saying that appeals to him. He cuts it out and pastes it on his locker. It reads, "Freedom is a state of mind!" He lives here six months, and it no longer appears true. So he amends it: "Freedom is *not* a state of mind!"

His instincts had preserved him to a degree from the American conviction that freedom is essentially freedom to consume, produce, manipulate others (poor and black especially), and to escape the consequences if one falls into excess in any of the above. But life here has prevented instinct from becoming conviction. Now he believes precisely what our mandarins—outside or in—want him to believe: Freedom is not a state of mind! It *is* a voiceless, immobile, powerless, convictionless slice of affluence. Paid for by the world's poor. They can let him go now—he is rehabilitated.

Hartford, Conn., October 1970

Two more days in court and no time to reflect. Days in court are like days in jail. And these were as tough as any I recall—boring, frustrating, exhausting.

The occasion is a preliminary hearing of Dan's and my class action against the government for denial of First Amendment rights for the some 21,000 federal prisoners.* It concentrated on two points—denial of permission in general to write for publication and in particular to circulate a sermon requested by religious leaders.

Dan and I left Danbury shackled wrist and ankle, and to each other, in a nervous little caravan of three automobiles, marshals to the head and rear of us. We did not understand why at the time, but the government was apparently uptight about intervention operations. We knew nothing of all this, so we could only fume at the marshals over the leg shackles.

The proceedings don't warrant detailed explanation; I don't have much confidence in their significance for the thousands of federal prisoners. The hopes we had were quickly tempered by the legal unrealities that unfolded before us, which reminded me of my three earlier trials. With rare exceptions—Constance Baker Motley's Martin Sostre decision† (which freed the prisoner from the Hole and granted him permission to read Black Panther literature, as well as write and publish)—the courts have exhibited narrow conceptions about deprivation, abuse and injustice for prisoners. Could a judge appreciate the sterile, brutal kennels to which he commits people for punishment?

As for our lawyers—devoted to us though they are, energetic and competent—they are *still* lawyers. They believe entirely too much in the law and in the courts, and they fail to remember that

---

* The class-action suit was an attempt to relieve federal prisoners of censorship in First Amendment areas: to permit them to write freely; to communicate with newspapers and magazines; to publish without government censorship; generally, to be able to freely express religious, moral and political opinion.
† The decision was later overruled.

legality's real function acts more to buttress the status quo than to provide justice for the poor and out.

We would prefer those who treasure their wisdom and courage more than their knowledge of the law to represent us. Our lawyers know, from knowing us, that prisoners are stripped of rights just as they are stripped of their street clothing at the gate. They know that prisoners are "rehabilitated" by punishment, and that punishment stretches from insensitivity to brutality, that men are processed like marketable goods in order to return them to "freedom" passive, anonymous, conformist.

They know these things, but seem not to be convinced. And so they accept the court's image of itself as a forum for justice. And they play the court's rules, questioning, as the court does, the right of 21,000 prisoners to their own minds, speech, writing, associations, political convictions and expressions, relevant religious practices, uncensored mail, and so on. And neither the court, nor the lawyers' deliberations with the court, nor the interminable and grudging pace of redress—if there is to be any—could in the slightest affect *the* fact that the men are treated like objects.

Surely we would not be cursed with such jails if we were not cursed with such courts. Both are worthy of the society that allows them and the State that sponsors them. Society and State will pile up their injustices faster than token redress can heal them.

It is impossible to know the outcome of all this. Far more important to avoid idle speculation and to work instead with the now and the possible. Given two days of suffering in that court, might they have done something to humanize it, might they have preserved some of its elements from progressive concessions to injustice, inhumanity, death? One feels very helpless. I say to myself: "Avoid harming others and wait for a moment to affirm a trust in people, even the bureaucrats who appear most lost."

Danbury, October, 1970

Dorothy Day has written that "we ought to fill the jails with our young men." One must remember that Dorothy's hope is in the Kingdom of Christ and not in any Great Society. She lives her life around the belief that one builds justice by being just, and by allowing God to make of it what He will. There is no other way to eliminate injustice, she asserts, except by accepting it joyfully and positively and by giving it a chance to heal itself at every turn. Catholic Workers therefore have little interest in telling society what it must do. They consider it to be far more important to do what *they* must do.

But practically speaking, the government is not about to fill its jails with young men. It wouldn't even have the support to do so, since this war itself hasn't any popular support. Also, its jails are already filled—though not with war resisters. And building more jails might jeopardize the government's already diminishing popularity.

This is not to say that I want the jails filled from the antiwar movement or that imprisonment by itself is a mark of serious resistance. Perhaps we could say simply that no militant can solve the problem of consequences without accepting them in the course of events, that a person is truly of the Movement when his resistance has become indifferent to jail, separation, loneliness, humiliation, loss of financial security and career satisfaction.

There is jail on both sides of the walls. One treats the street as a jail, therefore, and acts to free it. One cannot avoid action in order to avoid prison, since one is already in prison. The thing is to act against prison wherever one encounters it.

The Lord's admonition inspires this ramble, the "for My sake" means for the sake of humans, because Christ is human, the Body of Christ is the body of mankind. To paraphrase: If you dare to be a man by taking the cause of man (the majority of men historically have been oppressed), you will be jailed, brought before officialdom, hated and perhaps killed. Why? Because you threaten the domination of the powerful, who have won their domination at the expense of the poor and the slavery of everyone. Especially themselves.

"Be on your guard"—the classic Gospel admonition of alertness, waiting for the Lord to manifest His need in the need of another—and particularly in a suffering brother, in the contemporary version of the prostitute, publican, leper (black, woman, addict, homosexual, Vietnamese student). But waiting for the Lord requires not only alertness but also a clarity of mind and a resolution of will, an integrity in one's person that is capable of "telling the Good News" to the powerful—to those who live lies and punish with more lies.

November 1970

A professor from Cornell has read the sermon Dan and I wrote calling for nonviolent resistance and supporting our suit. He loves us, he writes, too much to condemn it, but he finds it angry, strident and extreme. We feel it was understated; The Bomb is real, Indochina is real, the ghettos are real, we are in jail.

He feels different. He is gentle, self-effacing, agonized. He advises, kindly and gently, that the war has destroyed language, among other things, in a discreet reference to our reckless use of it. We in turn offer the conviction that real experience with this society is impossible of elegant expression. The matter goes beyond language. How does one talk about genocide? How does one translate Hiroshima, or multiply its probability? How does one put starvation in print, or the colossal habitual waste, or the public conspiracy to crush the poor? To succeed would be to explain our lives. And this we cannot do.

He finds our attempts crude. He seems piqued that we trust people enough to make demands of them—daring them to forge their own ways rather than merely follow our examples. He feels, I guess, even more lonely because we do not share his despair or settle down with his impotence. When the frightened gather, they can do little more than cling dolefully to one another, like children in a haunted house.

We are a pampered and faithless people. Is there neither spark nor residue left of the twelve who died like their Lord, or Paul, Justin Martyr, John of the Cross, Thomas More, or Alfred Delp? Not much, it seems; the lives of such men are rejected by contemporary Christians almost categorically. And because they are, they reveal the dimensions of our alienation—from God, nature, brother—in exchange for the massive apparatus that satisfies our material needs. Alienated men are weak, broken and fragile; they are not the free, but the conquered.

Awareness is not entirely lacking, but real response seems to be. Most people are passively sensitive to urban blight, foreign war, domestic tragedy, and general social insanity, but they feel helpless to respond. They do not call events into question or take proper control of their lives.

In a sense, we have already decided to die, and the society we inhabit has about it the stink of a mortuary. It must prove itself by war. But our money is unsound, our unemployment rises, our cities crumble, our air and water are rank and putrid. But new life accompanies death, as gently as the entrance of the Child into our world and bloodstream. A new civilization rises from the wretched of the earth, and from those who admit their spiritual poverty, and from those whose deprivation and grace will make the New Man.

As a modest proposal, it strikes me that Christians ought to trade in their current despair for a more constructive and positive fear—that they will *themselves* put out the light. Of our alliance with the forces of darkness, there can be no question. Yet in spite of us the light holds and is inextinguishable. "The light shines in the darkness, and the darkness has never put it out."

From the despair that we might be putting out the light, we might come to appreciate its guidance and warmth, might savor it and value it. Might judge it to be ours, even as the Light of the World is ours, if we want Him. Might offer it to others as our best gift; might resolve to destroy the darkness with it; might realize, whatever the cost, Christ's incredible compliment, in which he expresses a hope that only God could have—*"You* are like light for the whole world." "Nobody lights a lamp to put it under a bowl; instead, he puts it on the lampstand, where it gives light for everyone in the house."

November 1970

From one view, offering a Christmas message from prison has its incongruities. Friends requested one because they concluded that Christmas was about becoming free. And that Dan and I ought to know something about that.

We may or may not. Freedom depends far less on what has been done, and far more on what is being done. For us Catonsville was a corner turned, but it is not the last one. It is perhaps not even the most critical one.

The point is that no one, in prison or out, personifies freedom, even those jailed for the most noble motives and deeds. One might break an inhuman law, might free himself from criminal support of a criminal state, might receive jail for his pains, only to weaken and regress so in prison that on release he is a different man, a reluctant friend of the State, "rehabilitated" in the conviction that resistance is too lonely, too foolish, too expensive. Precisely the lesson intended. To paraphrase an old parable: The State devours a human, labors, and brings forth a mouse.

John says, "The light shines in the darkness, and the darkness has never put it out." His magnificent soliloquy on the Word made Flesh crowns the grandeur of the Christmas liturgy. If one were to look for a capsule of revelation, and indeed history, here it is. "He came to his own country, but his own people did not receive him." God's inner life; His love for us; the gratuity of His Son; the Word's condition as man; toil, anguish, rejection, death, life. The Gospel only confirms in more detail the mystery of God, and the mystery of what we are and what we can be.

November 28

Today's *New York Times* relates that J. Edgar Hoover, before a Senate subcommittee, has charged Dan as co-conspirator with myself and five others to kidnap a high government aide and blow up heating utilities serving government buildings in Washington, D.C. He has claimed that we lead an "anarchist" group called the "East Coast Conspiracy to Save Lives." Superhawk obviously wants something—$14 million in appropriations to support another thousand agents. So he uses us to create a need, then makes his request confidently.*

A heavy business! Edgar has jeopardized Dan's and my First Amendment class-action suit indicting the government for denial of free speech to prisoners, as well as my appeal for reduction of sentence. He has laid a threatening "psych" upon peace

---

* On November 27, 1970, J. Edgar Hoover, Director of the FBI, went to the Capitol carrying 27 pages of prepared testimony for the Supplemental and Deficiencies Subcommittee of the Senate Appropriations Committee. He was asking for $14.5 million extra for an additional 1,000 agents. The testimony cited a number of statistics, discussed the mounting danger of subversion by the New Left, and then went on: Willingness to employ any type of terrorist tactics is becoming increasingly apparent among extremist elements. One example has recently come to light involving an incipient plot on the part of an anarchist group on the east coast, the so-called "East Coast Conspiracy to Save Lives."

This is a militant group self-described as being composed of Catholic priests and nuns, teachers, students, and former students who have manifested opposition to the war in Vietnam by acts of violence against Government agencies and private corporations engaged in work relating to U.S. participation in the Vietnam conflict.

The principal leaders of this group are Philip and Daniel Berrigan, Catholic priests who are currently incarcerated in the Federal Correctional Institution at Danbury, Connecticut, for their participation in the destruction of Selective Service Records in Baltimore, Maryland, in 1968.

This group plans to blow up underground electrical conduits and steam pipes serving the Washington, D.C. area in order to disrupt Federal Government operations. The plotters are also concocting a scheme to kidnap a highly placed Government official. The name of a White House staff member has been mentioned as a possible victim. If successful, the plotters would demand an end to United States bombing operations in Southeast Asia and the release of all political prisoners as ransom. Intensive investigation is being conducted concerning this matter.

militants—"Cool it or else!" J. Edgar has not been chary about playing God from time to time, as both citizen and President have discovered. " 'Justice is mine. I will repay,' saith the Lord." He gets his way with a kind of ruthless ease. He convicts us without trial, leaves us with no effective way to respond, and issues the manifesto that those responsible for present terror will be responsible also for future justice. If there is to be any justice. "Doubt not, question not. Only have faith!"

My first reaction is, "Oh, no! I'm never gonna get out of this joint." But the second is, "Theirs won't be the last word. Neither will mine. We'll grit it through in the darkness and see what the Lord disposes."

December 1970

Somebody once wisely wrote that temptations tell us where we are—they fit the quality of one's life.

I recall the Lord's temptations before He began his public ministry; they encouraged Him to materialism, presumption, and tangible power. At the end, as He hung dying, the temptations were far more fundamental and far more threatening. They assaulted His faith, causing Him agony far surpassing physical torture ("My God, why have you abandoned Me?"). One wonders what He could have hoped for at that point, with his faith so besieged.

On an infinitely lesser scale Dan and I experience temptations against faith and hope. How could it be otherwise? Apart from the loneliness of the position we have taken, which is shared by only a handful in jail or in jeopardy, there is the radical sickness of unfaith. (It is not that other ages believed better; it is that ours may not survive unless its belief in God comes to life through belief in itself.) But faith is nonetheless pecked away by a rhetoric that has no life, and by spurious pietisms, and by the various hypocrisies of expedient religion and churches.

And one's hopes suffer proportionately—disappointment, loss, early and late death. One begins by hoping in one's country, until one discovers that nation-states are cruel and empires conspiratorial. One hopes in the Church, until one discovers—by the very simple yardstick of performance—that the Church is neither Christian nor Church. One hopes in the Movement until one discovers that Americanism more than human concern rules the Movement. Finally one rests one's hopes in people, or a tiny number of them. There hope rests and becomes real.

Faith allows for survival. But against faith are ranged three insidious accommodations (enemies)—weariness, slackening fervor and incipient neutrality. People die needlessly, and one becomes used to it and outrage weakens. It is not so much that one can stomach quitting. It is rather that a genius develops for tolerating injustice as a personal and social constant, as present as hangovers and smog.

Official crime no longer outrages me as it once did. No longer do I think, speak, write, and act at white heat, incandescent over the immorality, stupidity, viciousness, inhumanity of American power. Does this indicate exhaustion, boredom, mellowing or wisdom? Does it suggest one or the other, some or all? I don't know.

Now the administration justifies widening the war by charging mistreatment of American captives by the North Vietnamese. The tactic, crude and devious, proves one thing—we intend to win in Indochina, we will remain, and we intend to lie and bully as may be required of us.

The duplicity is so patent and cumbersome (we have never lied with the flair and cleverness of the British), but so often endured that I find myself yawning and enervated. After all, what could be more stupid, insipid, gross than lying about the deaths of thousands of innocent victims? It gets to be such a damn bore, so appalling. It numbs one.

The numbness frightens me. It implies a blunting of sensibility and a weakening of resolve. It means getting used to the lies of others, getting used to lying to oneself. To slacken resistance would be to lose a grasp on one's tools and one's life. It would mean that death is winning and that life is losing.

Today, as more and more indictments come down and more militants go into exile, underground, or to jail, people question whether the revolutionary spirit can be sustained. Most conclude that it cannot. I am suspicious of that answer, but I have, God knows, no evidence that resistance can endure.

Yet I do cling to this: faith accepts God as the source and sovereign of life. And Christ as the model and donor of life. "Even as the Father is Himself the source of life, in the same way He has made His Son to be the source of life." Life and revolution, therefore, might very well mean that we place less confidence in our own experience and more in God's. "Our human duty is not to interpret or to cast light on the rhythm of God's march, but to adjust the rhythm of our small and fleeting life to his" (Kazantzakis). John the Baptist had it precisely right, in referring as he did to Christ: "He must become more important, while I become less important."

December 1970

A vacuum of a week here. But outside, controversy over us erupts. Congressman [William] Anderson extols us in a speech to the National Council of Churches, and Vice-President Agnew accuses him of political expediency. From loyalty, our friends won't leave us alone; from self-interest, our enemies can't. Astonishingly, we have become a goad to the national conscience —an unwelcome property it can neither accept nor reject. Around us it thrashes with its ambivalence, guilt, and desperate goodwill. Perhaps time is running out or sanity still exists.

Dan and I continue to discover each other. Periodically he hears my confession and I hear his. I learn that he has no fears for himself, but is desolate over me. His anguish is palpable: Why should I have to go it again alone, get chopped up in court, receive another lavish sentence and internment in a maximum-security prison? What rhyme, reason, or justice is there in this? There is none; we both bitterly know this. We question the insanity of official power, so it responds by enveloping us too. Or me alone —with Liz, Eqbal, Neil, Joe, and Tony.

In all likelihood, separation will hit us soon after my conviction; they will have greater cause to break us. And that will be another great pain whose meaning must come from the Cross.

Sister Jogues Egan refuses to testify before a grand jury in Harrisburg and the judge hales her off to jail in York. Her statement is admirably cool and to the point. The provisions of immunity, she claims, are unconstitutional, and the FBI has illegally gained information from phone taps in convents in New York City and in Rome, at her Order's Provincial Headquarters, and at its Generalate. Finally, she expresses obedience to a higher court than one of the United States.

Christmas 1970

A few weeks ago I had a long and intense discussion with a Canadian in my dormitory who was offended by something he had read: "Most, if not all, white Americans are racists!" He disagreed very vehemently, but when I told him that I agreed with the statement, he asked me if I was a racist. His question floored me; I had to think about it. Finally I said, "Yes I am." As I would have to answer to a parallel question, "No, I'm not a Christian!" (I'm trying to become one. Just as I'm trying to become a man.)

Theologians speculate, largely in vain, about the post-Christian state of the West. Or, with less reason, of the world. Their smugness prevents them from admitting that, in any real sense, Christ was the last Christian, and that mankind became post-Christian at His ascent to the Father. Numbers have nothing to do with the assertion—even a billion Christians. They merely demonstrate the human faculty for deviousness about Christ's meaning and their own. And so the most misunderstood words in nearly all languages and cultures—particularly Christian ones—are "freedom" and "love."

What will Christmas mean to Christians this year? Probably what

84

it has meant before. A mysterious, almost magical peace will seize us, partially suspending our intrigues and furies. The season casts a spell of sorts, declares a moratorium on the perverted energies of man, causes a euphoric release from guilt and unfounded hopes, and strengthens the sentimentalism in believer and nonbeliever alike—for hours, a day or two, for a week. Then normalcy resumes as we return to our chief tasks of cheating, alienating and destroying one another. We stamp our own inverted meaning on Dietrich Bonhoeffer's phrase "One must live in the world as though God did not exist." Or as though Christ had never come.

December 1970

Dan and I are brothers, priests, convicted felons, and—in J. Edgar Hoover's estimation at least—co-conspirators from jail against the United States government. It's a heavy trip that we're into—to the extent that taking it for granted could become a most tragic mistake. Our relationship has to be worked at.

Our fortunes within both Church and State have taken us on different, if parallel, roads. We have our respective religious societies and have been deeply engaged in their work—Dan's has been generally educational, my work has been involved with blacks. Circumstances have taken us to different parts of the country—Dan literally around the world. But more and more the parallel roads converge in the struggle for peace. Whatever the roads, they have led to federal prison, and it is unlikely that they will ever again separate.

Unquestionably we helped each other to prison. Most likely we will help each other to stay, or return again, or risk another jeopardy. Our lives have now assumed a determinism that is at once rigid and fully free. According to our lights, strength, or grace, we may not turn back, and that means pushing even further the limits of freedom. Who knows?—we might even become free enough to be killed for it. The thought no longer disturbs us.

Much history is woven into our relationship. Dan is my older brother, the first son to enter religious life, and as such, according to a certain traditional Catholicism, the first son to find himself clearly and irrevocably. He had made a commitment to God and to man, and the nature of that commitment seemed to exclude retraction. The rest of us, two younger as well as the three older brothers, played with our vocation, whether it was to be war, marriage, raising families. Dan had found his identity early while we were searching for ours.

This made his influence upon us, especially on the two younger boys, enormous from the start. Moreover, to commitment he added talent—a balanced and acute mind, incisive humor, deep scholarship, varied experience, stunning literary gifts, love of the Gospel and the poor, a horror of falsehood and violence and injustice. For his five brothers, themselves hearty, stubborn, altruistic, he cut an impressive figure, one worthy of choice—for or against.

Erikson* writes the following about Gandhi's tie to his father: "It is in fact rather probable that a highly uncommon man experiences filial conflicts with such mortal intensity just because he already senses in himself early in childhood some kind of originality that seems to point beyond competition with the personal father. Often also, an especially early and exacting conscience development makes him feel (and appear) old while still young and maybe even older in single-mindedness than his conformist parents, who in turn may treat him somewhat as a potential redeemer. Thus he grows up almost with an obligation beset with guilt, to surpass and to create at all cost."

Elements of this apply to our family's relationships with Dan, and particularly my own. Without great pain, with minimal guilt and frustration, I had coolly analyzed our father and found him wanting—a man whose charm, energy and power were shockingly nullified by a kind of neurotic sentimentality, pique, and egotism. I simply concluded that he could not help me, and while maintaining a kind note of filial piety, I nonetheless turned to others— my mother and my older brothers especially. They made more sense, for they had something to teach me.

* *Gandhi's Truth*, W. W. Norton Co.

When Dan entered the Jesuits, he quickly superseded everyone else in the family in impact, becoming in fact a substitute father. It is impossible to explain in detail why this became so for me especially. I was searching for ideals and direction, and he supplied them. His life struck me as eminently worthwhile; it had a warm and lofty quality about it, yet it was not so remote as to be inimitable. I held him in awe, in the sense that the more I faced him, the more I had to face myself. The gap in quality between our two lives was so wide as to be intolerable. I could not endure myself and do nothing about myself.

After the army I entered training for the priesthood, the best formula we Catholics were familiar with for sacrifice, service, self-perfection. Moreover, Dan had tried it—and look at the man he had become!

No need to retread the ground walked on since. We have learned, I suppose, that following the Man of Calvary was more than we bargained for. We learned eventually that personal or institutionalized virtue was sterile unless applied in public; and on the other hand, that death to self was vain and pompous unless it invited ridicule, risk, prison, death itself. In sum, we learned that the virtuous man was also a public servant who articulated the fact that one might have to die for others in order to live.

Dan had rare talents to help him with such conclusions. Though an academician, he did not fall into the trap of academia; he did not teach one set of values and live another, and he was Socratic enough, or Christian enough, to insist that teaching and living were one experience and one obligation. His other talents—writing, speaking, organizing—remained consistent with one theme: one did what one thought and said. I saw him giving wholehearted affirmation to Gandhi's "God never appears to you in person, but always in action."

As for myself, one factor contrived to save me from clericalism, or the type of forlorn schizophrenia that most clerics live. I lived with black people. I could not turn away from the abuse done them in history, and in spite of that, the beauty they retained, without self-contempt or even self-damnation. And as I tried to confront

the accretions of privilege that supremicist whiteness had burdened me with, I discovered this: The state of white America is
such that we were compelled to have our niggers all over the
world. And that defined the American Empire as well as I knew
how to do it.

This led to peace/war issues—issues of the nuclear-arms
race, the Cold War, and inevitably Vietnam. It led me to the
knowledge that the great American experiment was not an experiment at all but rather a brutal, calculated enterprise, as bleak and
unfeeling as the change in one's pocket. There lay the core of
our problem—the conviction that our relationships to God, to nature, and to neighbor had been reduced to a disgusting matter
of "business." More than that, we Americans had stubbornly set
about proving this, staking our billions, our laboratories, our young
men, our "sacred honor" to remake reality as we wished it—a
disgusting matter of business.

Black people taught me this, they and their brothers in Vietnam.
And my own blood brother did too—by giving his time, love, and
understanding. I never found him wanting; never did an occasion
arise when he didn't offer help generously as requested (or as
perhaps altered by his own acute grasp).

I began to organize in Baltimore against the war, following
the slow, arduous course, mounting protest as government, goodwill, and credibility were found more and more wanting. I followed
a simple formula: as Washington escalated the war, I knew that
peace people must escalate protest. I felt that they should bear
the main burden of the war—not the Vietnamese, nor the American GIs (more and more of whom were coming home dead, in-
jured, embittered, deranged). I still feel this, even while better
understanding the Movement's incapacity for doing so.

Of the two of us I went into civil disobedience first, believing
it to be a moral, political, even legal duty. (A democracy worthy
of the name will, under certain conditions of misrepresentation
and voicelessness in the people, sanction civil disobedience as
essential to the health of the republic, as literally the only measure for an equitable redistribution of power short of violent
revolution.) Dan, concentrating on campus resistance and the

wider education of audiences, came later to civil disobedience. His is a more complex and far-ranging mind, presenting him with more questions than my own. In any event, Catonsville had brought his search to an end, or had begun it in a far more radical way.

When I arrived from Lewisburg to join Dan here at Danbury it had meant building a relationship quite new and quite strange for both of us. He had arrived fresh from his nearly unqualified success in the underground, where he had repeatedly scored in favor of resistance and against the FBI. He had had four months of playing underground fox to the FBI hounds, repeatedly revealing their gumshoe ineptitude by moving about confidently, scoring from media and pulpit appearances—an audacious, hopeful figure to many apprehensive people. I had arrived fresh from two weeks of fasting in solitary that had climaxed a bitter struggle with official-dom at the penitentiary. I think it is true to say that we both found this compound more like a reform school than a prison, with a quasi-permissive, mediocre staff, and a population so mixed and short-termed that it appeared at first nearly impossible to work with.

And four months' work did pass with discouraging slowness, if one compares it with work outside. Yet a great deal happened, in spite of our critical views of our accomplishments. We had initiated our First Amendment suit against the federal government; we had begun a class in humanism and political science; we had invested many hours in counseling and in friendship. Finally, we had clarified what we are to each other, coming to a level of understanding previously elusive.

I confess to harboring hobgoblins in my mind concerning Dan. As he put it, I had a "younger brother" difficulty with him, and as another friend told him, "You're more dramatic than Phil." Both observations are precise. The early dependency reasserted itself in a totally unexpected way after I had been used to running my own show, used to my own independence and even arrogance. I became adolescently envious and jealous, began to fabricate ambitions and injustices on his part that were quite nonexistent. I accused him of liberalism when he was merely trying to work with possibilities; I accused him of egotism when he was merely trying to be himself; I accused him of center-staging for trying to introduce joy and humor into discussion.

We had it out, very painfully and sorrowfully. He took my generalizations, my ill-conceived and threatening allusions with courage and restraint, though none of it made sense to him, nothing struck him as being indicative of anything but trouble in me. A week later he returned to our talk, asking me to substantiate my accusations. I could not; they seemed mostly a jumble of nitpicking.

I am better now, and I think he is better for that. And the very least, he will have less worry about me. As for my gain, it has been tremendously liberating. I realize better my need to build, and the amount of building needed.

And I understand that in a setting as unnatural as this one, or in fact in any setting, to consider oneself as a psychic and emotional muscleman is the most terrible of delusions. One is vulnerable in the best of communities; how much more so here. Saint Paul used to speak of the necessity of arming oneself with truth, justice, love. He might have added: good humor.

January 1971

It cannot be said that Dan and I had no warning whatsoever of Hoover's awkward and vengeful accusation of November 27. The Beast was giving signs of turning ponderously on critics and naysayers.

Elizabeth, on her visits to Danbury before late November, had told me of intensified federal surveillance and of her suspicions that the Feds would indict her and others for raids in Delaware. Something was appearing on the wind; we were all sniffing for it.

Naturally, before that time Dan and I had discussed events at Lewisburg, just as we had discussed his four months underground. I had told him about Boyd Douglas (the "inmate" who had passed many letters for us and had been a trusted ally) and of our hopes for him. We had gone over the main ideas about citizen's arrest and the tunnel proposal, and I had voiced my reservations about the grandiosity of the first and slackness in the second. Dan had no major objections to either idea, but he shared my misgivings that neither was practical, given our resources.

To be perfectly frank, we had always thought of both these ideas as exploratory—hopeful and necessary, but mere explorations.

Neither of us had caught the news on the evening of November 27, 1970; we had got it secondhand from friends on the compound. As I recall it, the evening was cold and snowy—like our hearts. For purposes of security we walked on the handball courts to discuss Hoover's bombshell. Reasons? (1) The FBI's incapacity to prosecute in the draft-board raids. (2) Dan's impudent and effective underground. (3) Hoover's sagging reputation. They were the best we could think of. I had not dared conclude at that point that Douglas had betrayed us.

William Kunstler appeared the next day—the first of our lawyers. He compared Hoover's fantasy to the Reichstag affair—a setup, an entrapment. I recall that neither of us particularly liked the statement he had prepared and felt the need for more reflection before getting into purple rhetoric. But we felt very grateful to Bill for his appearance. We suggested some revisions to do with the absurdity and spite of Hoover's charges, ending with a put-up or shut-up invitation: prosecute or retract.

A ponderous gloom invaded us. I fought to reconcile myself to the idea of life imprisonment. My experience, however, served me to some extent. I had been boxed in before, to no lasting ill effect. I knew what they could try; but I also suspected that they could not accomplish much against resolute nonviolence.

It took a week to get reconciled to the worst. But lest this appear casual or offhand, I confess that I asked over and over: What will God ask me to do? How many prison years will be required, years of resistance to penal corruption marked by solitary, fasts, the possibility of being shipped from one institution to another?

Others, apparently, had not been asked to do that much, or they had rejected doing anything at all. Thus the reasoning—and the temptations. In the end I banished them and tried to go on.

I remember thinking too, with astonishment, "Wow! They've finally got me!" If they had ever known what some of us had done, it would be all up with us. But now they know. And there's nothing quite like their anger and vengefulness in knowing; prima donnas at heart, they rage like rejected mistresses.

And then, I thought of the others. Thanks to me, they were in deep trouble. However I, because there had been letters written and received, might excuse myself, however they might excuse me, however people might rally to my defense, the fact is that I had been guilty of imprudences and shallow judgment, had asked for concern and services that few would have had the arrogance to expect—information on the Movement, requests for advice and speculation, etc., etc. I had no rational or justifiable right to risk myself, let alone them. I had written out of my own need.

January 19

The reality of the indictment is now a week old, and most of the novelty and some of the shock have worn off.* So

* On January 12, 1971, the Justice Department made public an eleven-page indictment that, according to its press release, named the Reverend Philip Berrigan and five others as having plotted "to blow up the heating system of Federal buildings in the Nation's capital and also to kidnap Presidential Advisor Henry Kissinger. . . ." The five others arrested were the Reverend Joseph Wenderoth, the Reverend Neil R. McLaughlin, Sister Elizabeth McAlister, Anthony Scoblick and Professor Eqbal Ahmad. Listed as co-conspirators were Father Daniel Berrigan, Sister Jogues Egan, Sister Beverly Bell, Marjorie A. Sherman, a former nun, Paul Mayer, a married priest, William Davidon, a physics professor at Haverford College, and Thomas Davidson, a conscientious resister and peace activist.

Aside from the seven counts, which included conspiracy to obtain maps and diagrams of the tunnels under Washington, D.C., government buildings, they were charged with conspiracy to "seize, kidnap, abduct and carry away . . . Kissinger . . ." Conviction on the kidnap conspiracy was punishable by life imprisonment; the general conspiracy charges carried five years' maximum imprisonment. In addition, Sister Elizabeth McAlister and Father Philip Berrigan were charged with three attempts to smuggle correspondence in and out of Lewisburg Prison, where Berrigan had been an inmate. Each of these charges carried a maximum ten years' punishment.

ﬄ

has the tendency to fantasize about victory in the courtroom, about defeat to the government, about new breakthroughs into peace that would begin with our trial.

First, the shock—a kind of mental and emotional numbness. I had already felt the government's vindictiveness—the preposterous sentence of six years for the Baltimore Four action, interminable from many points of view. Now this indictment seems like God answering an appeal from hell with "Continue until expiration!"

There is no panic; I have long ago learned the extravagance of that. But reason tells me that between the government and myself there is a one-sided vendetta, and that I must face the possibility that for a long time my dialogue with power is to be from behind bars.

My faith bears me up—or what I like to call my faith for want of a better name. I realize that when push comes to shove with Christ, no one but He defines the Cross or predicts its outcome. At this point one accepts or not, because to insist on meaning where none is possible amounts to rejection of Him. One obeys. Though the command comes from a silent Lord and Brother, He is worthy of far more trust than I can ever give him.

Anyhow, fantasy accompanied the shock, because the numbness required a hyperactivity of the mind as complement. For several nights I could not sleep; my being required a purge, a release of everything trapped within. My mind raced at precarious speed, anticipating frantically the courtroom struggle still months away. Hope *had* to be created, for I was fighting my way back from a kind of despair. And despair, if acute enough, can impair sanity.

And so an ego trip ensued, amusing upon recollection, yet apparently necessary at the time. I reviewed facts mastered years before, all but forgotten, and expounded them—facts about the Vietnam war, the arms race, imperialist economics, military carpetbagging; moral arguments from Jesus to Aquinas to Gandhi; legal points drawn from the Constitution, from international law, from Nuremberg. Through it all, my moral offensive was invincible, my geopolitical analysis devastating, my logic lucid, my subtleties and humor embarrassing to prosecutor and judge alike.

In the end, before I could fall asleep, vindication would come for my friends; hope and vigor for the Movement; pause for the government. The government would have learned caution—not a moral lesson, but some version of modus vivendi, because upright and strong resistance is *not* to be dealt with hastily, *not* to be steamrolled, *not* to be cast aside arbitrarily. A great lesson for power. Then I could sleep.

It was a fantasy, but a salutary one, which drained the unreality of hate and resentment from me, and was therefore beneficial to sanity and survival.

I have a card on my wall, its message brave and fanciful, much like my hallucinations. "For sure the hour for which we yearn shall yet arrive, and our marching steps will thunder: WE SURVIVE!"

January 27

Another momentous day. I receive a detainer from the U.S. Marshal's office in New Haven—the government's oblique way of announcing its new charges—and I learn that my custody has been tightened from "medium" to "closed." I have once more incurred Big Brother's displeasure. One would have thought that being here indicated the lowest common denominator. On the contrary, there are doghouses lower yet—and if there aren't, Big Brother will build some.

Harrisburg, February 1971

The marshals plucked me out on a Sunday morning; I was feeling weak and miserable with a persistent cold that had hung on grimly against all remedy. Three of us, two black guys and I, stuffed ourselves into the rear seat of a new Buick

Riviera. None of us was that huge, but crated chickens have more room. The car must have cost $4,500—making our transportation very expensive indeed. As well as very uncomfortable.

I checked the appointments as we rode; nearly everything was extravagant and delusory. These incredibly complicated, dangerous, superficial, tranquilizing tin projectiles, plus fuel and pavement, are the core of domestic prosperity. People talk about lockups. Here's one for you, and a national hobby at that.

En route I ask the marshals about my fate, since I hope for meetings with defendants and lawyers. They put me off airily. "These guys [the blacks] go to Lewisburg. We gotta get more orders about you."

I don't believe them. An escort of state cops picks us up as we cross into New York. A depressing thought occurs to me: there is always enough money for more cops, abroad or at home. And for their hardware. Will we yet see the day when America will turn against itself, one man watching another, all in the interests of justice, freedom, and peace? Luke wrote: "From now on a family of five will be divided, three against two, two against three."

We cross into Pennsylvania, pick up new cops to replace the old. And the marshals give me a laconic message. "We're puttin' you in the town jail in Bloomsburg [Pennsylvania]. We'll take these guys to Lewisburg, and then come back. Takin' you down to Harrisburg in the morning."

So it was. The Bloomsburg town jail resembled something prepared to frustrate the British in 1812—massive limestone walls, battlements and turrets. Yet within, everything was oddly cheerful and bright, an exception to county jails. Without ceremony, the sheriff took me to the second floor and locked me into a spacious, clean room with bath.

I begin to get some control on the cold with the help of penicillin. Sleep and a little exercise help. Ultimately, I suppose, the body's own defenses must be prodded to fight off the invading bugs.

They rout me out at five the next morning, and we start for Harrisburg in heavy snow. Another car of marshals joins us. Three cars now—federal and state cooperation. The plan is to whisk me into the Federal Building in Harrisburg before newsmen or sympathizers can arrive.

Locked in the marshal's cage, I have time to ruminate on the facile manipulations of which power is capable. Seeing it operate —seeing its men, muscle, weapons, money, machines; seeing its awesome apparatus—one can wonder how it ever can be changed, humanized, restructured. One consoling thought: Bureaucracies are like unpicked fruit—they get ripe, rotten, and finally die. Essentially the national bureaucracy is already dead; the husk just hasn't gotten that chilling message.

Our lawyers come, led by Kunstler the Irrepressible. The judge will receive them in moments, they will request a postponement of the arraignment, so the defendants can meet first.

The lawyers leave, and marshals lock me up again. I have an hour to reflect on the prospect of meeting the "defendants." Overwhelming. Eqbal Ahmad I had seen over the holidays with Sister Elizabeth and Sister Jogues. Tony Scoblick and I have not met in nearly eleven months. My last sight of the two Baltimore priests Neil McLaughlin and Joe Wenderoth had been at Lewisburg in August, just before my transfer to Danbury. But since official wrath has come upon us, no communication, oral or written.

The marshals unlock me; my friends have arrived. For a time we are like kids with unexpected presents. Our joy is unrestrained, we are silly and quite incoherent. A grimmer reality. I discover from my friends, who have the opinion of informed and alarmed friends, that the government from the White House down is committed to our conviction. If such a threat extends to us, it must be leveled against all who question the criminality of the arms race, the Indochinese wars, the whole record of our brutality, waste, and ineptitudes.

In this setting, civil liberties may be a larger issue than ordinarily argued—life and death. The oppressors are gambling for something rare and almost unprecedented—thought control. Already they have seized on body control through the domestic police apparatus of courts and jails. And word control too; those who join rhetoric with action, those who suggest that analysis leads to resistance, are speedily crushed. Now, through human and mechanical informers, the powers seek to smoke out those who indulge in the treachery of rebellious thought.

Our press statement attempts to deal with the issue: "Throughout history, citizens of conscience have engaged in discussions as to how to oppose the overwhelming power of unjust governments. In such discussions, the problems of violence and nonviolence have been aired, and an infinite variety of strategies and tactics examined, accepted, or rejected. Such discussion is part of the tradition of free speech in a democratic society, protected by the First Amendment. When our government moves against some citizens through wiretapping, secret agents, and conspiracy laws to turn this constitutional right into a crime, free expression is endangered for all Americans."

More and more Americans sense or realize that the government has "brought the war home," that it is prepared to war against its own people. Its mandarins intend to have their own way. And they intend to employ power as they have gained it —ruthlessly.

Americans, though not their leaders, are becoming afraid of murder. The society smells like a gas chamber. One cultivates a nose for death. What to do about it, however, is a different matter. (Here, perhaps, death takes its greatest toll.) The psychology of death is nearly pervasive. Americans despair of doing anything about it, for compromise (as complicity) has stunted our capacity to reject the death we are asked to endorse.

Some have tried. Increasingly the young refuse to fight— though the poor have less choice; and a majority of Americans say they favor unilateral withdrawal from Vietnam. Still the mood is despairing and feeble. Anthony Lewis put the case well (*New York Times,* February 13, 1971): "The relative silence that has greeted this latest non-expansion [into Laos] is not a silence of approval. It is a silence of despair. What else is there to do but despair if one does not believe in revolution, when peaceful

assembly and the democratic process and protest and polls showing an overwhelming public desire to get out of Indochina uncon-
ditionally produce no political result?"

We get to more immediate concerns, the need for decision on a
legal team. Almost without exception, people are opposed to the
inclusion of Bill Kunstler as a trial lawyer. They fear his so-
called flamboyance, his Chicago Seven image, his melodramatic
performances in the courtroom. If the imperative is to win, one
does not unnecessarily endanger one's case with a political
liability like Kunstler: so the arguments go. All defendants agree,
except me.

I imply no criticism of five friends here. They, however, have no
friendship with Kunstler, and I do. They have less acquaintance
with his courage than I, less evidence of his love for people.
(Several members of the Chicago Seven have not yet recuperated
from that exhausting and brutal trial, while Kunstler hardly broke
stride over it.) Dan and I have seen more of his ego than they, but
also much more of his love.

Both Dan and I wanted him for the following reasons: (1) His
exceptional service to the Movement, matched by no one American lawyer, save Charles Garry perhaps. (2) Our confidence that
he could help us counter this grotesque indictment with a creative,
radical defense. (3) Our friendship with Bill and love for him,
stemming from his defense of us at Catonsville, and even before.
We feel these considerations far outweighed misgivings about
Bill—concerning public reaction to his flamboyance, his casual
attitude toward trial preparation, his inability to fit into a legal
team, his tendency to relish publicity. Furthermore, we resented
the opposition to Kunstler generated by the lawyers who were already on the defense team, and by the liberal marginals. From our
standpoint, it was the right of the defendants to decide on Bill—
without outside interference or advice.

Our position was apparently not practical. The defendants,
harried by a multitude of personal and external pressures and
bombarded by the advice of lawyers and intimates, decided
against Bill. At several meetings Dan and I had fought long and
strenuously—first, for the inclusion of Bill as a trial lawyer; and

when we failed to accomplish that, for a compromise position for him as legal coordinator, or as legal liaison with the press. We pushed the last with sad hearts, knowing it was an implicit insult.

Bill took it with admirable grace. On the one hand, he never relaxed his insistence on inclusion as major counsel; on the other, he never pushed himself to the point of exasperating us or compounding our difficulties. At one point he said, "You must speak for yourselves. Your experiences are your lives, and lawyers can't tell about them."

Going to the dock from jail had got to be an immensely arduous and draining experience, as I had discovered at Catonsville. Second, how could we possibly gain a collective decision on the matter—having committed ourselves previously to majority decision? Third, the case revolved around Sister Elizabeth and myself; she had good reasons for opposing a defense that would separate us during the trial. Fourth, could we win support from the legal team, which already possessed widespread influence over our decision-making? By a majority, the defendants decided to accede to a legal mentality, which doomed Kunstler's offer.

Despite these practicalities, Kunstler was right morally and politically. If this war is criminal, and the government that sponsors it is illegitimate, then government courts should be resisted, and indictments like ours confronted as savage lies. So goes the abstract politics of the case; but the human politics is sometimes less bright and brave.

I take some satisfaction and hope from the belief that the defendants did the best possible under the circumstances. We could have done much better; we could also have done infinitely worse.

February 1971

Still, we talk rationally and lovingly, we six. It is normal for us to be together again, given the times and their unutterable tragedy. In a sense, the dead will it, even as the living require it. That says enough about God's will.

We go to the arraignment. The judge is conciliatory and tense. Poor man, perhaps he senses that the pompous, archaic chant of a bailiff is insufficient to guarantee his legitimacy.

The marshals lead me back to Dauphin County Jail, on the outskirts of Harrisburg, for a supper of macaroni and tomatoes and a cup of Kool-Aid. Then a bed in the corridor of a cell block; no room in the inn. At best, American jails are deplorable. Local jails are usually worse, and prisoners on the road, or waiting, are at their merest mercy.

By a concession, we meet once again in the marshal's office in the Federal Building. I begin to get the feel of our predicament and of our opportunities. One point strikes me as ominous, and this feeling grows. The government's case is weak unto death. Is the government ignorant of that fact? Hardly. What then? We agree that the indictment rests totally upon Douglas, the informer from Lewisburg. Given that assumption, and given his lies, what must the government do to prop him up? Other informers may be brought forward, even more contrived than he.

The marshals end our discussions at 3 P.M. Back to the county jail. What about return to Danbury? I can get nothing definite from them. For reasons of security or whim, they remain vague.

We have a cozy chat. I tell them of my disillusionment with county jails; I'm prepared to have my lawyer issue a press statement about mistreatment; I will back up my convictions with a fast until I am moved to Connecticut.

I have touched tender sensibilities in the chief marshal. In a humane gesture toward the human revolution, he promises a quick trip on the morrow. He also promises that the warden will give me a cell.

He is true to both his promises; we leave for Connecticut in the morning. I enjoy the ride thoroughly, in spite of bleak and wintry scenery. But our marshals get lost in New Jersey. For all their traveling, they seem oddly casual about planning and efficiency. I suspect that their attitude has something to do with years of stalls, wrong turns, detours. Bureaucrats, for all their love of the bureaucracy, for all the horror they feel at attacks upon it, are noneless intent upon beating it. So life becomes a simple formula: minimum service, survival politics, maximum take.

Friends here welcome me back with genuine greetings and real questions. They recognize the government's put-on, but at the same time realize our real danger. They worry about me and offer to help.

They have helped just by asking. The loneliness becomes less acute and the air less rarefied.

Danbury, March 1971

Since arraignment in Harrisburg, the government has given us enough cooperation to make us thoroughly suspicious. It has lowered bail, relaxed travel restrictions, and given us comfortable meeting space here. What does all this signify? A weak case perhaps, a stealthy attempt to make us careless and unwary, to set us up. Or maybe they want to cooperate. Cooperation costs them nothing, and it may gain them critical information —if we're that foolish.

Eqbal, Liz, Neil, Joe, and Tony arrived yesterday with Bill Bender, one of our lawyers, and today again with Bill Kunstler.

Some days before, Liz and Eqbal had seen [former Attorney General] Ramsey Clark and had left with the impression that Clark sees the case far differently from the way we do. Apart from the problem we all have with his liberal politics, we would have further problems with accepting him (as we thought he saw himself) as the central figure and strategist at the trial.*

Nonetheless his generosity (no fees) struck us, plus his political courage (perhaps sacrificing whatever presidential aspirations he may have for 1972). But does he have humility and

---

* As Attorney General, Clark prosecuted Benjamin Spock, Marc Raskin, among others, also the Milwaukee Fourteen. He had also prosecuted Philip Berrigan twice as a result of the Baltimore Four and Catonsville Nine draft actions. Since Father Berrigan had stood for trial, Clark of course had had no choice as a government prosecutor.

flexibility? Can a man of his family, prominence, and reputation forget his own interests and favor ours? Can he say, "I'm here for you people—to lift your jeopardy, to communicate your issues, to resist with you"?

At about the same time Neil, Joe, and Tony had interviewed Paul O'Dwyer. O'Dwyer, a New York trial lawyer of competence and passionate reputation, had impressed them far more than Clark had the others. Mainly, the difference lay with politics. O'Dwyer, it appears, has seen something different in the Beast's entrails. He sees terminal cancer; Clark calls it indigestion.

Whoever joins with us must also join with what we aim for in this trial. We aim to call attention to the real conspiracies: conspiracies to ruin this country through neglect; to suppress legitimate aspirations and human rights; to continue the institutionalization of greed, racism, and war; to terrorize the world with war crimes, crimes against peace and crimes against humanity (genocide).

We want to clarify the realities of government repression, contempt for civil liberties, determination to suspend rights once they become troublesome. We aim to prove invasion of privacy and private communication, and the use of human and mechanical informers to threaten a people already subdued and passive.

We intend to suggest that the real criminals are not in this dock but in Washington, in the Pentagon, on the boards of the multinational corporations, all of which are war manufacturers.

Maybe Harrisburg can become the first of several national Nurembergs to answer the questions: Whose law is broken? And by whom?

March 1971

Clark surprised us with a visit. We hadn't expected him. The guard let him in; he came toward us quietly and a trifle self-consciously. His lack of ostentation impressed me, his sobersides Texas manner reminded me of my years in the South and the earnest "red-necks" I knew there.

He is a big man, well over six feet, lean and erect, with a tired puffiness of face that comes from too much work and too little sleep. A shuttle from Washington, a car at La Guardia; he had come alone, no fanfare, no entourage.

One of our lawyers briefed him on where we stood. (I should more properly say, where the lawyers stood, since every meeting but a couple have so far been legal meetings, at which we, the defendants, have been a privileged audience.) Lawyers are like water, always seeking their own level. They are inflated, pompous, and, in political cases, frequently useless.

It is only fair to add that we had our prejudices, or our realisms, with regard to Mr. Ramsey Clark. But here he was, at our service. He began by rejecting any intention of vendetta with Hoover if he were to enter the case. Then he began a monologue on truth, which I found extremely interesting in light of backgrounds and circumstances. "You must believe in your truth," he said, "even as I must believe in it. . . . Our objective in this trial must be the truth; the American people must know the truth. You serve people best by giving them the truth. I'm a believer in facts, because without them the truth cannot come out." And so on. As a discourse it was impressive—not for its content, but because the man so obviously believed in what he said.

He asserted that our object in this trial must be acquittal. But acquittal, with the Justice Department emotionally and tactically committed to conviction, would be a massive job, requiring exhaustive investigation and deft coordination. An energetic and competent lawyer had to pull things together, had to know everything about the over-all human and legal picture.

Rumor had it that he saw himself as coordinator and strategist. We asked him if he would serve with others. He answered, "Most assuredly!" I inquired about available time, since friends of his had reputedly already opened campaign offices for him for '72. He admitted that he was busy; nonetheless he would devote to the case whatever it required. We told him of the controversy over Bill Kunstler's presence on the legal staff. "Do you object to working with Kunstler?" we inquired. "No, I do not!"

We found him honest, attentive, strong. He suggested one or

two young legal investigators, men who had worked with him on civil rights cases. They would, he said, be glad to work for us, and possibly undertake the coordination of the case as well. We shook hands at parting. He told Dan and me "God bless you," and left.

At this point I would favor taking him on. One cannot underestimate the weight he would bring to our defense or the experience and dignity he would lend to the proceedings. Such would be my hopes. But the decision is not mine entirely.

Daily our "affair" becomes more mysterious, bizarre, hilarious, tragic. Contradictions abound, and we, along with our friends, are becoming signs of contradiction. The men of power cannot leave us alone, liberals are at once fascinated and repelled, there is a scramble on all fronts to take sides.

Somebody remarked, "It's because there's nothing else happening!" True! And if one strives to imitate the Lord, one necessarily becomes a sign of contradiction.

First Sunday of Lent 1971

Sometimes I write simply to gain fortitude. Writing helps me grip reality and sanity a little more firmly. Perhaps that's all fortitude is—a tenacious grip on sanity.

It has both a rational and a faithful aspect to it. Reason asserts that life is conflict and that one becomes most alive in nonviolent struggle *for* life and *against* death, *for* man and *against* his debasement. Faith asserts that Christ is Man because He was first God, and that in Him humanity becomes possible. A professor of theology might put it that way. But I need to relate to experience. I am into my eighteenth month of jail, with recent confirmation of a six-year sentence overriding an appeal in Richmond. As further proof that my leaders love me, there is the prospect of indefinite sentence, perhaps life imprisonment, if I am convicted at Harrisburg this fall.

So I submit to myself that it is one thing to know in one's head the ponderous vindictiveness of federal justice and another to live with it year upon year behind bars. Periodically my whole being rebels against such a present and such a future. I vomit it up emotionally and psychologically, trying desperately to swallow my nausea of spirit. I need to think that our technocrats enjoy only tenuous control (despite the evidence).

Today is the first Sunday of Lent. Lent recalls a number of happenings from sacred history: the forty days Moses spent preparing himself for the Law; the long Jewish exile in the desert; Christ's prayer and fasting before His temptations. And above all, Lent gives life to the grandeur and portent of Christ's prophecy. As Luke writes: "We are now going up to Jerusalem; and all that is written by the prophets will come true for the Son of Man. He will be handed over to the foreign power. He will be mocked, maltreated, and spat upon. They will flog him and kill him."

A question seldom squarely met (Americans, Christian or not, have perfected a facility for avoiding difficult questions): What does "going up to Jerusalem" mean today? And what of another passage, this time from Matthew: "This very night all of you will run away and leave me, for the scripture says, 'God will kill the shepherd and the sheep of the flock will be scattered.' "

Most Christians say they will travel on request, and most will promise, like the disciples, to be there when the heat comes down. But "being there" must mean some defense of others, some loving risk for life, some purposeful tragedy like His, some death like His.

I take it that what Christ had in mind was that we be human, even as He was. But how does one act like a human—and not like a lemming—when mankind faces extinction, when there is a scarcity of humans? When one's country is the planet's Public Enemy Number One?

Common sense tells me (so does faith) that word and act are only human when they are one, that "mystique" is also "politique" (to borrow Charles Péguy's phrase). Common sense tells me that the profession of life is an unalterable resistance to the high and mighty, who pose as patrons of man while they destroy him. Resistance, common sense reminds me, is essential. Without it one cannot realize humanity in oneself or in others, only illusion, euphoria, comfort, escape.

Resistance will outrage the high and mighty, who tolerate such convictions neither from Christ nor from any of us. Dissent they will ridicule smugly; impetuosity or passion is forgivable—at least the first time. If contrition is not forthcoming, however, an apparatus more frightening than ridicule is trucked out—indictments, exorbitant bail, arraignment, collusion between prosecution and bench (conspiracy of common interest), an automatic conviction, punitive sentencing. If dissent remains inflexible and unsubmissive, the power will invade even the penitentiary—monitoring rebellious thoughts and words, presenting the wretched rebel with new charges, new courts, new trials, new convictions, new sentences. In this setting Jerusalem becomes Atlanta, Leavenworth, Lewisburg; and Calvary becomes a permanent cell. And from these places one makes whatever resurrection one can.

A somber view? Perhaps. Or is the somberness built into the society? Whichever, most of us will probably see worse days before better. And a few will see the worse days from a prison cell.

So, we *do* have the naked character of American power to deal with, and we *do* have the Lord's words to offer the relevant questions. "We [the disciples and I]," the Lord says, "are going up to Jerusalem." *But* "He [the Son of Man alone] will be handed over to a foreign power." If "He," why not the disciples as well? Again—is this government automatically *our* government, simply because we are citizens? Can *this* government be anything but a "foreign power" to a Christian? What is more normal for a Christian than to be handed over to a foreign power? Or what is more abnormal for a Christian than a truce with a foreign power, the illegitimate State authority?

So faith tells me. Which is not to say that it is ahead of, or behind, emotions or psyche. They are probably joined together. I perceive it and I labor to respond. Millions of dead Indochinese and Americans have a voiceless request—that we come alive and stop the murder, that we indeed live like humans by living for humans. And if that means rebirth through a prison cell, where life is incubated for succeeding generations—then, right on. How else shall we see the twenty-first century?

"And be on your guard, for men will hand you over to their courts, they will flog you in the synagogues, you will be brought before governors and kings for my sake, to testify before them and the heathen. But when you are arrested . . ."

"And be on your guard. For if you break a war law, or a privilege law, or a money law (they're all money laws), the fuzz will hunt you down and bust you." One gets a response from the Movement similar to that the Lord got from his disciples— not enough. Hearts and guts are not there, not then. Not yet.

Until peace people master fear of themselves and other people they have no hope of creating a movement, much less a revolutionary movement. When one fears himself, he fears others, oppressor and victim alike. Maybe this is why the Lord asks repeatedly, "What are you afraid of?"—implying of course that what you fear isn't there, it's not real. And it's not worthy of you, if you intend to be human.

Or look at it another way. When peacemakers fear dishonesty in their rhetoric more than they fear consequences, their fears will have become human, inspiring a clarity of passion and a style of genuine service. Camus put it well: "What is needed is a grouping of men resolved to speak out clearly and pay up personally."

But in the concrete, one cannot speak about fear without speaking of its focus in the Movement—fear of consequences. Everywhere one turns, in jail or out, with prisoners, with Movement people, with militant clergymen, dove politicians, well-meaning bureaucrats of all denominations and hues, the big question is, "What will it [action] cost me?" Rarely is the question turned around to become, "What will it cost me if I don't act?" The lunacy of present life inspires the question, and usually the answer.

Inmates ask us, "Why did you people at Catonsville stand around for arrest?" Movement people will concede, "Do your thing, stand around or surface later, go to trial if you choose, but don't go to jail!" And political prisoners will admonish, "Don't come to jail, you can't organize here. It's a bore, a waste and a drag."

Incongruous! Inmates, especially recidivists, have infinitely less fear about returning to jail for the same nonsense than returning to jail for political activity; Movement people fail to see that fear of jail neutralizes them far more than jail itself would; and political prisoners organize as little, or as much, in jail as on the streets. To me all three judgments spring from cultural attrition—unrecognized and unresolved. One rests content in the belly of the Beast, and is there digested.

My brother, when he was a "fugitive from injustice," wrote that his aim was to "demythologize the police"—certainly a gallant and deeply needed effort, with Big Brother striving to quiet the restless natives with various innovations. It was, moreover, an endeavor that evoked quick sympathy from harried liberals and militants.

But, by the same token, we must demythologize jail, in spite of the reaction its very mention provokes. For the same attributes that threaten a man with jail are those that can build a movement —historical sense, reasonable risk, communal action, tactical ingenuity. These are the only qualities that are capable of educating others and that can break the slavish manipulation imposed upon the thousands of decent people who must be brought to the struggle.

More concretely, how can the poor be freed (a Movement objective) without sharing the legal jeopardy under which the poor must live (police overkill, repressive courts, indescribable jails)? How can military politics be changed if one does not counterbalance the risk of young GIs who go to possible injury or death for overage death merchants? Above all, how can the bloodshed in Southeast Asia possibly be stopped if one refuses to accept, in some small way, the danger and death faced by the Vietnamese? In every instance, breaking the law, with the possible consequence of jail, does not begin to match the danger lived by those chewed up by domestic and foreign politics.

The Movement ought to divest itself modestly of frantic rhetoric and untimely slogans as a major first step into reality. "Power to the people" is, at this stage, unreal enough to be pathological, simply because there are pitifully few resources around to realize it. "Equal jeopardy" ought to be the substitute, jeopardy equal to that suffered by the poor, by GIs, the Vietnamese, and Third World people—partly because the Movement, too, allows profit, falsehood, and terror to prevail.

March 1971

Of necessity, I've been delving into the idea of conspiracy. I have as much success understanding it as I would trying to understand a mad psychiatrist's casebook. Jurists admit that no definition has really been found. Or if one exists, it could go something like this: a sprawling, elastic legal net, cast to ensnare those innocent of more substantive charges—radicals, political dissenters, organizers of the poor, blacks, Chicanos, Indians, and working classes.

Conspiracy stems from English medieval history and the reign of Edward I. Ironically, early statutes on conspiracy were intended to forestall unjust and malicious prosecutions. If a person was judged innocent before a court of law, those who had wrongfully accused him were subject to a conspiracy indictment. In the seventeenth century the infamous Court of the Star Chamber perverted these statutes from their original intention of the protection of human rights. From 1611 on, the essence of conspiracy has lain in an agreement to commit a crime—not in the performance but in the planning. Clarence Darrow offered an absurd example: If a boy steals candy, it's a misdemeanor; if two boys plan to steal candy but don't do it, it's a felonious conspiracy.

Politically, conspiracy is a tool of pacification, victimizing some dissidents to warn others. The Philadelphia cordwainers case is notorious. In 1806, journeymen shoemakers agreed to strike (withhold their labor from their masters) for better wages. The courts convicted them: a group had *agreed* to use criminal means for criminal ends.

Closer to our time, the government used the Smith Act during the paranoiac McCarthy era to accuse, indict, convict and execute leftists for conspiracies to overthrow it. No act was performed, nor were any plans unearthed; the bewildered and overwhelmingly innocent victims were convicted of conspiring to do something threatening to the national Pharaohs. Even when their convictions were reversed on appeal, they escaped prison on technicalities. The higher courts never faced up to the conspiracy laws themselves.

By way of tragic exception, the Rosenbergs were killed and Morton Sobell served eighteen years of a thirty-year sentence, with no better evidence against them than a flimsy alleged conspiracy. The conspiracy trail is strewn with a few deaths, more imprisonments, and a multitude of broken reputations and ruined lives.

Etymologically, "conspiracy" means "breathing together" or "acting in harmony." In the Christian tradition, it suggests a union of minds and hearts for humane purposes—for contemplation, community, public service, political resistance. It is in this last category that conflict with the State develops. We believe conspiracy to be conscientious; the State believes it to be illegal. We believe conspiracy is a profound duty; the State believes it is rank treason. We believe conspiracy is the ultimate service; the State believes it to be subversion. We believe that without conspiracy the State will destroy itself; the State believes that with conspiracy unchecked, the State will be destroyed. We believe that without conspiracy the State becomes a tyranny; the State believes that with conspiracy, society becomes anarchic and law becomes chaotic.

Obviously the State feels it must monopolize the thinking on conspiracy and stop those who define it differently. Conspiracy is forbidden by the State only to some. The power elite can do what others cannot. The State acts with impunity, and forbids the only defense against *its* conspiracy, the moral conspiracy against its intentions.

While the State bombs Indochina back into the Stone Age, kills people or resettles them by kidnapping, it charges us, my co-defendants and me, with conspiracy to bomb and kidnap.

Where are those who will conspire for life against the State conspiracies of death? Where are those who will brave the State courts to educate gently with their conspiracies and indict the State for its conspiracies? Where are the peace criminals to try the war criminals, the peace conspirators to oppose the war conspirators?

War conspiracies, many of them blossoming into war crimes, are bringing Americans to their senses and perhaps to their knees. A few of the more notorious of the last twenty-five years:

1) President Truman's conspiracy, backed by Secretary of State Byrnes and Secretary of War Stimson, to use atomic weapons on Japanese flesh.

2) The same gentleman's conspiracy, with fervent amens from advisers and scientists, to spawn hydrogen bombs.

3) The conspiracy to risk World War III twice over Berlin, once over Suez, and once over Cuba, under Presidents Eisenhower and Kennedy.

4) The conspiracy to make atomic weapons available to the French during the Indochina war.

5) The conspiracy to assassinate Fidel Castro under President Kennedy.

6) The multiple conspiracies to launch preemptive atomic strikes upon Russia and China by the United States.

7) The conspiracy, later a war crime, to replace the French in the Indochina war.

8) The conspiracy, later a war crime, to spawn bacteriological and chemical weapons, and to employ the latter in Indochina.

9) The conspiracy to develop MIRV and ABM.

10) The conspiracy, later a war crime, to make Indochina the most heavily bombed area in history.

11) The conspiracy to invade Cambodia and to "incurse" upon Laos.

12) The conspiracy (most of us share this crime, of indefinable

proportions and grave culpability) to make America an aggressor empire and a warfare state, a state whose very prosperity is forged by economic and military exploitation.

"A conspiracy is proved often by evidence that is admissible only upon assumption that conspiracy existed" (Justice Robert Jackson).

After the indictment, police tactics degenerated further— grand jury intimidation as a substitute for real investigation, plus furious snooping at Lewisburg by FBI watchdogs. With a case so slender, the FBI must supply the flesh. Our valiant Bureaumen are attempting to make a case against singular noncooperation from the defendants.

The whole debacle argues palpitating egos in high places, pique and vindictiveness, a virulence of self-righteousness that can come only from enormous guilt, and a violent, unattainable desire to wring from dissidents the acquiescence necessary for the stability of the republic.

But another chapter in conspiracy is still to be written. People will breathe together, will act in harmony, will gather against the modern cavemen, whose civilization extends only to a technology of fang and claw. The new conspirators will dispense with the Nixons, Hoovers, Mitchells, Lairds, and Kissingers, not because their malevolence is crafty or resourceful but because their mediocrity is distinct and hence dangerous.*

April 1971

The government's libel concerning their ideas of the relationship between Sister Elizabeth McAlister and myself is not in the least astonishing. It has the vicious consistency of

---

* This was written two years before the revelations of Watergate that revealed a mass of interwoven conspiracies at the highest level of the government to defraud the American people of their right to vote in free elections, and to rob them of their constitutionally guaranteed civil liberties.

all the efforts to fabricate a case against the Harrisburg Six. Now the government brands two of the defendants as charlatans who stealthily denied their religious vows.

Our relationship lies, of course, outside the scope of the indictment against us. So it would seem irrelevant to "answer" such allegations. We have nothing to confess, nothing to deny, no cause for shame. We have done no violence to conscience, nothing to scandalize or injure others, nothing to violate trust in ourselves.

Had we in fact so acted, logic would have dictated that we abandon service and resistance and avoid risk and prison, that we flee the country before my incarceration and become safe spectators.

Pope John once wrote that governments are held to the same morality as individuals. Our lives speak for themselves. We welcome a comparison—by the Church and by the American people.

One is supposed to develop operational rules of thumb in prison, borrowing them from an inner survival kit. In matters of security, for example, the old Quaker axiom of "truth and openness" is suicidal. Already we are a nation of snoopers and informers, and prison society has always been a specimen of what larger society has become.

Another rule of thumb has to do with energy. Precious as energy is, we've found it wise not to talk seriously to too many people. We listen to everyone, keep it friendly, give advice when it's sought, and maintain a light vein. But we don't get heavy—not anymore!

April 1971

One man had seemed to be an exception to the rule. Perhaps prison had opened his eyes, or the bombastic bull sessions so common in jail, which are frequently precise in their politics. Or maybe the shock of being imprisoned had deepened his awareness of failure as it had stung his pride. Whether from one thing or a combination, he came awake and began to connect.

What struck me about him was his honesty and enormous goodwill. He tried. He now understood what he had been, a wretched and cheap little crook, with the mind of a rat and the heart of a rabbit. And he wanted something better—which means he was already trying out definitions of manhood.

He stopped me one day abruptly and desperately, very much unlike his usual self: "The captain asked me if I wanted a round-trip ticket." I looked into his wretched face and tried to remember his history. Three months before, the Bureau had transported him from California—sixty days on the road or in lockup, no mail, no legal contact, no friends, no available family. A number, who is also a person, is packed up and moved, almost as anonymously as a prime steer in a cattle shipment.

Here, however, the carrot awaited him. His family lived nearby in Bridgeport and could visit him weekly. I noticed them frequently in the visiting room—his chubby, pretty wife and four vibrant, towheaded kids. They used to wave to Dan and me, and once we met his wife. A warm devoted picture, a powerful, human reason for his staying nearby.

He had given concrete shape to his new sense of worth and manhood. He had been agitating about the little things that assume exaggerated importance in an inmate's life—poor food, harassment from guards, crowded dormitories. In effect, he had gotten off his knees, had stopped groveling for the hideous little favors for which men in prison trade their dignity. He had quit the ranks of the creatures who are bought, sold, or rented for a few "good" days, work release, a parole promise. One thing had led to another; he had criticized work conditions and then had refused work.

Now he was back in the factory, depressed and defeated by the captain's clearly put ultimatum: "Do you want a round-trip ticket? Work or get shipped." The captain had reminded him of who was who, who jailer and who jailed, who had the keys and the muscle and who had nothing. And the captain had reminded him that he had no time for bullshit rhetoric on human rights and democracy.

He smartened up; he accepted the captain's point of view. He had nothing going for him but a lot of purity and mouth. They weren't enough; if he persisted in using them, they would cost him visits, letters, all the sweet insulation that helped him tolerate the locks, bars, keepers, as well as the overriding contempt for one's fellows ("people I wouldn't be caught dead with on the street").

I had not the heart to blame him. He had stumbled on reality precipitously, as though it were something readily digestible. He found that it wasn't, as we have all found that one's guts curdle on such a diet, and that it takes only a tough cop's threat to bring on nausea, to excise one's gonads, and to shiver up self-respect and identity. Work stoppage equaled transport equaled separation from family. He couldn't pay the prices in this store; he'd wait for a better time to buy.

No better time will come—or if it does, it will find him with the same essential dilemma. But his predicament makes me think of freedom and slavery, of penal control and social control, of the old-new desire of most men (their original sin) to dominate others, to make choices for them, to whistle them back and forth like dogs, to structure the differences between ruled and ruling, to play Olympian to the earthbound.

Here a handful of men keep seven hundred fifty others—many of whom possess unusual physical, mental, and professional gifts—under astonishing control. In fact, most of them are immeasurably more tractable than our friend who was threatened with being shipped. To be so docile, prisoners obviously must prize something slavishly that the Man alone can give them.

Americans are conformists not because they do the same things but because they desire the same things. These desires build the basis for social control whether it is public or penal. They are the reason that Americans tolerate their country's barbarity in Indochina and why they tolerate Richard Nixon at home. The fact is, what they want is control; it is more real, more critical to them than peace, or equality, or economic justice.

So it is here in this compound. Inmates bring a cultural slavery with them, lives that revolve around irresponsible desires mainly concerning property. They bring with them our common myths:

DANBURY FEDERAL CORRECTIONAL INSTITUTE, 1971

1) property is scarce; 2) property is the reward of toil, or craftiness, or unscrupulousness; 3) property is a gauge of human worth; 4) property brings happiness; 5) property is worth defending, and therefore demands police and military.

Cain was the first capitalist; he had an exaggerated attachment to flock and harvest. And because he did, he offered to God what he thought of as "his." This perverse attitude led to murder. Men jailed for violence against people have invariably been disoriented by a sick relationship to property. A genuine reverence for things cannot but engender a reverence for people.

Nonetheless the convict has made his own rules about property. But if, as ethical justice asserts, ownership beyond reasonable need is theft, many of the legalisms protecting property also protect theft. If this is so, the convict becomes merely one who steals extralegally, while nearly everyone steals "legally." Attitudes toward property do more than provide a basis for social control: these attitudes *are* social control.

When prisoners gain release they look back with loathing on their prison time; they make profound vows to themselves and others that they will never return. Some honestly intend to avoid recidivism by keeping to the rules, by becoming card-carrying capitalists and by stealing legally. But most anticipate an eventual return to the old excursions. As one inmate put it, "The trip is a bummer": one leaves more manipulable than when he entered.

Bad as they are, American prisons are still relatively luxurious by world standards. Their claim to superiority in comfort, however, is not the issue. Much less their claim of successes in rehabilitation. More to the point is their accomplishment in preserving the myth of property value. The penal system further entrenches the myth that property is valuable enough to lie at the core of all laws and institutions, and of society itself—valuable enough to have police, armies and courts to protect it. Indeed, if men believed that "this" was not "mine" or "ours" but "everyone's," what would happen to government? What would happen to the distinction between ruled and ruling?

From time to time inmates have announced to me with some pride, "The men run this joint!" Indeed they do—in all things save

116

policy. But they also "run it" in a far deeper sense than any of the men possibly imagine. Inmates in fact mollify, enervate, and pacify one another by craving above all "freedom" outside. They tug restlessly at the leash of punishment.

This becomes clear when one discusses the reasons for conviction and imprisonment. With impressive grace and good humor (So I got caught!) men will accept jail on account of theft, manslaughter, rape, con games, hard-drug dealing—only to be shaken by the suggestion that a man is a fool and a dupe to come to jail for any other reason than for opposing abuse or slaughter of human beings. One young "head" said, "It blew my brain, man. This cat was tellin' me that comin' here for shootin' horse was adolescent bullshit, and that my life might depend upon coming next time for doing something real, like rippin' off a draft board! And you know something? The snotty bastard was right!"

In 1922 thirty thousand Indians were in jail under Gandhi's leadership. Even so, the British hung on until the late 1940s. Obviously the British jails were freedom schools which, more than any one element of foreign injustice, invigorated and matured the movement for independence. The struggle for independence in the U.S.—independence from the totalitarianism of wealth, from the coalitions of economic, political and military interests—can hardly expect to flourish differently.

Easter 1971

The Lord is risen. Alleluia! "Then the disciple who had reached the tomb first went in too, and he saw and believed; until then, they had not understood the scriptures, which showed that he must rise from the dead." So says John.

Once again hope is renewed with the Lord's resurrection. One notices it as spring refreshes the air and land, as heads go up and people smile, as vitality and concern come alive outside. Winter, unconcern, selfishness and death are under siege and in retreat.

From Latin America, where political tyranny and poverty have sparked a Christian renaissance, comes the new language of a theology of liberation. Christ is "animator" of the universe, Who "conscientizes" His people through the Church and through events. Peace is not "development" (as per Pope Paul), with its Western connotation of "foreign aid," "technical assistance," "rising standards of living." Peace is liberation of spirit, deeper personal identity, and especially resistance to the curse of oligarchical tyranny.

We have the example of Christ, Who became man and, as man, victor over death. "Jesus came and stood among them. 'Peace be with you!' He said, and then showed them His hands and His side." In brief, the gift of peace depends on His Passion. To reject the gift is to choose insanity. It is to become not a man but an executioner.

"Jail has its good sides; only one warden, whereas in free life there are many; no worry about food; work keeps the body healthy; no 'vicious habits'; the prisoner's soul is thus free. . . . The real road to happiness lies in going to jail and undergoing sufferings and privations there in the interest of one's country and religion" (this was Gandhi, quoted by Louis Fisher in *The Life of Mahatma Gandhi*).

For most inmates jail is an embalmment; for a few, a rebirth. Most accept the jailer's proposition that jail imprisons both body *and* spirit. A few do not, perceiving that bars and locks have nothing to do with the state of one's soul.

Liberation will draw its best paradigms from the prisons, the military, and the seminaries, where men have learned to say no to bureaucratic excess, and yes to human life.

Professor Gilbert Murray of Oxford wrote about Gandhi: "Be careful in dealing with a man who cares nothing for sensual pleasures, nothing for comfort or praise or promotion, but is simply determined to do what he believes to be right. He is a dangerous and uncomfortable enemy, because his body, which you can always conquer, gives you so little purchase over his soul."

One test came with a six-year sentence. Now another has arrived. I may have to give the remainder of my life. I don't know how much purchase the Powers have over me, body or soul. I try not to care. The issue is to be faithful, faithful to Christ and to others. From that comes peace, a peace that Gandhi would call equability, quoting the *Gita:* "Hold alike pleasure and pain, gain and loss, victory and defeat."

April 1971

The Harrisburg grand jury has reactivated its search-and-snoop operation, subpoenaing people from the entire Northeast. At last count, thirty-two have been summoned, and already a number have indicated that they will not testify. It appears that Anne Walsh, Paul Couming, and Joe Gilchrist, among others, have been cited for contempt.

What's the government's strategy? William S. Lynch, the chief prosecutor, a righteous and energetic Roman Catholic, has already warned of superseding indictments. Indictments for doing what? In my case, conspiring to destroy Selective Service systems in Philadelphia, Rochester and Wilmington.

Two aspects of the new maneuver strike me. On the one hand, the present case limps horribly. Our friends in government (who remind me of bounty hunters) realize they will lose the kidnapping-bombing fiasco either before a jury or on appeal. So they beef up their charges, counting on the fact that a jury (especially a Harrisburg jury) is apt to convict us of *some* crimes, since we are charged with *so many.*

On the other hand, if the government feels a greater need for caution, because the possibility of conviction is lessened, superseding indictments will lend them flexibility. The government can bob and weave with our legal countermoves; it can drop charges, add new ones, delay proceedings, ease out of the whole case if it wishes.

It is essentially a cat-and-mouse thing. Certain ruling Toms would take unholy joy in giving me a permanent cell, or, at the very least, one nearly permanent enough to suggest contrition and penance. But the cat it fearful, harried, paranoiac. He is no longer fat, sleek, confident, facing as he does dispossession from the house to the alley. As for the mouse, he's no strong hybrid—there's merely more of him, enough, in fact, to take over the house slowly. Less and less can the cat tolerate its squeakings and droppings, its contempt for his position.

As in Vietnam, he's thinking of claiming victory and then getting out.

May 20

The government has reindicted us. The news arrived Friday. And with me (and I with them) the same five defendants, plus Mary Cain Scoblick and Ted Glick. Meanwhile the government drops Dan, Paul Mayer, and Tom Davidson as alleged co-conspirators.

This time I am beyond shock. All of us had expected more nonsense, so when it came, there was only relief, grim amusement, and contempt. The big boys never learn; they finish one disaster and plunge into another—Spock et al, the Chicago Seven, now us. They blunder in their courts just as the military blunders in Indochina, bullies of "justice" and bullies of "goodwill."

It is hard not to fulminate about the Ogre, his power, his "justice"; hard to cultivate an attitude more human than rage. As national affairs deteriorate, as the country sinks into an uneasy stupor of shame and apprehension, the Ogre replaces bad leadership with worse, relying more and more on force to convince the people that the opposite of what is, is. And out of this comes a message that more and more Americans understand: "If you don't like the way we're running things, keep quiet, leave the country, or go to jail."

In any event, the Ogre realized that his earlier case was evaporating (it had its greatest substance in Hoover's ego). Rather than drop the case entirely, it beefed up one conspiracy with others—conspiracies to disrupt Selective Service in Philadelphia,

Rochester, and Wilmington—diffusing and broadening the case while retaining the original indictments. As embellishment, the Ogre attaches "threatening" letters between Sister Elizabeth and myself regarding Kissinger. Finally he shamelessly poses a contradiction: several defendants have already publicly acknowledged disruption of Selective Service. Now all of us (including Eqbal Ahmad) face charges of conspiracy antedating the fact of disruption.

It reeks: abuse of the law and offenses against human rights— electronic and human bugging, intimidation of witnesses and defendants, smear tactics, strong-arm investigation and prostitution of the grand jury. One of our lawyers, experienced in political trials, confesses to being shocked at the excesses of the prosecution. "It [repression] is really happening here," he says sadly.

May 1971

At our weekly meeting yesterday (four lawyers came with the defendants), Sister Elizabeth tells me of a big *Life* story in the works, by Lee Lockwood, probably for next week. She has the page proofs along, and I skim them quickly. Sections are quite bad—saccharine, opinionated (liberal), inaccurate, and insulting.

The government's release of those "letters" between Elizabeth and me has inflamed publicist imaginations. The story appears fantastic at one look, credible at another. It even has a dash of sex—our "relationship" in the Movement, vague enough to allow consideration of an affair, or latitude for "an intense friendship."

Supposedly, Liz had cultivated a hero worship for me following my first troubles with the government in 1967. Supposedly, too, we conversed far into the night after a New York City rally in early '68; she became a convert to "the way" after that. Plus more of the same, adding up to distortion of a very rank sort. Contrary to the picture of empty-headed discipleship that the article conveys, Liz is noted, among us hard-headed individualists, for creativity and independence.

Beyond such criticism, the piece is slanted wrong; it is a puny, lightweight miss. The author is not entirely to blame, but the fact is that he cannot deal with us if he separates us from the war and the moral and structural rot it has accelerated in our midst, or separates us from a dedication to the Gospel and community. Since he doesn't understand such concerns, he cannot deal with them.

Most distressing to us, it is a friend who wrote the piece, and in its preparation we feel he has deceived us about it, promising publication of a more precise and serious version and then settling for the present copy. Yet it is predictable that any mention of a breach in trust will upset him.

We have not yet confided in a writer who we feel is trustworthy and knowledgeable. Unfortunately we have confided in some we feel are not, one of them the author of this *Life* article. It strikes me that professionalism severely compromises the humanitarianism of most writers. Like most professionals, their trade is absurdly competitive; sales and income truncate integrity and true relationships. And our friend reminds me of an egg farmer—he sells us as a consumer item.

I've just finished two marvelous accounts in the paper by Kate Webb (May 13 and 14, *New York Times*), who was recently freed by NLF troops after being captured in Cambodia. She testifies that she learned more in three weeks with her captors than during the previous five years of reporting the war. Something momentous reached that woman during those harrowing days of danger and hardship (infected feet, exhaustion)—the courtesy and humor of her guards. She emerges with the truth; indeed, she says she understands the war for the first time.

What we would request from our writer friends is not a "sympathetic press" but a common human footing. Their lives do not allow them to interpret *our* lives. Talking to them is much like Abraham talking to Dives—"a vast gulf separates us."

Kate Webb could write as she did because her integrity was engaged by a gallant little band of liberation fighters whose spirit was uncowed by American military might. Her integrity grew because the experience liberated her and gave her a new reverence for truth. As she left them they shouted after her, half in request, half in warning, "Tell the truth about us!" It was superfluous. She had no choice.

May 1971

Elizabeth McAlister and I married on April 7, 1969, in St. George's Episcopal Church in the Bronx. In a conversation that evening we had become certain of a love we had long shared, and we accepted it joyfully and gratefully. We married for life and welcomed what life together might entail.

We accepted each other as adult, baptized Christians, and exchanged our consent. And marveled at what God had given us, as gratuitous as grace. No one else was present, and at that time no one else knew of our decision.

I was free on bail then, following seven months in jail after a draft action. Resistance to the Asian war was not so much a passion as a way of life for me. Elizabeth perceived this, supported it, and shared it. Had not her Order threatened her with ejection, her involvement and conflict with the law might well have matched mine.

From the outset, therefore, there was a profound, largely unspoken agreement on the nature of our marriage. When we accepted each other, that included acceptance of our work in resistance and its consequences: discipline, risk, separation, jail. We understood this. It was unnecessary to discuss it or to make explanations, requests, plans. We had married each other, but before that we had married all who suffer in consequence of war, poverty, racism. Now, we believed the two contracts (to humanity and to each other) were complementary and mutually enriching. From the start we looked upon our marriage as a religious and political act.

Neither of us considered abandoning our vocations. We had great sympathy for those who had left their vocations and those who had been forced to leave on discovery of love for another. But that was not for us. Why leave? We had a fundamentalist Gospel sense of Christian conscience, of freedom, of social responsibility. We had experienced firsthand the rigors and riches of celibacy, having lived it for many years. But we also felt that God had given us our love not that we should sacrifice all we had known and loved and lived, whether Church, vocation, or community, nor that we should insulate ourselves from suffering jeopardy, and jail. No, He had given us our love to open up for us vital new areas of conscience and service—within our vocations.

That is to say, we tried to decide in favor of people, but no less in favor of the Church. It had nurtured us, educated us, given us the Word and the Bread of Life. Neither of us, as our lives testified, was a stranger to freedom of conscience, and we owed even that to the Church, however imperfectly it realizes freedom in practice.

In our view, and according to the rights of conscience, priests should volunteer celibacy, if they choose; or marry, if they choose. But marriage does not nullify their priesthood. By the same reasoning, a nun should be accorded similar rights. The issue is not marriage or celibacy but mature fidelity to the Gospel, in contemplation and loving witness.

We believe that the choice we have taken can contribute to a more intense service for the victims of war, exploitation, color. We believe that married love can embrace people everywhere, and that a wider love can renew and restore married love.

Our marriage, it seems to us, addresses questions to both the Church and to married Christians. To the Church: When will optional celibacy be accorded priests and nuns? When will non-violent resistance to war (and not the constant preparation for thermonuclear war) be encouraged by official example? To married Christians: Is it Christian to exclude love for mankind and service of mankind because one has taken a spouse? Can one be truly married in Christ without being married to His brothers and sisters?

These were questions we believed we should face. Our decision to marry offered good Gospel sense to us, good human sense, good politics. We found it severely demanding, but profoundly rewarding as well. We denied ourselves frequent meetings, we never considered leaving the country or evading prison—even though such alternatives were tempting and possible. What helped us, without a doubt, was discipline—another gift from the Church.

Questions may arise about a decision to delay announcement of our marriage for over two years. Certainly it has puzzled the government, which has tapped our phones and invaded our correspondence. We regret the frustration inflicted. But the fact is, neither of us could have survived in the Church three years ago if our marriage had been revealed. Now the announcement raises the question once more, with new urgency.

We had been married only a year when the Supreme Court refused to review the Catonsville conviction. Eight of us had been given April 9, 1970, as a date of surrender, and five of us had rejected it and gone underground. I knew at the time that this would destroy my chances for a reduction of sentence.

Elizabeth never opposed my refusal to surrender, cost us what it might. Nor did her spirit fail her once I was in prison. She worked for peace harder and more effectively than before, becoming more conspicuous and unpalatable to the authorities. Two questions occupied her: If the war in Indochina cost billions of dollars and millions of lives, what, then, must be the cost of peace? And what must Americans pay for the horror and death we have sown in Indochina?

Now we face a trial in Harrisburg for conspiracy to bomb, kidnap, and disrupt the Selective Service system. Whatever the outcome, we will wish to inform both Church and public of our marriage. It is a duty perhaps too long delayed. And we—a man and a woman of the Church, for *its* honor subject once more to the rigors of court and prison—wish hereby to offer that love to others.

But as we offer, we also ask. We ask the Church to allow us our ministry—not grudgingly, but with a sensitive understanding of prerogatives of conscience and in awareness of our efforts for nonviolence and peace. Moreover, what we desire for ourselves we request for others—that reinstatement to ministry be granted to those who wish it, and that celibacy be optional for both priests and nuns.

As for the public, we wish Americans to reflect on the issues of freedom and peace implicit in our marriage. We love each other deeply, but that fact will not deter us from the sacrifices required for peace. So we pray our country will choose peace, and will gladly and freely pay the price of peace.

The future remains obscure for Elizabeth and myself. I am serving six years for destroying a few hundred Selective Service files—government hunting licenses. Elizabeth is threatened with jail—how long a sentence only time and the ambiguous character of American "justice" will tell. (That "justice" ignores American war crimes, pins medals on those who kill, exonerates its Medinas, gives immunity to the architects of genocide, and imprisons those who resist and refuse to kill.)

If Elizabeth goes to jail, our separation becomes complete, relieved only by the "privilege" of writing (under government censorship, of course).

None of this will be news to us, none of it particularly unsettling or depressing. We foresaw it, anticipated it, and sought to prepare ourselves. But neither prospect nor reality has made it less costly.

Elizabeth and I have been separated over many months, and many others for longer. However long our ordeal, it is our present contribution to peace. The separations of war must be matched by the separations for peace; those profiting from war by those sacrificing for peace; those dead tragically by those alive responsibly; those licensed to kill by those imprisoned for not killing.

May 24

En route to Harrisburg for tomorrow's arraignment. Phase 3 of this bizarre case.

All of us consider that it would be unconscionable and servile to plead to the indictment. The law, which we have tortured internationally to validate our debacle in Indochina, is now raised against us, domestic "naysayers," as President Johnson used to call us. One is counted with the enemy; arms and indictments are the weapons.

The marshals who escort me are old acquaintances, men grown middle-aged and mellow in their depressing work. Both remind me of sausagelike, grandfatherly types in shape and demeanor.

They have a kid with them who escaped from Allenwood three months before, supposedly to see a cancer-doomed father for the last time. The Bureau of Prisons, he told me, allowed either a bedside visit or attendance at the funeral. He wanted more time with his pop, so he calmly walked from the reservation in central Pennsylvania and hitchhiked to Connecticut.

I write this from Bloomsburg County Jail, from what has become my private suite every time I come through, a large room and bath. It is habitable and quiet. I can walk and exercise and meditate. Given the abomination that most local jails are, I like it.

Before leaving Danbury I say goodbye to Dan, recovering from an ulcer in the prison hospital. It's his first trouble in four to five years, oddly set off by the removal of a tiny growth on his tongue which had begun to cause discomfort. The medical people here gave him a painful local anesthetic and crudely cut it out. That done, they stitched the incision in an equally callous way. Such an experience, following an especially nauseating goulash for lunch, sent the ulcer into rebellion.

He is at once extremely susceptible to pain and extremely resilient under it. He is graceful with life, accepting it joyfully as it comes. Part of this quality is his reluctance to worry others, part is a view of pain as opportunity and grace. Under considerable suffering he is capable of a dazzling performance of insight and humor. The afternoon following the operation, with tongue and ulcer rankling, he chatted and joked with visitors as though pain were alien and millennium near.

I don't go alone to Harrisburg; his spirit accompanies me. And he will be present with us in that sterile courtroom, tomorrow and later. He is still very much in the case.

Scranton, Pa., May 26

Everyone is tolerably well pleased with the way the arraignment went yesterday. All eight refused to plead to the new indictment. Judge Herman responded with good enough grace, entering a plea of "not guilty" for us, though he refused to let us read statements. Nevertheless he allowed them into the court record, and we made them available to the press. He also reduced the bail of five defendants.

Really our gathering was more a celebration than an arraignment. I met the elder Glicks, and Ted's wife, Sarah, also the young people arraigned the same day on criminal contempt charges—John Swinglish, Paul Couming, Anne Mentz, Terry McHugh. Their solidarity with the defendants and with life was complete: having refused to testify before the grand jury, they then refused to plead to criminal contempt indictments.

I watched, with astonishment and delight, the pulsations of intelligence and love in our crew—defendants, lawyers, co-conspirators, and young people—and knew them to be invincible. And a feeling arose that we finally have a handle on this case, and the means to respond to the government's treachery and harassment.

I write this from the county jail in Scranton. Amazing old fortress of a place, forbidding and silent. But unlike most local jails, clean and well administered. Temporarily my apprehension and distaste vanish, and I find myself relishing the eighteen hours here.

Undoubtedly much of my satisfaction is traceable to the people who come by and talk. Both guards and inmates exhibit an unexpected sympathy and interest, astonishing in a city like Scranton, ethnically grouped and largely Roman Catholic. It quite takes me off balance.

A husky Marine veteran of Vietnam settles in my cell for a rap. He tells me he is serving a year's sentence for breaking a man's jaw in a barroom fight. It was a first offense, but neither that nor his military record saved him from the rancor of a self-righteous judge. Before dismissing him His Honor remarked pointedly that he must "learn to unlearn your military aptitudes."

"You know," the ex-Marine said, "they taught me to kill, and I got to be a great killer. Real professional about it—a Silver Star, two Bronze Stars, three Purple Hearts. But where's the education to unlearn killing? They don't give any. They just told me I had a lotta hostility, and that don't go over well back in the States.

"I understand now that they don't give a shit about me. In fact, they never did. When I was killing for them I was just doing the job of a cop, a goddamned cop, so that the slope-heads would understand, just like blacks understand, that to screw around with Whitey is to be dead.

"You know what they say when I start asking about trainin' and jobs? Go back in the Marines. They don't wanna lose a good cop!"

It's a familiar sad tale. His awareness delighted me. He seemed to comprehend why he had gone to Vietnam and who had decided who was to live or die there. Nevertheless awareness was emasculated by hostility; he would never act on what he knew. Or if he did, it would be as he acted in the barroom—impulsively and destructively. His hostility was real, and granted, he had ample reason for hostility; he had been used as no one should be used. But to take abuse and fashion it into a grudge apes those for whom he had killed in Vietnam.

He is a poor man now, a cast-off mercenary, a case study in how the rich manipulate and live off the poor: at one turn crushing other poor; at another fastening on them like parasites in the ghetto.

I met, as well, a middle-aged Polish guard named John Koski. He had fought with the First Armored in Africa, Sicily, and Italy, and had made his own study of war.

"You know what I call those people in Washington? Dollar fascists! They live dollar lives and practice dollar politics. They're so goddamned greedy. I saw it with Roosevelt in '42 and I see it with Nixon in '71. The economy stagnates without war, and they say there ain't any other way. There ain't for them, that's for sure; they like being fat and comfortable and with their boots on other people's necks.

"That's why we're in Vietnam, and that's why we ain't about to leave. Some say two hundred rich men run this country and half the world's business. As far as I can see, it's closer to fourteen families.

"You know who's wakin' up? Working people like me. They tax us more and more, and we just scrape along. The working man—he's getting fed up. They take our kids for war and give us more empty promises than we can keep track of. And if you don't like it, they'll bug you and spy on you and trouble you and call you a traitor who deserves nothing but jail. But you know what? They aren't scarin' me! I'm with people like you and Mr. Kunstler and Rap Brown and that young Rennie Davis."

John Koski bade me good-night and went his way. I thought of the fourth beatitude: "How blest are those who hunger and thirst for justice; they will be satisfied."

Danbury, May 1971

I've been reading again the translation of Gandhi-isms. On the Satyagraha pledge in 1919 he wrote, "Even such a mighty government as the Government of India [British] will have to yield if we are true to our pledge. For the pledge is no small thing. It means a change of heart. It is an attempt to introduce the religious spirit into politics. We may no longer believe in the doctrine of 'tit for tat'; we may not meet hatred with hatred, violence with violence, evil with evil; but we have to make a continuous and persistent effort to return good for evil. . . . Nothing is impossible."

Jail is a good place to ponder the effect of such a pledge, and the hartal it promised, on the United States of today. The hartal was a favorite moral and political tactic of Gandhi's: a moratorium on business—stores, factories, banks, and offices shut down, ship cargoes not loaded or unloaded, trucks and planes immobile. Commerce stops, the marketplace empties and becomes silent. People turn to prayer, reflection, fasting. In one concerted, peaceful but vibrant act the people declare their spiritual and political freedom.

Gandhi made whole revolution. He knew that a resister's values, tactics and politics must differ qualitatively from the oppressor's, as profoundly as life differs from death. He knew that the first step toward making a revolution was the realization that men have forged their own chains and that the rich have welcomed the arrangement by adding links of their own.

Those who point out the differences between imperial India and imperial America tend to emphasize them only on one level. True, we must consider an industrial as against a technological society, a village people against an urban one, almost total impoverishment as against relative affluence, a foreign domination as opposed to a domestic one, religious prejudice as against racial persecution. But always people who truly desire justice and peace, wherever they are, have much more in common than the things that distinguish them. If Gandhi's Satyagraha (truth force) was human enough to seize India (and indeed the world) with longing, hope and effective peacemaking, so it could here too. We will have to take Satyagraha, preserving its fundamentals, and adapt it to our circumstances so that we can "offer" it (Gandhi's word) to our people. Without that we will reap nothing in this country but violence. First it will come in repression, then there will be chaos.

In 1919, in Bombay, after there had been sporadic outbreaks of violence, Gandhi said, "If we cannot conduct this movement without the slightest violence from our side, the movement might have to be abandoned. It may be necessary to go even further. The time may come for me to offer Satyagraha against ourselves." He had often made the comparison, "Violence is the law of the brute, as nonviolence is the law of our species."

It was not an exact observation. Violence is unknown in the brute world; what is loosely called violence are acts of survival or efforts to relieve a given environment of overpopulation. But man is violent, though it assaults his nature both individually and corporately—as a son, as a brother—and unmans him.

"I have always held that it is only when one sees one's own mistakes with a convex lens, and does just the reverse in the case of others, that one is able to arrive at a just relative estimate of the two," he wrote.

I need to keep the convex lens on myself and my mistakes. These have been enormous; only a powerful community has kept them from becoming disastrous. I trusted the FBI's hired hand, and Elizabeth and others trusted me. My reasons for trusting him were not that good, not good enough to risk critical people and their work. It is no excuse to claim the whole thing has come about through injustice or repression by the Justice Department. Nor live on the lame hope that the experience will toughen community and radicalize the Movement.

When Gandhi's hartal resulted in scattered violence, he publicly admitted "a Himalayan miscalculation." A few of his Satyagrahis were unprepared for the test, and he held himself responsible. I was unprepared for the test at Lewisburg, and I must hold myself responsible. There will be other mistakes, which (hopefully) I will admit in turn. This will do for a start. Yet . . .

"When there is a choice between cowardice and violence, I would advise violence," Gandhi wrote. When violence is a way of life, it is inevitably thought to be an answer, a solution. In effect, what most Americans find thrilling, pragmatic, reasonable and worthwhile is mere violence. That violence works is a moral, cultural, interpersonal and political assumption.

To juxtapose violence and cowardice, though, is imprecise; cowardice is itself a form of violence which falls under sins of omission. What Gandhi meant was that it is better to practice violence against injustice than to do nothing. Doing nothing is acting in a cowardly way.

It is terribly unsettling to learn that violence is unworkable. And it is fearfully demanding to learn that nonviolence is workable. To experience this, and to know that it requires a sort of moratorium, is not cowardice but active re-education. What we need is compassion for all of us who must relearn our ABC's. It is excruciating. What does Bonhoeffer say? "We must learn to regard people less in the light of what they do or omit to do, and more in the light of what they suffer." He died in a Nazi prison.

Gandhi in an article, "Tampering with Loyalty," for which he was convicted of sedition and sentenced to six years, in 1922, wrote: "I have no hesitation in saying that it is sinful for anyone, either soldier or civilian, to serve this government. . . . Sedition has become the creed of Congress. Noncooperation, though a religious and strictly moral movement, deliberately aims at the overthrow of the government, and is therefore legally seditious. . . . We ask for no quarter; we expect none from the government.

"We must widen the prison gates, and we must enter them as a bridegroom enters the bride's chamber. Freedom is to be wooed only inside prison walls and sometimes on gallows, never in the council chambers, courts, or the schoolroom."

Gandhi knew that entering Indian politics meant entering British jails. By 1930 one hundred thousand Indians were in prison, including most of the first-, second-, and third-rank leaders of the Indian Congress. Even so, independence did not come until 1947, and it came with the stain of partition, a terrible compromise of thirty-two years of Gandhi's work. The nonviolent price paid by Indians was great, but it was simply not enough.

In this matter, how generous are Americans? A few hundred, mostly resisters, will accept the consequences of civil disobedience and go to jail. Thousands in exile cannot bear to face their country's judgment, or else they judge it not worth facing. Meanwhile institutional leaders mouth the empty rhetoric of liberalism as they live comfortable, sterile lives. Can one imagine a Catholic bishop going to prison for breaking immoral laws, a judge for conspiring against illegal laws, a politician for actively resisting unsocial laws, or a university president for condemning untruthful ones?

Much of America's trouble flows from our system (trouble at the top). Mediocrity and bureaucratic guile are the credentials for advancement. When the people have no leaders, they raise up their own—men of service, vision, suffering, peace, men who have come from resistance, jail, second birth. Or they raise up demagogues.

June 1971

Hannah Arendt once wrote that political power ceases to be power insofar as it ceases to be moral. In the United States political power is a public mouthpiece for technological and military empires—profoundly interrelated and symbiotic. The technocracy it represents controls over half of the world's riches, while the war machine has disposed of over a trillion dollars since 1946, becoming in effect the most profitable element in the economy, even as it secures, in exchange, practically laissez-faire immunity for domestic and foreign investment. History has seen nothing to match it.

Having no moral base, this government rules rather than governs through patronage, surveillance and repressive force. With increasing momentum, control is shifting from the reward system—even the rich can no longer ignore the corruption of the environment or fiscal oscillation—to repression. Power is helpless to do other than fend off the threats, and confesses its bankruptcy at every stroke.

The first curb on American power is itself—its immorality as reflected in its structural contradictions. Even if it had neither internal nor external stresses placed upon it, even if the poor and students and the lower echelons in the military were not in ferment, it would have no long-term viability. The cancer has long ago fanned out from the heart, and now races throughout the organism.

The second curb on American power is the Vietnamese people, who have burst the myth of our military invincibility and of moral and political probity. Historically it is virtually an unprecedented achievement; the Vietnamese have matched the American blacks in teaching us, by their blood, what this country is and, largely, what it always has been. To paraphrase Churchill's glowing tribute to the RAF, "Never did one people owe so much to another." Our future rests literally upon how fast and how well we learn.

The third curb on American power must be the Movement. It does not yet exist. Movement implies willingness to resist and to change the forces capable of Hiroshima, the Cold War, Korea, and Vietnam, foreign exploitation, racism, polluted environment, antisocial poverty and chronic unemployment. Movement implies revolutionary movement, and only a few hundred have clearly stated their intention to undertake this. Only a few have asked the questions worth asking: "Does the country need revolution?" and, "What kind of revolution does it need?" Yes to the first, nonviolent to the second.

Peacemakers have far more responsibility to stop and then smash the American war machine than Southeast Asians. We sanction it until we struggle against it with our bodies as well as our minds and mouths. The war is not between Vietnamese and Americans; it is a few Americans and most Vietnamese against some Americans. The price in the struggle has been largely paid in Vietnamese blood. Upon the Vietnamese question will hinge the struggle for survival.

Writing just before his death, Ammon Hennacy, in *The Catholic Worker,* quoted Robert Frost saying the only revolution that has ever happened is the one-man revolution. Obviously both men spoke honestly from their experience—advocating a kind of purified Ayn Rand individualism, compromising to any real notion of Christian community. Nevertheless **both** clung to the idea that revolution began by spiritual conversion, which obligates one as brother and servant of the exploited. And Hennacy lived his conversion publicly and with astounding purity—voluntary poverty, repeated jailings and fasts.

He was, however, a supreme individualist, taking his own line rather than the desperately slow, painful work of community. And in that measure failing the communal aspect of revolution, which seems destined to be both catalyst and prototype of the new society.

If men disagree fundamentally on the nature of theology, not understanding that theology is revolution, that God is God of the living; or if they reject such a theology, which teaches that God's revelations have to do with the evolution of human beings into New Men, they will have a lopsided view of man's spiritual vocation. To one degree or another, the balance will tip either in favor of individualism without public responsibility, or activism without personal responsibility. The peace movement exhibits both extremes, reflecting faithfully the cultural strengths and liabilities of the society itself—idealistic, spontaneous, vocal, divided, paranoiac, philosophically scrambled. Little wonder that the Vietnamese, despite their tolerance, find us astonishingly egotistical and sterile. Through bitter experience they've discovered how little they can count on peace people in this country.

June 1971

An event attacks whatever equanimity I've recently found and shakes me to the marrow.

After lunch, one or two friends relate a vague story about Dan getting sick in the dentist's chair. "They're taking care of him now," one guy tells me. The news doesn't sound too urgent, but I hurry to the hospital nonetheless.

The entire hospital staff is gathered around him. The doctor is taking a cardiogram, three technicians apply oxygen, another drains a bottle of glucose into his arm. He is conscious, but laboring hard to breathe, while his pulse races at a tremendous, shallow pace. I look at the faces hovering around him, trying to read a sign of reassurance, or relief, or hope. It is useless—they are anxious, drawn, pale. Everyone is frightened, mainly because of their powerlessness.

I slowly grasp that this is no spell of weakness, no fainting fit. It is something immensely more serious, serious perhaps to death. I stand by in utter helplessness until it occurs to me that I can pray. So I pray, and watch him struggle for breath, his fingers blue with cold, twitching as if in protest. And I dumbly realize that he is beating back dark oblivion.

I also understand, without any trace of dramatics, that losing him would be like major surgery without cause. I had simply never imagined life without him, without his understanding, humor, vigilant love.

The doctor leaves to phone a specialist, and I follow. When he has ordered an ambulance and completed his business with a local cardiologist, he begins to tell me his impressions. Before he gets far, however, an inmate bursts in. "Dan wants you!"

I rush back. The oxygen mask is off his face, and he's chatting with everyone. Weak as he is, and still in shock, he nonetheless worries about his friends and the anxiety they feel, especially me. I lean over him to talk and he seizes my head and kisses me resoundingly on the cheek. He gives me another lesson in the love that binds us.

My chin begins to quiver and my eyes to fill. I have not wept, secretly or otherwise, since my brother Jerry left the seminary in 1954. But now I come precariously close to crying.

Later the doctor explains that two heavy slugs of Novocain, administered in close succession, had sent him into heavy shock. They had concluded that his heart was affected and had given him adrenalin. The anesthetic combined with the stimulant and sent his heart into paroxysms of overexertion. Simultaneously his lungs became paralyzed; he could not catch his breath nor utilize the oxygen given him.

The ambulance arrives, and Dan wants me along. But the specialist has left orders: "No visitors." Later the doctor tells me that he's resting comfortably.

June 1971

I get permission to accompany the prison doctor to see Dan. Actually, our head jailers handle the affair humanely. Since being indicted by J. Edgar, I have "close custody," calling for cuffs and guards whenever leaving the prison. But now I stroll off with the doctor as if we were going to a clambake.

It is an unexpected consideration, which reminds me that the authorities are uptight with us both and—in the manner of law-and-order men—are troubled by the prospect that heads might roll (theirs) if Dan should worsen. But it also reminds me that they secretly admire us and take vicarious pride in a variation from their own drabness. So I welcome the kindness as I welcome the growth in them.

I discover Carol and Jerry at the hospital. They had heard the news the night before and had come immediately. We find Dan weak, but lucid, cheerful, amusing. Best of all, there is no evidence of damage to heart and lungs. He has already begun a recovery, and as Pop would have said, we can only give thanks.

June 1971

An old friend comes in, and during a conversation she quotes another old friend, Gordon Zahn, a Catholic pacifist and professor of sociology at the University of Massachusetts. Gordon wrote a classic study of the Catholic Church under Hitler, as well as a life of Franz Jagerstatter, an Austrian peasant and Catholic who chose execution rather than service in Hitler's armies.

She tells us that Zahn now speculates that the American Catholic Church, in its official passivity before the Vietnam war, has passed the point of default achieved by Roman Catholicism under Hitler. If the German bishops had been less nationalistic and more humanitarian, they would have faced heavy penalties from flock and State alike. Mob action, imprisonment, or death would have been likely. In the United States, episcopal opposition to war and racism would be constitutionally protected and would enjoy popular support even from within the government.

The comparison points up the extent to which the American hierarchy has betrayed its magisterium and its charism. Like the government, the Catholic episcopacy has lost authority in the critical questions of life and death. While the majority of men live under the threat of imminent death—war, starvation, poverty, political tyranny, natural catastrophe—the bishops have offered neither voice nor presence for these men; they have neither taught nor acted in concert with them. But the biblical notion of authority rests upon service, service even to death.

Zahn's conclusions are nothing new, nor do I find them especially profitable. I have preached similarly, and have found American Catholics largely unmoved. Their cultural asphyxia has left them with little enthusiasm for risky explorations into moral and political responsibility. From every indication, they care little that Rome and the German Catholics had sold out Church and country—including six million Jews—and that they themselves have sold out. I had sometimes surprised a flicker of understanding in Catholic eyes, then fear, then impassivity. Defenses come down only for instants.

Yet I shrink from criticizing Zahn or his patient, sensitive illumination of our religious and social predicament. He is an exemplary man and Christian, and an outstanding social scientist. But I think we should put things into perspective. To break a law that directly supports the American war machine means jail. But in the process a public forum is available through the courtroom, sympathetic publicity, wide-scale popular support; and there are comparatively comfortable jail conditions for such dissenters. War resisters do not suffer that much. In fact, they suffer mainly from the realization that virtually no one will risk even the little they have.

In many Communist and Third World countries things are quite different; dissent can mean death or worse. In the Soviet Union troublesome intellectuals are classified as insane—indefinitely. South Vietnam has Con Son and its tiger cages, Brazil its torture rooms, Guatemala its White Hand, Indonesia its anti-Communist bloodletting. In such countries, and in many others, one does not dare dissent without first having accepted death.

In America people are selectively prosecuted for civil disobedience; thousands of young men have refused military induction and still walk free. Some who have faced the courts receive an agonizing hearing and a moderate sentence. Still, Americans will not dissent. We are pampered, soft, morally sterile, frightened. Most of us are willing to remain controlled as long as control guarantees us our comforts.

June 1971

Foreigners often cannot understand how the values of our society stunt our humanity, emasculating and pacifying us. They can merely observe the effect with astonishment and shame. One night, in a conversation with a Dutch priest recently returned from Indonesia, this had hit me with stunning force.

With a group of liberal priests, we were talking about politics and about personal responsibility. The issue had narrowed to this: If one's society is intent upon destroying itself and is therefore hopeless, how does one create hope for oneself and others?

The liberals floundered. The Dutch priest listened intently for a while. "I have a question," he remarked quietly. "Why don't you Americans dissent?"

Dead silence greeted him. "Let me explain. I have worked in Indonesia nine years on fishing and farming cooperatives. Naturally I know something of the regimes of both Sukarno and now Suharto. You've heard a bit, I suppose, of the anti-Communist bloodbath after Sukarno was thrown out. But not enough; the Western press has lied. Over several years a million people died—your newspapers said four or five hundred thousand. Many who died were my people. They died not because they were Communist, whatever that is, but because they believed in justice. Justice they didn't have.

"Justice meant enough to eat, seed for the ground, a fair price for their crops and fish. They had hope for this under Sukarno, for all his faults. And then the terror began, and they were hunted down like jungle animals. The streams and rivers literally ran red, and bodies were everywhere. When they killed my farmers they killed their families too. When they killed my fishermen they machine-gunned them and sank their boats. The sea is vast, and there are no survivors—you see?

"And now Western investment comes back, especially American. Dissent has been crushed, and they can begin again to bleed us.

"Do you understand what I'm saying? My people are dead because they asked nonviolently for what belonged to them. But you Americans, you upset me. If you protest seriously—and you should, because no one is more responsible for tragedy in the world than you—you are indicted, you get a better trial than in most countries, trials from which you can at least speak to educate others. And then you get a few years in jail. So I'm puzzled. Why don't you dissent?"

He got no answers, not even any attempts. We are among the most unfree people in the world because we are so high on the hog. High enough, in fact, to get the first cuts with the sharpest knives. Even in the Movement—already renowned for ego-tripping, acid, grass, easy sex, booze, all when one wants it. And the rhetoric. My God, the rhetoric! We have our own credibility gap; the distance between mouth and performance is wider than the government's. Can one wonder, then, why "peacemakers" cannot face the music? When you mention consequences, people look at you as though you'd spoken an obscenity.

July 1971

This week Dan and I will go before the Parole Board. In one respect it is an event; Dan has waited eleven months, and I twenty-two. In another it is a nonevent; our future, *ad nutum regis,* is quite out of our hands. Caesar will decide whether we must do more time or enjoy, under heavy supervision, the ambiguous freedom of the streets.

For many months now I have witnessed the psychological

141

havoc that parole and parole boards create in prisoners. Parole becomes a prize only slightly less precious than one's life; it can save one from as much as 60 percent of one's sentence. The attitude toward parole, therefore, amounts to continually frustrated anticipation and suspended desires, a limbo of expectation and wild fantasy. One discovers, by experiencing it, the outrageous value one places on the fleshpots of Egypt (or bread and circuses).

I am not arguing that inmates should see prison in a beatific light or should politicize the experience into unreality. But parole is a psychological thumbscrew, a con game that exacerbates the destructive self-interest so common among prisoners. It leads them to make oracles of caseworkers, to plot and connive and lie, to cheapen and demean themselves by making every circumstance connected with their freedom a matter of interminable diagnosis, compulsive reflection, and extravagant hope. I have seen men embalmed in acute anxiety for two months waiting for word from Washington, and in nearly suicidal despair at rejection.

One day recently I heard a front-office inmate, privy to administrative scuttlebutt, announce to an intent circle, "Federal joints is packed. They gotta use the Parole Board. This last board cut loose fifty percent." His words were hungrily received, men listened and grasped at hope because they needed to. Their needs fed their credulity, and their credulity made them accomplices in their own punishment.

Punishment is the business of miserable places like this. And parole is a significant part of the punishment. In regard to our own parole, we will have an answer from "executive" session in Washington in eleven days. Inmates without our support or notoriety sweat for a decision for four to nine weeks in literal agony. We will have ours in eleven days so they can obscure what is the normal policy of making men wait until they are half mad with anticipation.

The men realize what is being done to them. Privately they curse and rage over it, maintaining meanwhile a placid and courteous slavery to officials. This is the apex of punishment, and they know it. They know parole is the ultimate weapon of degradation, that in fact all the emasculation the penal system so subtly exacts finds its culmination there. They know this and speak of it with hatred. They even try to draw hope from it, telling how they intend to reconstruct themselves and nullify the damage they have endured. Yet such hope is mostly an illusion; the damage is usually irrevocable.

To place one's hopes in the parole system is like believing in Richard Nixon, or believing in the ultimate justice of Pentagon politics. Yet this does not preclude an understanding of federal expediency, which can be marvelously and insidiously flexible at times. (Witness the President's resolve to visit Peking, to cool it with our favorite devils these many years, even in face of Russian and Taiwanese alarm.) Dan has excellent medical reasons for release, so the Powers might prudently decide to free him, rather than endure a storm of criticism. For similar reasons they might decide to free me, perceiving that their rhetoric (eventual withdawal from Indochina) and my "crimes" (civil disobedience opposing the war) happen to coincide roughly in the public mind. That is to say, many people will ask: "If Nixon really wants to get out, and if Berrigan destroyed draft files as a way of saying we must get out, why does Berrigan have to stay in jail?"

Looking to 1972, if Nixon has liabilities, they are the war abroad and the war against dissent at home. (The first naturally necessitates the second.) If the image for '72 is to be "a man of peace," a certain amount of credibility in that title may be lost with peace activists in jails.

Perhaps such reasoning grants our leaders too much. Their slavish preoccupation with "power solutions" makes it increasingly difficult to imagine doing right things even for wrong reasons.

I would like to get out again: that's a fairly sane and modest admission. All the moral and psychological discipline that one can apply to the reality of prison does not make it easy to accept. I would like to get out again—to see my mother, my family, the people I love. I would like to work for peace again, not as a symbol of repression, but as a peacemaker with a more human and durable life formula than the war-makers offer. But those are my views and my desires, not necessarily God's. I have already accepted the prospect that much of the remainder of my life may be spent in prison. I do not welcome this nor relish it. I accept it in the hope that the means to live it will be there when it is needed.

If one considers oneself in the light of the Indochinese, one's contribution to structural change and the outlawing of war is pitifully small. Those people have paid for peace with their blood, with the decimation of their families and friends, in the incredible squalor and despair of the refugee camps, under the shattering terror of American firepower. I pay with a few months from an otherwise mediocre existence. No big deal.

July 1971

I sit outside of Control (the institution's communications center) awaiting call for a visit. A black guy bursts out suddenly, shaking off the clutch of a guard. Then the black races off, shouting that he intends to see his parole officer. (He probably meant his caseworker.) The guard watches his retreat disgustedly, obviously upset. Then he ducks inside to reappear with another hack. Together they start off purposefully after the inmate.

The scene is like a one-act farce. Next comes a medical technician, worriedly standing in the doorway. I know him as a good guy—straight, unpolitical, but conscientious and sensitive. "What's the rhubarb?" I ask him.

He laughs apologetically. "That black guy checked in with a urinary discharge. We took a smear and looked at it. He's got the clap."

Now here's a new twist, I thought. This place isn't Saigon. "I don't get it. What's he running away for? You can clear up the clap easily, can't you?"

"Sure! But we've gotta isolate him before he infects somebody else. He's gotta come to the hospital."

"Yeah, but he's scared. What's he afraid of, punishment?"
"Naw, he knows we won't punish him. He's a Muslim, and Muslims frown on this kind of nonsense. If he comes to the hospital, they'll wanna know why, and they'll learn he's been messin' around. And they'll take some measures."

Prison and war, I reflect: those twin abuses of the spirit, twin refinements of abused sexuality. One comes to both from a culture that markets sex as though it were a new garden hose. And one builds upon that unreality during the prison or war experience. In either a man becomes expendable.

Obviously the sexual climate here is a derivative of that outside. Sex is sold under the illusion of scarcity. But in prison scarcity has a hopelessness attached to it; scarcity is total, it's a drought. Therefore vicariousness must be complete, fantasizing must be total. And to accept vicariousness and fantasizing as normal (most prisoners do) heightens the dangers of both. For the most part, inmates do not comprehend the dimension of escapism, or that vicarious sex is the main escape.

Inmates have no hope of access to their women—or to any woman. There is nothing to give substance to their fantasies, made more furious by the pneumatic and plastic females in *Playboy, Penthouse, Evergreen,* and by some hard-core pornography. A few practice total abstention, being critical of masturbation or homosexuality and resolute in what is for them a code of honor. Most masturbate and defend the practice. Some bring their homosexuality with them, others find it here, becoming homosexual for the duration or maybe longer.

The contempt and ostracism to which habitual and extracurricular homosexuals are subjected intensify their problems, which are psychological anyway, because they originate in feelings of exclusion. Here, as elsewhere, the dominant sexual character is macho, sexist, aggressive, violent, and anticommunitarian. Sexism will disappear only when the profit motive loses its hold on us.

July 1971

Dan and I are still looking for *one* reporter who knows the basics about life and resistance, who does not have holes in his ego, and who will not sell our confidence for a buck. As I say, we're still looking.

Like most professionals, reporters come in combinations of pluses and minuses. Why shouldn't they be a very mixed bag, caught up as they are in the ambivalent business of fulfilling themselves personally and economically? They do their own thing, with a sometimes frightening mixture of dedication and competitiveness. And we fascinate them, people who risk life and liberty for the anawim, the poor.

Fascination, however, is not understanding. Not when understanding means a challenge to suspend their egos and to learn patience. So some reporters are adequate students of the Movement, deeply appreciating nonviolent militancy, yet they will use one arrogantly and betray confidence for a price. Others are ignorant, but strangers to success and firm in their own identity, and therefore trustworthy. Rarely do we find one who is knowledgeable and honest.

Our experience with the press, since the government has begun trying to impale us on legalities, has been a series of disasters. One can understand stupidity, or facile manipulation of facts, contempt, or the use of innuendo. One can forgive clumsy conjectures about past or future possibilities. But what does one do about deliberate breaches of trust, broken agreements, and betrayals of confidences that suddenly appear on the newsstands? After these experiences, one dare not give any information to reporters. Even the possibilities of friendship with them no longer exist.

On three occasions in the last six months reporters dealing with us allowed, in effect, their greed for reputation or money to overwhelm agreement, friendship, the truth itself. In two instances they broke their word, publishing inaccuracies they had agreed to correct and publishing when they had promised not to. Their duplicity reminds one of our Brahmin policy-makers, who, under certain pressurized conditions, deny today yesterday's press releases.

The latest incident is only the most recent in a series. Two men from a West Coast newspaper, highly respected muckrakers, had asked Elizabeth McAlister to cooperate with a story on her relationship with me. Liz remained cool to the idea but agreed to discuss it. Finally it was decided that (1) the account would merely paraphrase speculation that was already published in *Life* and elsewhere; and (2) nothing would appear without her prior clearance. Throughout negotiations she made clear her opposition to any further unraveling of a private matter that is subject to our control alone. They agreed to honor the conditions. On a visit here she appeared satisfied, spoke of the respect in which they were held and of her own confidence in them.

All this time, it appears, our newsmen were keeping creatively busy. They picked the brains of people in our confidence (probably defendants) and obtained the following information: (1) that we were seriously planning marriage; (2) that we had a statement addressing Church and State to that effect; (3) that we would not disclose our plans prior to trial, not desiring to "upstage" the government. In a word, they gained from informers everything that we wished kept temporarily secret and under our control.

On July 18 our friends released their story, and it appeared syndicated around the country. (Local papers around Harrisburg, the area which will supply the jury, all covered it.) The story was unimaginably bad. I felt raped.

One of the ways really to learn basic civics is to be forced to feel in your bones and heart the corruption of government. Our leaders have done their utmost to smear and ridicule Liz and myself; they have shadowed us, seized our correspondence, bugged our phones, sent their agents to gossip about us like hags over a back fence, leaked allegations to the press of our "squalid" affair. Despite their efforts, however, we had regained some measure of control over our love, in the hope of disclosing it later with dignity. Now control is ours no more. Friends, both defendants and reporters, have collaborated with our enemies

147

and picked up their predatory habits. Our friends have done a bit of whoring. They have picked up with Mother State as one picks up with an ex-wife for a night of pleasure.

Where Liz and I go from here, in a way useful to Church and public, is anybody's guess. But we will find it richer for the experience of having been blocked. We will proceed hopefully with more wisdom regarding newsmen, and more love regarding defendants. In a real sense, security doesn't rest on much else.

July 1971

A letter came in yesterday from one of our young friends released two months ago. It was the first substantial word we've had from him, and everyone felt glad.

His view of the Great Society was a somewhat sobering one. His parole status forced him to take a job; he lives at home, and keeps his life straight and very, very narrow. He has no reluctance about telling us these things. While he was an inmate here we helped him reclaim his life, and he responded with such abundant intelligence and goodwill that he became one of the staunchest and most lovable guys on the compound. When he left we had high hopes that he would dig into peace and continue his experiments in peacemaking.

He found this impossible, apparently. He had no community to connect with, nor did he know enough to form community. There was no one but old friends, and he soon lost interest in them, for they still clung to the childishness he had once shared but had abandoned in the course of his prison experience. The trouble was that he had decided to become a man, while they were still trying to make up their minds about that.

The trouble also is that we have no community outside that awaits him, capable of responding to his needs. We have no extension of what exists here, no fellowship of concern, understanding, dialogue, spirituality, activism. We must provide that, and the logical people to do it are the men here. A loose community of ex-cons responsive to one another, to the poor, to militant nonviolence, to civil disobedience, to a great society of the free and responsible.

Late July 1971

        This was a day of some anticipation, with decisions on our parole hearings promised. We analyze all expectation and arrive at only one certainty; we will know far more at the day's end about ourselves.

Two of our lawyers, Paul O'Dwyer and Father Bill Cunningham, arrive. They plan to call a press conference for tomorrow. Accordingly, we give them statements contingent on Parole Board mandates: (1) both of us released, (2) Dan released and me held, (3) me released and Dan held. As lawyers do (this seems to be part of their professional mystique), they have their hopes cresting, feeling at the very least that Dan will be paroled.

At five-thirty Dan and I are called out of quarters to Control. Washington has spoken! It strikes me as odd that they would formally announce bad news to us; most of officialdom here would prefer seeing us freed (more normalcy for them). Perhaps it's good news?

The chief of corrections and parole, along with the associate warden, kindly sit us down. "We want to give you the news before it hits the radio. Dan, you are to continue to expiration. Phil, your case will have a review in January 1973." In more graphic language, Dan was told to "wrap it up and bring it all home!" For me a sixteen-month setoff and a progress report in early 1973. If I mend my manners and learn more institutional groveling, I might make it then.

Reflections of various kinds are in order, but above all, thoughts on the nearly absolute corruption of the government. Out of this comes the intransigence we have seen carried to an absurd degree in Indochina. If the government could carry on that choice bit of pathology since 1949, with its consequent rape of rationality and decency, this refusal should not be surprising.

There is nothing to do here but pick up the struggle again. One of our mistakes is the operating assumption that being in jail is enough—enough for us, enough for the Movement, enough for the American people and the Indochinese. Obviously it is not enough.

August 9

I recall that Martin Buber said that life is relations; Thomas Merton called it connections. So I connect up with the Danbury Five, who are in hospital solitary for their resistance last Friday. They were thrown into the Hole for posing questions, on parole boards, political prisoners, and war. They are fasting from solids.

I connect with five more young guys and pass out the Friday statement. The guards reluctantly arrest us, and we proceed to the Hole amid applause. We have let loose a floodgate. The men here are, as a group, educated, touched, moved. They refuse work by the droves, and by the day's end thirty to forty prisoners are in the Hole, fasting with us.

August 10, 1971

Our friends in the Hole are beginning to slip in their support, trickling back to population after the captain sweet-talks them in court. The five who came with me hang in; we leave court and go back to solitary and fasting. It is easier now; yesterday was a bitch. Apparently one has to adjust psychologically as well as physically. I have stopped smoking and that helps.

I read Luke last night: "Happy are those who hear the word of God and obey it." It strikes me once again, almost as much as the first time, that obeying God's word is very likely to get one killed. It accomplished that for Christ, who was God's word, and whose actions were his words. God's word is a living force, and it will insure life if it is lived. But it also provokes death, meets death in confrontation, and invariably (if only temporarily) loses. Let those who hear God's word and try to hear it better, along with those who obey it and strive to obey it more perfectly—let them be forewarned. It can kill you—or rather, it can get you killed.

August 11, 1971

I should explain the reasons for our protest and fast. The Parole Board is a smug, bloated, overpaid, immune circle of bureaucrats, whose share of the pork barrel is individually $32,000 to $38,000 a year. They rule over the sentences of 21,000 federal prisoners. An inmate who goes before the board can neither view the data by which he is resentenced nor know the reasons for resentencing.

This provided a locus for our protest. Parole Board machinations affect the lives of every federal prisoner, among them political prisoners. Moreover, political prisoners have their counterpart in Indochina, particularly in the notorious tiger cages of Con Son Island. Despite the furor over them created by Congressmen Anderson and Hawkins, the tiger cages are still filled, and more are contracted to a San Francisco firm.

Some have questioned why this protest must be centered on Dan and me. For several reasons: (1) A protest, to be viable, must be personalized. (2) It must deal with obvious injustice. (3) Preferably it should be constructed around those already publicly known.

Springfield, Missouri

AUGUST–SEPTEMBER 1971

August 12

This diary can't keep pace with events. Last night, about 5 P.M., the administration made good on its threats to transport the fasters to "adequate medical facilities." They acted with astonishing speed and an efficient mobilization of manpower. We were not consulted nor given a choice. Our "processing"—collecting our personal effects—took half an hour, and then a calvacade of some seven cars of guards and federal marshals drove us to the local airport. It was in fact a military convoy, similar to those we run through enemy territory in Vietnam.

Once at the airport, guards manacled us hand and foot, and we shuffled, chain-gang style, to two small chartered Beechcrafts. On the plane we remained handcuffed and helpless in case of an accident, though our leg irons were taken off. The Beechcrafts cruised at 170, so it took over six hours to reach Springfield, Mo. —a thousand miles away. The press awaited us. We walked through blinding lights to a prison bus.

At the hospital, which suggests a junior version of an Ivy League campus, we were speedily processed and led to an airy, pleasant wing, given individual rooms, and bade adieu. It is nearly 3 A.M. We reflected happily that our government can certainly move when it has to, and do it with a certain devious skill.

August 14

We weren't shipped because of health endangered by fast. They shipped us out secretly and precipitously because we had awakened the Danbury compound to its true situation, and because this awakening threatened an enlargement of the protest, and even a danger to prison industries and their huge profits.

Here the lie is given to their pious solicitude about our health. If that was the only reason for our removal, then why our total isolation from other prisoners, why the twenty-four-hour guard

155

outside our locked doors? We feel the familiar credibility gap, and I once more reflect sadly on the separation of government from people. How can it be frank with people when its main line is war, nuclear supremacy, arms traffic, global profit, and government of, for, and by the rich?

August 16

It is a dull, sullen Monday—the most sluggish day we've had since we started. A week ago we handed out our statements, got busted, went to solitary, and began our fast. It has been a packed seven days.

I feel strong and clear-headed despite a weight loss of fifteen pounds. No big deal, I can afford it. Last night I dreamed of food all night—or so it seemed. This is my fourth fast of a week or more (Baltimore City Jail, Baltimore County Jail, Lewisburg Penitentiary, now here), and I don't recall such hunger pangs or such dreams.

The local bishop, William Baum, pays a pastoral visit (probably what he would call it). I bring him up to date, and he listens patiently. At one point he interjects mildly, "You see this as your witness, don't you?" Obviously he didn't see "my" witness as his also, or possibly that of other Christians.

He is one of the new breed of bishops gingerly appointed by Rome. They generally know speculative theology, relish the Scriptures, are kind and not dictatorial men. But they are criminally ignorant of history, other cultures, the poor, entrenched power, human tragedy and triumph. Their mystique has no politique, and is therefore doomed.

They recognize no flex in the Gospel, no pain, no dialectic. They know as little of naked power as the rich know of morality. And so they have little grasp of what underlies death or desolation in Pakistan or Indochina, no yardstick to gauge our common responsibility by. Bishop Baum made it clear that he would publicize no judgment on me or our position. The genius of a successful churchman is to remain neutral even over life and death.

And yet Bishop Baum would and did visit me; most American bishops would not, given the opportunity. They offer a commentary on the American hierarchy more astringent than any I could possibly make.

August 20

A limbo day, perhaps the first real one we've had since arrival. It is not that people are weak or depressed. There is merely no information from outside, the best stimulus possible to have.

I am reading a remarkable autobiography, *In God's Underground,* by Richard Wurmbrand. Wurmbrand and his wife were Jewish converts to Christianity. He was also a Lutheran pastor. When the Communists took over Romania after World War II, Wurmbrand was imprisoned for his outspoken teaching of Christian principles and his opposition to the regime. Fourteen years of imprisonment, torture, solitary confinement, and degradation followed. He contracted tuberculosis, and was the only man to emerge alive from Tergal-Ocna's "Death Room." His wife, Sabina, experienced her own ordeal in forced-labor camps, narrowly escaping death.

Three characteristics of Wurmbrand attract me—his intelligence, his faith, his compassion. Some of the exchanges he had with his jailers and with high party officials imprisoned with him are wonders of humanitarianism and political wisdom. He knew, as few Christians know, that Christianity faithfully lived is politics enough. He had no time for ideology, or for the murderous abstractions of the irresponsible.

August 25

The guards at Springfield prison call out Ted Glick, my co-defendant, and me for a visit. We are overjoyed to see Liz McAlister and Bill Cunningham. We soon discover, how-

157

ever, that they have more on their minds than joy and solidarity. They arrive somewhat upset by two developments. The first has to do with our shipment from Danbury; that event has deeply shaken them and they conclude that a like jeopardy threatens us here. The second involves the initial reservations about the politics of our strike.

At the start both defendants and lawyers had disapproved of our politics and tactics. They felt we had sacrificed solidarity and trial preparation, and had offered the government further provocation to lean hard on us at Harrisburg. They were learning, however, that like Olaf, there was some shit we could not eat—that Con Son and Springfield are not far removed; that parole is a favorite psychological club used on prisoners; that indictment and parole denial are twin fists of repression. Liz, Eqbal, the Scoblicks saw this immediately; it was hoped that all defendants were beginning to see it. Liz and Eqbal were working very hard at publicizing these issues, and at explanations for the lawyers.

What impresses me is the humanity of their difficulties, the defendants and lawyers. How can they understand that our fast is the best security against further shipment; that our community of eleven is strong, resolved, and confident; or that prison, with which they are so unfamiliar, can radicalize people with astounding speed? However staunchly we might pursue these points, understanding comes slowly.

August 28

I have neglected this journal mostly because of voluminous letter writing and long tactical meetings. Here's how it went. Thursday night had brought a letter from Jerry dwelling on Dan's health—more frequent fits of depression, pain from the hernia, missing us all very badly. Carol and Jerry had gone home deeply worried—and they are not people to shout wolf unnecessarily.

I realize that when one receives such news in isolation it is more apt to strike with peculiar and painful force. One can't qualify it with other opinions or other news. So my thoughts whirled in angry and abrupt fashion. I concluded that our month's fast had been a mistake. We had not asked enough of the authorities (Dan's release), or of ourselves (water fast to the death). Reinforcing that, I suffered horrid visions of Dan eroding mentally and physically, ruined by an unjust confinement, deserted by his brother and his friends. We fasters began to talk, however, and reason prevailed. We could hardly begin a water fast without Dan's consent; it might destroy him as much as us. We couldn't ask our supporters to accept this without consideration. Ted Glick and I could not have ignored the effect of such a move upon the other Harrisburg defendants or upon the impending trial. So we have concluded that our fate depends much more on what is done outside than on our actions. We have done our thing and must now rely on them even more strongly. Dan, I'm sure, would agree with this wholeheartedly.

August 29

Bill Cunningham and Liz returned far more optimistic than before. They have called friends in the East, who report a continued momentum for support. Two are lobbying with Congress to begin an investigation of the Federal Parole Board; others are preparing for a large press conference; Dave Dellinger is agitating for a national demonstration at Danbury in early October. Consequently our visitors feel able to encourage us.

Our tiny group of valiant men remains cheerful, resolved, optimistic. I observe them slack-jawed—they are that astonishing. Seven of us—John Phillips, Jon Bach, Tom Hosmer, Deven Jones, David Malament, Ted Glick, and myself—are in prison for political resistance. Four others—Mitchell Snyder, Ed Gersh, John Halloran, and Tom Ireland—are in prison for assorted rule-breaking, from embezzling to narcotics traffic. Needless to say, they have learned a better way.

159

I have worked with many activist communities—in fact, some of the best, if one is to measure quality by risk, balance, generosity. But this bunch is unique. Some short months ago two or three of the nonresisters were hung-up guys who would have been benumbed by a generous thought, while some of the resisters were frightened people who couldn't explain why they had come to prison. And then something hit them—history, tragedy, a few good books, a few good men, grace, a cause, a need, a lot of things. And they became men—who together could do marvelous things.

Individually we are not that much, but we've known uplifting, renewal, fortifying—a rare experience. And this experience we must digest and pass on to others, making it an educational form capable of attracting others, attracting others to new life through resistance. In a word, we must learn to become architects of community.

Monday, August 30

Today is Black Monday, the day of the Attica tragedy. As I write, thirty-nine people are dead, with an almost certain prospect of several more. But the uprising has been put down, the colonials have been quelled, law and controlled disorder re-established. And power is content.

Two questions occur, one of them already dealt with by Bill Kunstler in a postmortem press conference. Why couldn't the State wait before crushing those inmates, before forcing the murder of those guards? Why couldn't Rockefeller come and talk, when all the negotiators agreed that he should? Several reasons: (1) Americans will not negotiate from parity. (2) Americans will negotiate from strength, but only briefly. Why possess strength if it can't be used? (3) Lives are expendable, but what isn't expendable is an abstraction, namely, stability in the state prison system.

Second question: Why couldn't amnesty be granted by the State? In one breath it acknowledges its default toward the men of Attica and its implication in the death of the first guard by bowing to over twenty demands. And in the next breath it rejects a plea for amnesty because a guard died from the first outbreak of violence. The State will not share the responsibility for the uprising and for the death of one of its own guards. This is to say, it will not admit to the violence that caused the desperation behind the riot.

What we have is another example of a war exported, only to return. As many observers remarked, "It was war inside that prison." Tear gas, assault guns, and clubs are solutions to people when people become problems. In Indochina we drain the ocean in which the fish swim: we rid ourselves of the problem by ridding ourselves of the people. At Attica the methodology was essentially the same: eliminate the people (even the guards had become the enemy) and you will eliminate the problems. (News has just arrived that the nine dead hostage-guards had been killed not by slashed throats but by gunshot wounds.)

Which, finally, constitutes a lesson for prison guards as well. If ever men are expendable, it is they. The barons of power sacrifice them without a qualm of conscience, without a flicker of remorse. A few San Quentin guards got the message and quit rather than do their sickening work in an "unsafe" institution. Perhaps our prisons will change for the better, then, as it becomes more difficult to get jailers. But many men will have to die before that.

August 31

One of our men, Tom Ireland, has abandoned the fast. He left us tonight for the hospital. For five or six days he has suffered steadily and acutely—weakness, cramps, nausea, depression. His worst affliction, however, from which the others arose in part, came from guilt over failing us. I feel personally that the rest of us have had a much easier time of it because of the sufferings of this one man.

In one of his letters the apostle Paul wrote of supplying in his own flesh the suffering lacking in the Body of Christ, the community. The law of redemption holds: we do not become adult or godlike without suffering freely chosen. Christ did not become Son of God and Son of Man until he had drained the chalice of suffering to its lees.

In some mysterious way our bodies failed to suffer in this fast. So Tom filled them up with his own suffering, and in answering our need eased our pain.

September 1

For nearly a week now we have been writing some thirty-five Congressmen and ten federal judges about our experiment and the underlying issues that brought it about. None of us expects a startling response. Some will never see our mail, some will be frightened by it, a handful will answer, one or two will inquire further.

But we have finished doing that and need a new project. Time hangs heavy, people waste precious energy at TV or other nonsense. One friend suggests we get on with our political education for an hour a day, starting with "Political Organizing in Prison." Everyone agrees.

I won't say that agreement comes hard, but it must be worked at. Some of our guys are quite new at the political game, short on ideas and shy to voice them. Weakness, too, enters in. None of us can any longer stand long periods of intense reading, thought, or even conversation. But we agree to try nonetheless.

September 2

We get word that Tom Ireland feels better, eats solid food, and will soon join population. It is a great relief to us.

We have decided to quit the fast after thirty days. One group enters its fourth week today. We pick September 7 as the ideal cut-off date—thirty-three days for the first group, thirty days for the second. Other items must be decided: court action to return us to the East (preferably Danbury), adequate publicity, demonstrations if possible.

September 5

Bill Bender, one of our lawyers, and Tony Scoblick and Joe Wenderoth visit us—a heavy, four-hour session covering the fast, self-defense at the trial, cohesion between lawyers and defendants, and more draft-board raiders arrested in Camden, New Jersey, and Buffalo, New York. A number of them are fasting in Camden to protest outrageously high bail; John Grady had an initial $150,000 slapped on him.

Today completes twenty-four, giving us six days to go. We all remain comparatively strong physically and have normal mental energy. Betimes our young doctor berates us for "starvation," but our experience proves only how grossly we Westerners overeat, how much dangerous fat we carry, how weak and indulged we are. Once strength is regained I will get a better regimen on food going.

With the trial in view, I am reading *Ecocide in Indochina: The Ecology of War*. Most of the material it contains is two years old or more, which would indicate that it is now understatement. The destruction of that land and people is so much more advanced.

I can bear only an hour or two of it a day—it sickens me to the point of nausea, literally. Which is interesting, because I have been reading similar material for six or seven years. There's no schooling oneself to monumental insanity.

Items:
Pilots commonly refer to bombing victims as "crispy critters."

The "Food Denial" Program, really a campaign of starvation, has destroyed rice supply of one million people in order to deny food to twenty thousand Viet Cong. Little wonder that over 50 percent of Vietnamese children don't reach five years of age.

Seven million people have been rendered homeless by the war—nearly half of South Vietnam's population.

Indochina contains enough bomb craters to cover an area far larger than the state of Connecticut—most massive excavation project in modern history, exceeding the excavation of both Panama and Suez canals.

Anticrop attacks have ruined 3.8 million acres of arable land in South Vietnam.

Ninety percent of those killed and wounded in South Vietnam are civilians; and of these, 60 percent are children.

Culturally we Americans are narcoticized by statistics like these; they have no meaning for us or, if they do, we run from them. Chief among our domestic narcotics is not heroin or amphetamines, but violence.

September 6

Today is number twenty-nine for me and four others, thirty-two for five. Technically we finish tomorrow night, but for a variety of reasons we will break fast at Tuesday noon. We have a statement for press release, several defendants and lawyers are expected, and (hopefully) there are plans for much soup.

We want a restraining order to be filed so that the government can't shotgun-scatter us after recuperation. We have directed our lawyers to sue the government for punitive transfer, abridgment of free speech, and cruel and unusual punishment. We want to force the Bureau to return us to Danbury.

September 7

Today is the thirtieth and last day of a fast we began at the federal prison in Danbury, Connecticut.

During that time many events have occurred. First and foremost, Washington's war of extermination against the Indochinese continues with unabated fury. B-52s continue saturation bombing of three countries; fighter planes and helicopters provide fire support for mercenary troops; and naval vessels shell the Vietnamese coast incessantly. Computerizing the war, it is clear, has not made it less savage. Contempt, misery, starvation, forced relocation, and death are the lot of a people we are claiming to save.

Moreover, George Jackson has been killed in San Quentin prison—a proud and courageous victim of a racist, vindictive society. Killed with him were five white guards and inmates, victims no less of the violence and brutality condoned by those in power. As in other prisons around the land, inmates at San Quentin will know more punishment than rehabilitation, more humiliation than justice.

Tragic happenings most certainly—but they are made even more ominous by a no-see, no-hear, no-action government. Washington refuses to consider the humane and reasonable Vietnamese seven-point peace plan in Paris. Indeed, it has ridiculed the plan's true significance, diverting public attention from the war to Nixon's China trip, and to wage and price freezes against an inflation provoked mainly by militarism and war.

In a similar manner, the government has ignored the issues raised by our fast, displaying again its rigidity and imperviousness to legitimate request. For lack of official response, we can only conclude that Washington has an economic need to pursue its Indochinese war; has a political need to build more tiger cages at Con Son and to bury American dissenters within its prisons; has a bureaucratic need to sanction corruption in federal parole boards. Very simply, it judges Vietnamese political prisoners, as well as George Jackson, Angela Davis, and ourselves expendable.

This behavior is utterly consistent. It is consistent with the new feudalism—government by and for the wealthy and powerful. It ignores human rights, aspirations, and potential—and to that degree is virtually illegitimate.

We end our fast unaffected by official insensitivity. In fact, we are heartened by public support and by new signs of nonviolent resistance in Camden, New Jersey, and Buffalo, New York. It is our hope that such beginnings will swell to a movement capable of confronting official waste, terror, and death.

We ask our countrymen to consider this: Washington's war has now burst its frontiers, invading every aspect and sector of American society. It is now war upon you—psychological, economic, environmental, political. Unless you resist nonviolently and powerfully, expect the contempt, repression, and death accorded Vietnamese, blacks, the poor, and political prisoners. For the ultimate victims of total war are those silent at its obscenity.

September 8

We began eating yesterday; after thirty days it's bound to be a disturbing experience. Temperate as we were, some of us felt distress, and one or two guys were up most of the night, burping at both ends. We thought the doctors would descend on us like French governesses, clucking of soup and bland food. Just the contrary; they kept their distance, and sent in the ordinary, heavy, greasy institutional food. But nearly everyone exercises faithfully, and I expect we'll conquer the indigestion.

Liz and Bill Bender came yesterday, a particularly joyous sight for Ted and me. One of their many services to us is a measure of tough, blunt talk about the trial's complexity, about the welfare of defendants, about relationships with lawyers. Having Ted and me here fasting has activated some and weakened others. Whatever the situation, unity in the case is currently transparent and fragile.

Liz had seen Representative Kastenmeir of Wisconsin, who heads a House subcommittee on prisons. He knew nothing, I mean nothing, of conditions in federal prisons, let alone Parole Board operations. But he appeared open and willing. Congressman James Symington is expected tomorrow. And on the weekend, [Congressman] Bill Anderson.

A lot of this work is attributable to Liz. It is not because of my involvement that she works so hard. Her performance is the same with any issue or project.

Danbury Federal Correctional Institute
(Connecticut)

SEPTEMBER 1971–JANUARY 1972

September 1971

We return uneventfully except for ground fog, which prevents a landing at Danbury. The pilot finally gets into Westchester County Airport, where a top-level entourage from the prison meets us for safe-conduct back to Danbury.

We all know the jailers who come to transport us, yet a professional impersonality prevails. There is no hint of recognition, no greeting, no inquiry about our health. We could be chickens crated for market. The explanation would be, of course, "doing my job." And doing one's job may not include gestures, amenities, courtesies.

No phrase takes a more accurate measure of the moral failure of this society. We are offering new sophistications to the Nazi rationale, and the generation most guilty of them is the one whose purifying violence swept the face of Europe clean of Naziism. Now the same empty abstractions, sterile loyalties, crippling fears and hates bind us also. If enough people fear and hate, one finds as commonplace people who are "doing their jobs." As they say in our prisons, give penal personnel a week's crash program and they'll run gas ovens for you.

But, more happily, we return to a prison community much changed by the fast. The men knew that two among us had lost parole over their witness, and though the majority might not understand or share this generosity, they respected it. But paroles had at the same time multiplied because of the impact of the fast. Administrators had approached inmates to inquire about improvements; prisoners had a little less fear, a little more confidence, more courage. Much of this was a by-product of the rebellion at San Quentin and Attica; functionaries struggle to change only when it becomes too expensive not to change. But generally, new hope seemed to have arisen because people here knew *us* and knew what we had done and recognized that our return signaled a nonviolent victory. Every sign of hope is a victory over darkness, a victory for all men.

September 1971

I just came across a fascinating little parable attributed to the late Rabbi Abraham Heschel. "Once upon a time in a kingdom long ago and far away, it happened that, after the grain crop had been harvested and stored, it was discovered to be poison. Anyone who ate of it went insane. The king and his advisors immediately took counsel as to what should be done. Clearly, from other sources not nearly enough food was available to sustain the populace; there was no choice but to eat the grain. 'Very well,' the king decided, 'let us eat it, but at the same time we must feed a few people on a different diet, so that there will be among us some who remember that we are insane.' "

"Some who remember that we are insane." If such a kingdom could stand as a microcosm of the world, then such a handful might emerge as the saviors of their mad fellows—"some who would remember that we are insane."

Contemporary translation: How to convince our leaders that they are insane? The king, the establishment in that tiny kingdom, wisely and humbly expected insanity, asking only that there be a few to remind them of it and to check them from destroying their subjects and themselves. Who among our leaders would admit the possibility, or ask and expect that his people would resist him in the worst manifestations of insanity? John McNaughton when he was Assistant Secretary of Defense wrote a memo to Robert McNamara in 1967: "A feeling is widely and strongly held that the establishment is out of its mind." McNamara would not accept McNaughton's candor or precision. He and President Johnson, as well as Secretary Rusk and the Bundy brothers, preferred to rely on the most terrible delusion known to man—that power can create a new reality, a new order, a New Man.

September 1971

What did Springfield mean to Harrisburg and the trial?

I think the two have a very mysterious but a very real relationship. Which is to say that the struggles against overblown power are reducible to one—the problem being to make connections between one aspect and others of it.

It is imperative to reject Washington's definition of "felon": felon under indictment (with the presumption of guilt), conspirator, bomber, kidnapper. It is imperative to reject such contemptuous interpretations, to state by resistance that one is none of these things, but a great deal more. It is imperative to express kinship with political victims in Siberia, in Greece, Brazil, Iran—and especially in South Vietnam. It is imperative to see parole board abuses as the same kind of institutionalized violence that led to tragedy in Indochina—control boiling under an altruistic public-relations stew.

There were meetings with defendants just before August 6, when we had already scheduled the first group of six to pass out leaflets to the population, get busted, and begin the fast. It simply did not register. For reasons quite comprehensible— "We had to prepare for trial, remember?"—it simply did not register.

On the following Monday a second group, which included myself, repeated the performance of August 6, commemorating both Hiroshima and Nagasaki. The Hole filled up—thirty-five to forty men refusing to work, some of them fasting with us. The situation became precarious for the administration—men like us fasting in segregation would endanger "industry" and the false peace of the compound. By Tuesday the warnings had become pointed— a continued fast would mean shipment. On Wednesday night threat became reality, and that's when we were plucked from our cells, bundled into waiting cars in a heavily armed motorcade and flown to the medical center at Springfield.

So we spent about five weeks at Springfield in a segregated wing, and all the defendants visited us at least once, plus several of the lawyers. I think it is fair to say that everyone overreacted to our resistance and the official response to it. Yet the discomfort associated with a long fast, and the patience with which we heard our visitors out, seemed to us a source of reassurance and even liberation. In the end, all sympathized, and Eqbal and Liz worked like dogs to publicize our attempts.

Ours was the first challenge within memory to the Parole Board, which, the next time around, handed out paroles as if they were going out of style. Liz was instrumental in awakening a House subcommittee on federal prisons, and though its efforts at investigation were halfhearted and superficial, it was another first. But most important, we acquainted federal prisoners with the idea that resistance to the Parole Board's psychological abuse was a good part of valor and a better part of politics. Before, it was unheard-of to knowingly reject parole. Several friends are now doing it. They're saying, "Take your parole and stick it!"

In a nonviolent way, moreover, I think we did help to focus national attention on the abominable American penal system. Meanwhile Attica had erupted, and George Jackson had been murdered in San Quentin. When it came to prisons (and much else), the press was interested in little but blood. Innovative nonviolent attempts to change the debasing character of our jails, repeatedly introduced throughout the federal system, have gotten insufficient notice.

Ted Glick and I returned from Missouri charged up, more than ever determined to confront nonviolently the disgusting conduct of government in this indictment. From somewhat successful measures to resist Parole Board repression we conclude that essentially the same resistance ought to guide us at Harrisburg. The government is colossally wrong; the government is violent; the government is employing its courts as a legal force to back up its military force. The government's barbaric war in Indochina needs Harrisburg. Its arrogance of power could end in an unresisted license to wage total war—and perhaps later, thermonuclear war. Of this we are convinced.

Of Gandhi it was written, "His menu for the growth of individuals was fearlessness. . . . He did not fear governments, jails, death—it would unite him with his God—illness—he could conquer it—and hunger, unpopularity, criticism, or rejection." And he had a profound respect for the promise dormant in people. "I have not the shadow of a doubt that any man or woman can achieve what I have if he or she would make the same effort and cultivate the same hope and faith."

What of our friends? All have broken the law, all have followed their consciences courageously, all have taken paths of resistance that have deepened intelligence and tempered resolution. Most important, at least half have had unusual experience with jail and have accepted its eventuality for themselves. Somebody remarked to me as we began preparation for trial, "You're blessed in one thing at least. You couldn't get a better bunch of defendants anywhere."

Perhaps. But the threat of life imprisonment does funny things to the most committed "head." So does a devilishly clever superseding indictment, the fears about the locale, the judge, a ruthless and vindictive prosecutor, and obviously, such an informer as Boyd Douglas, plus some two dozen letters of Liz's and mine that are in the government's possession. And so does the nightmarish prospect of a long trial (and possible conviction) for something that one thought about but did not do; that one discussed but did not plan; that one judged a responsibility rather than a crime. Evidence abounds that the government has brought out its big guns; that its machinery of indictment and punishment is methodical and unscrupulous; that it is determined to "get us" to save Hoover.

Entirely apart from comparative religion and politics in individual lives, the fact is Glick and I differ considerably in experience from the other defendants. (This is not to hold ourselves superior—we have had greater opportunity to realize our strength and the government's weakness.) For ten years I have fought the Church, and the State for over six. This is to be my fourth trial, and except for Ted, their first. As for Ted, he is an exemplary resister and organizer, fearless and self-sacrificing. Jail, moreover, decreases rather than increases our vulnerability—we have resisted there repeatedly. Naturally we present a different front to the trial from that of the other defendants. In addition, our politics are ratified totally by Dan, who possesses a similar history of resistance to Church and State.

It is not surprising, therefore, that our view of the trial clashes

175

radically with those of our sisters and brothers. If discussions remain abstract—i.e., Christian community, conspiracy, nonviolence
—agreement is automatic. But the concrete is a different matter—
self-representation, noncooperation, or even possible disruption
(nonviolent). It becomes painfully clear at these sensitive junc-
tures that six defendants have agreed on a conventional legal
representation, and that the legal priority of acquittal remains
uppermost. The framework for that has been set and bureau-
cratized with the lawyers. That decision, and that reality, has left
Glick and myself with two more alternatives—go *pro se* (defend
ourselves) and risk severance, or submit and remain with the
community. For obvious reasons I choose to stay; for reasons
just as clear Ted chooses to split.

Some defendants might consider that the resistance at Springfield will tend to benefit our defense at Harrisburg. I would not
necessarily agree. I feel rather that the thirty-day fast, undertaken with the full weight of indictment and prison upon us, renders
Ted and me somewhat unpredictable (even rash) in the eyes of
some of the co-defendants. I even feel that it mysteriously raises
the threshold of fear, and serves, to one degree or another, to
solidify opposition to my trial expectations. Though individual
expression differs somewhat, one can distingiush clear lines
of decision among the other six defendants—lawyers will engineer the defense, defendants will take a secondary role, acquittal will be the priority.

Reflections on the above are like hauling coals to Newcastle
or preaching nonviolence to General Westmoreland. But they serve
to illustrate the human and political differences between us, and
the phenomenon of community that holds us together. Hopefully,
they contribute aspects of clarity otherwise lost.

October 1971

A new month! New months are always greeted
with anticipation and relish, as though they constitute a rare
achievement in endurance. They say that one doesn't count time

when doing good time. But compromise enervates even the best of principles.

We have a memorial planned for tomorrow dedicated to the dead of Vietnam, of San Quentin and Attica prisons. The administration, apprehensive of similar trouble here, has tolerated an inmate committee, composed of delegates from the black, Spanish-speaking, and white communities. Meetings with officials commenced on Wednesday—slow, painful, exasperating work, what with the deviousness of our jailers and the inexperience of prisoners. But a few gains begin to register: the men hang in persistently and nonviolently, support grows, interest widens, and new hope takes root.

Ted Glick, my beloved co-defendant in the coming Harrisburg trial, leaves on bond after a prolonged wait. Possibly he has completed his jail for now; probably, however, he'll have ample opportunity for more later. We will miss him sorely. For his age (twenty-two), I have not seen his equal. Assuredly, people outside need him more than we.

The Memorial, October 1971

We are favored with top-heavy, mindless, over-armed and robotized "security" forces—National Guard, FBI, federal marshals, and prison guards. They constitute a redoubtable paramilitary force, with enough firepower to deal with Napoleon's Grande Armée.

As I write this a soldier of the republic stands atop the water tower, several hundred feet above the compound. He has binoculars, a radio, and (I'm sure) a high-powered rifle. From the opposite end of the compound, peering owlishly in, are three video tape cameras, ready to photograph any conspicuous gathering.

Our jailers would have both us and the public believe that change will spring magically from negotiations. But the firepower they pack displays their hypocrisy. Here as in Indochina the fact is that they're saying, "We have the guns! What do you have?"

We have nothing but a gesture. The few hundred demonstrators outside the walls, and a few hundred of us inside, have nothing but our gesture. Which we hope is more human, and therefore more powerful, than picking up a gun against one's brothers.

Memorial services begin in the auditorium, with the chairman of the prisoner committee offering some remarks. One has to understand the context of these remarks—he is memorializing the dead of Vietnam, of San Quentin and Attica, and a lot of political prisoners under the iron fist of Uncle Sam. Hundreds of people, maybe thousands, many from far away, have arrived to support us. Yet he begins by rejecting *any* political connotation in what we're doing, asserting that it is unconnected with any event outside. I try to make allowance; he is a well-padded lawyer from New York City who has nonetheless worked hard and selflessly for the memorial program. It is not an auspicious beginning.

We have agreed that I should keep out of it. Dan, however, rescues the proceedings with a few words of Saint Paul's "when I was a child, my speech, feelings and thinking were all those of a child; now that I am a man, I have no more use for childish ways." He tells of a custom, not unknown in the villages of contemporary India, whereby unwanted children are imprisoned in earthen jars, with holes cut in the bottom for defecation, in which they grow crippled and stunted and are freed only when the physical damage is irreparable. Then they can be exploited as beggars. So do most Americans relate to power—as spiritual beggars who cannot imagine themselves apart from the State handout. But the sign of a man is straightening his limbs by reaching out to a brother—breaking his own jar, so to speak.

The proceedings get better. Blacks read their poetry to the accompaniment of drums. Excellent! I go to a visit, and return to a slightly different spirit. These men, so many of them cheap grafters, who have never received a single worthwhile thing from community or achieved anything by a profession of moral and political ambition, have a new sense of themselves. The evening national news shows Ted Glick marvelous at the outside rally. So the day is a beginning—imperfect and schoolboyish. And quite beyond expectation.

October 1971

Yesterday was my birthday (forty-eight), my third in jail. People are embarrassingly kind and thoughtful. Frankly, I would have preferred to forget it.

A rumble begins in my dormitory, where seventy-five men live in uneasy truce. Overcrowding is such a burden that the enemy is not the Man, who stays out of sight pretty much, but the guy in the upper bunk or in the next one. *The Man* doesn't bug you— doesn't talk all night, doesn't snore, doesn't scatter his garbage, doesn't close the window when it's warm outside, doesn't steal from you, doesn't snitch on you, doesn't betray your confidence, doesn't curse you out. But in our dorm *the next guy* is likely to. Everyone is just too close.

In any event, this is a drug joint, and drugs—hard and soft— move despite measures to choke off the import. The other day, when returning from a visit and its customary strip-search, a guy said to me, "I've been here two years, and I've never seen them catch drugs by stripping people down. You know what I saw in the john the other day? Five different guys vomiting up drugs. They get 'em in a condom or a balloon from folks, swallow them, get back to their dorm, drink warm water, and puke them up. Then they shoot them, sometimes in broad daylight."

Such being the bare facts of dormitory life, rhubarbs and rumbles are predictable—indeed, inevitable. Mostly they center on cards and pools (cigarettes) and drugs (heroin). Now it appears that a young French-Canadian has gotten drugs from, or has dealt drugs to, some Puerto Ricans. There was, at any rate, some complicity, and the Spanish-speaking accuse him of ratting them out. He denies the charge vehemently, a fight breaks out, others umpire and quiet it down. But, alas, the Puerto Ricans return with a task force intent upon retribution, carrying pipes, two-by-fours, broomstick handles. They work over Frenchie in a brief, violent encounter, and leave him with his head split.

He is in the hospital now, not badly hurt. I talk with one of the whites standing by, suffering over one man going down under that vengeful little mob of Latins. The only lesson he draws is: "Them Spics are together, and we ain't!"

He's wrong, poor guy! The Puerto Ricans are not "together"; neither are the whites nor the blacks. Those who are together are the Nixons, Mitchells, Rockefellers, Mellons, Fords, who know no other way of life except lordship of the world, no other relationship to people except domination and control. What my poor friend does not know is that Big Brother creates "enemies" for the poor to fight—and they are invariably one another. What's the difference between a prison dormitory and 116 Street and Third Avenue? They're both ghettos. And in the ghetto one never resists the right enemies. They're not around—they're in the boardrooms, in the Bahamas or Nice, or in Westchester and in Greenwich, Connecticut.

So one turns on the brother, the one who bugs you with petty irritations. He doesn't overcharge you for squalid, rotten housing; he doesn't begrudge you the miserable subsistence of welfare; he doesn't raise and process the drugs overseas, and sneak them into the country through his craven, greedy slaves; he doesn't hate you because you're black or Spanish-speaking; he doesn't steal your sons for war; he doesn't hang a "cheap labor" label on you for your life's remainder; he hasn't decided that you are human offal, unworthy of dignity, incapable of feeling. The ones who do these things are not at hand; they have no desire to see their handiwork. So one rages against the brother and loses one's innocence terrorizing the innocent.

October 1971

The last World Series Game is on; my confreres are out to watch it, leaving the dorm oddly quiet. I sit on my bunk and try to pray over the Beatitudes. They are a synopsis of all revelation, Christ's manifesto and life formula, His revolutionary doctrine.

The translation I'm using has the fourth Beatitude this way:

"Happy are those whose greatest desire is to do what God requires—God will satisfy them fully!" My guts and my head react
and tell me: fine and dandy, if you want to die! Because desiring
what God requires means doing what God requires. (Desire
equals act: any other notion eventually leads to madness.)

What God demands are two dynamic processes. First, He requires the emptying of self so axiomatic in Scripture; and second,
identification with the oppressed. Moreover, the two are one, and
must constantly nourish each other. Contemplation is essential for
resistance, and resistance is essential for contemplation. The
model in all this is Christ Himself.

Without question, I have desires that purely and simply oppose
what God requires. These desires inspire fear; I fear their insistence, their clamor and tenacity. Above all, I fear their loss, and,
because I do, I fear death. Death to self, death by violence;
they are one, and I fear them.

The contrary of faith is fear. The Lord used to chide His little
band, so timid and frightened despite their bravado and ambitions.
He would ask them about their fears, exhort them to faith, give
them evidence for believing. My problem is essentially the same
as theirs—I fear death to self, I fear violent death done to me.
I fear liberation. For death, properly understood, is liberation.

November 1971

I remember somebody describing prisoners as
the most vulnerable people in the world. And so I receive a little
extra education in this.

Two marshals pick me up at Danbury for hearings on motions
in Harrisburg. Even as marshals go, they are a queer team—
gruff, taciturn, emotionally and mentally musclebound. And desperately unhappy. Why not? What a miserable, stinking job, trans-
porting men as though they were beef going to market.

One is white and one black. The slight human gain this might
have represented is nullified by the dour Tomism of the black,

who is apparently senior, and therefore in charge. For the most part he sits immobile in the front seat, issues bad road directions, reads the *Daily News,* or sleeps. By contrast, his partner scurries around with chains and handcuffs, does all the driving, and speaks only when spoken to.

The white makes our acquaintance first in the Danbury lockup, greeting us with the tools of his trade—a nine-foot chain and handcuffs. He wraps the thing first around me and then around a young black who is returning to court in D.C. Finally he handcuffs us through the chain. We are now secured to each other, while our arms are secured to our waists. I register this curiosity. The chain is utterly new to me, and I ask him what's going on. He grunts, "Regulations!" (His most intelligible remark of the trip.) Nonetheless he makes a point and he knows it: "Run and you're twice as good a target!"

He leads us to his Buick, all trunk and hood. I wince at the sight of it. Marshals are frequently so vain and style-conscious as to be contemptuous of an ordinary sedan. This monster has two thrones in front and an upholstered afterthought in the back.

Once we are crammed into the afterthought, he completes our bonds, putting on ankle shackles (in polite parlance; one never calls them leg irons). I suddenly recall going to Regional Market as a kid and seeing crated fowls and animals there. I feel a sense of identification.

First stop, Bridgeport—for another captive. With his addition, the back seat becomes more overpopulated, like India after receiving refugees from East Pakistan. Moreover, our chauffeur has the heater on despite the day's warmth.

A sardonic and interminable Calvary begins, lengthened by New York City traffic, a route judiciously chosen by the black marshal. A traffic jam on the Cross-Bronx Expressway costs us an hour. In that tiny back seat we can only squirm to a change of position before a neighbor's bulk and our chains remind us that there's nowhere to go. I feel myself going numb from the waist down, my circulation choked by shackles and lack of space.

In eastern Pennsylvania the marshals are hungry, and this wins us a little pity. Regulations require that they feed us as well. I manage once again a trick learned by practice—eating a sandwich and drinking coffee with hands manacled and fastened to a waist chain. Then one of the brothers gingerly suggests a nature call. Without a word our marshals drive to a nearby gas station. "How about taking off these leg irons?" I ask. "Whaddya mean," he retorts, "you can walk with 'em on!" We walk lockstep; it's either that or float.

By the time we arrive at the county jail in Harrisburg I have had it—I'm tired, numb, enraged by the viciousness of these two cops. I compare our experience with the cattle cars in Nazi Germany; better technology is available here, a late-model Buick and mass-produced chains. Which gives the illusion of advancing civilization. But the guards don't change.

I toy with the idea of getting their names and sweating them through our lawyers. But I dislike pulling weight; moreover, they may retaliate against the two youngsters still with them. I tear into them nonetheless at the jail's entrance, smiting them with evidence of their stupidity and violence. They take it dumbly, like two pouting children caught in a pantry raid. Again the white grunts, "Regulations!" and we part company.

As always, I'm grateful for such occasions—*after* they are over. They teach me, among other things, more about the pervasiveness of violence and its interconnection. The butchery in Indochina could not happen unless it was supported by an accompanying oppression of the poor, blacks, prisoners.

I tell the story to my friends, not to win sympathy but to make them think. Almost without exception, their faces pale in disbelief and horror. "Lord Christ!" I mutter; they still don't grab the whole point about genocide in Indochina, or Kent State, or Attica, or Rap Brown's "Violence is as American as cherry pie." They still don't understand that these horrors better describe our cultural guts than the dull gentility of middle-class life. They still don't grasp that where they touch down on the culture—courteous audiences, sober courtrooms, decent friends, comfortable beds, decent food and good highballs—it is not the culture itself, but merely its veneer.

Moreover, they dread learning further—*even as I do*. But learning must go on; when one stops learning, one stops resisting. And when this happens, one stops becoming a man, to the sorrow and loss of all men.

November 1971

I want to deal with the question of religion—what it's like here, and in prison generally.

Naturally it's very bad here. It has no quality worthy of mention; it is vapid, ambiguous, bewildering. Religion being a prime element of the general confusion, most men protect themselves by simply staying away. Religion at Danbury, and in most prisons, does not even possess the slight compensation of availability. Men rarely see the chaplains, or if they do, it is in the chaplain's capacity of hack correctional officer. Contrast this with the lavish attention accorded the powerful, particularly in government.

But what about *quality*? This neither the poor *nor* the powerful get. A visitation by the local bishop serves as example. He came last Sunday to offer the Eucharist and to preach. His sermon related a recent trip he had made to Italy and Poland. In Rome he had attended the beatification of Father Maximilian Kolbe, a Polish priest murdered by the Nazis at Auschwitz. In Poland he visited the notorious camp, in which perhaps two million died, and prayed at Kolbe's grave.

Briefly, Kolbe's story went something like this. In 1944 a work party returned to the camp one prisoner short. The Nazis haphazardly chose ten men to die if the inmate didn't return by a certain hour. When he failed to materialize, the officials passed final sentence upon the ten: death by starvation. Kolbe heard one of the hostages lament that he would never again see his wife and children, so he offered to take the man's place. Inexplicably, the official agreed.

The ten were locked in underground cells and died one by one. After all the others were dead, Kolbe still survived. Finally the Nazis poisoned him.

Obviously Kolbe's heroism had moved the bishop. But to what degree, and to what purpose? Undoubtedly Christ's sacrifice had moved him before—many times, in fact. But moved him where and for whom? Had Kolbe (or Christ) moved him to compare the then and the now; 1944 and 1971; two million dead in Auschwitz with two million dead in Indochina; Europe leveled and Indochina raped; 1.5 million tons of bombs dropped on Europe and 6.2 million tons on Indochina; political prisoners in Auschwitz and political prisoners in Con Son and Danbury? Where did His Eminence hook up? Hard to tell. His words and actions expressed no desire to hook up anywhere.

I don't mean to imply that Danbury is an American Auschwitz (though Con Son in South Vietnam is), or that the resisters here match Kolbe's sacrifice. And analogies are never exact anyhow. But roughly the point is that Kolbe asks the bishop real questions to which the bishop gives no real answers. His "answer" was to exhume Kolbe, canonize him, and get him reburied as soon as possible. The trick, then, is to make a dead memorial of a living spirit.

Two escape hatches are presumably available to the bishop. "I will spread Kolbe's message," he told us, "and I will pray to him." He encouraged us to do the same: "We must ask him to help us kill the Auschwitz in us, and to let the Kolbe live." So a noble sentiment at once becomes a dangerous and easy mystification.

What the bishop has done with Kolbe is what Washington has done with My Lai. In failing to apply the lesson of one man he absolves himself of complicity in murder, and invites us to do the same. To him Kolbe was not a wise man, a hero, a historical paradigm, a true Christian, but an abstraction. A noble abstraction, unrelated to the present, to life.

The bishop invites us for coffee in the officer's mess—with himself, the chaplain, the warden, and so on. Dan asks him if the other prisoners are invited, since several had asked to see him. He says, "No! I don't have that much time." So we decline, and he leaves to talk to his own. We discover later that he had spent an entire morning at a local rectory awaiting his afternoon commitment. So much for his lack of time.

And so Kolbe and the prisoners here got about the same treatment.

November 17

Today is Liz's birthday, her thirty-second. She visited us with Jogues yesterday looking like a gamine, her hair short, her face piquant and animated. She is back from two bruising weeks on the road in Texas and the mid-West—four and five talks a day, Feds all over the place. And on her return she encounters tough talk from me on indifference to the trial and sloppy priorities.

Like a cork in mid-ocean, Liz gets heavy seas from every side, most of it immeasurably more messy and painful than the weather. With me in jail, she has taken alone the veiled questions, arched eyebrows, and clumsy innuendoes arising from our relationship. She expects, and gets, pressure and criticism from her Order, her family, the defense committees, friends, defendants, lawyers, audiences. And handles it beautifully, humanly, nonviolently, gently insisting that the issue is the murder of innocent people.

Only rarely does the strain show; her clarity and patience weaken. She has splendid stamina—capable of immense, sustained effort—and an intelligent resiliency of mind, cheerful and comprehensive.

She is a striking woman, spiritually and physically. I have no illusions about her, nor she about me. We have experienced too much pain alone and together for that. Like the official horrors we face and resist, our relationship is a fact, and we are fully confident of it.

My politics make me difficult to know, even more difficult to know intimately. Sooner or later, torturous questions arise, and most people flee from them. Besides Liz, what other woman could, or would, accept and support me, wait for me, while carving out her own identity and independence? What other woman could accept our separation as more normal than normalcy, face jail with optimism and courage, cling to the Gospel and to people with a rare tenacity of faith, all without compromise, sentimentality, or dread?

Here is a resistance woman, a true Christian revolutionary. More may come later; she is the only one now. I am very blessed in her.

January 13, 1972

A fantastic day, unsettling but incredibly rich. Liz and I renew our vows, this time with Dan and all the defendants present. Everyone speaks to the event with hope and gratitude. All things considered, it was an audacious enterprise.

This morning federal marshals appeared and ordered me to pack for Harrisburg. When I protested that a meeting was scheduled and defendants were due from as far away as Chicago, they said emphatically, "Orders are orders." I refused to go, and they asserted that I *would* go, forcibly if necessary. The associate warden offered to call the others and tell them not to come. I backed down and went to pack.

An hour later, dressed and waiting for my captors, I hear the defendants are here, giving me some small grace. And so it happened. In the teeth of my departure, my separation from Dan and an imminent, torturous trial of three to four months, Liz and I renew our marriage vows.

Dan remarks that every significant juncture in his life has been marked by a marriage. Somebody else adds that such a sign of hope is a fitting preliminary to the trial, which *must be* a sign of hope to others. And another remarks that we ought to continue living life as it should be lived—that is, enough to embody the new society.

As everyone leaves at 3 P.M., I delude myself into thinking that the marshals, big on their own convenience and comfort, will leave me until the morrow. Alas! Within minutes I am haled into Receiving and Discharge and put on the road. I have no opportunity to explain to Dan or to bid him and friends goodbye.

One of our friends in resistance is fond of remarking, "Hope is where your ass is!" I reflect ruefully that this is so, and that one's ass, to be hopeful, has to be pinched. A rule of life, so to speak.

Friday, January 14

The marshals, like the government, have two formidable elements going for them—force and secrecy. Harrisburg is a four-hour drive from Danbury, but I am not fortunate enough to make the trip nonstop. One knows nothing of destination until arrival. Last night, accordingly, my carcass is unceremoniously dumped at Scranton City Jail. The marshals do not condescend to feed me en route. Vindictiveness for disrupting their schedule? I don't know—they appear affable enough.

As a federal prisoner, I go speedily to lockup. But the young guys, curious about my notoriety, and desperate to talk, drop around, huddling in the door of my cell. Most are fresh from their teens—burglars, addicts, car thieves, a few older alcoholics. Invariably they have histories of broken homes, foster parents, orphanages, delinquency centers and repeated arrests. And their lives speak volubly of abject, tedious failure—failure of their families, friends, institutions—of the Great Society itself. Indeed, a society is known by the quantity and quality of its culprits.

It is immediately apparent that none of them is into anything real. How could they be? The jail is a moldy, crumbling anachronism—it locks them up, feeds them, gives them canned music all day. That's all! It contains them as we contain rebels overseas, and with the same ruthlessness.

Today my young friends organize a fast. The food is ill-prepared and insufficient, no recreation, no work, no classes, no reading of any import. They ask me to join; the request leads to a rap on jail protest and organizing. They know nothing of practical politics. No matter—they will learn by doing. And I can miss a meal or two to support them.

At noon news arrives that a young inmate has been shot while running from court that morning. Handcuffed to another prisoner, he had sprinted directly into a downtown crowd. Miraculously, no bystanders were hit, while he received a superficial wound in the back. One can commend the responsible officer only on his luck.

In any event, the news stiffens my young friends, and they resolve to continue.

On my way out to meet the marshals a young New Yorker makes an insistent request—can he talk with me? I discover he's a graduate student and a lapsed Catholic—atheist, he calls himself. He passionately disputes my fidelity to the Church, which he regards as capitalist, racist, antipoor, silent in the face of war-making, etc. I attempt to explain, and he becomes somewhat more calm. "What's your sentence?" I ask.

"A year," he admits.

"First conviction?"

"Yes."

"For what?"

"Robbing pay phones. I didn't feel I could demonstrate. And this, at least, was doing something!"

Commenting on that was useless. No point to my feeling that he could do something better for justice and peace. *He* had to feel it. I promise to write and leave him in somewhat better spirits.

Saturday, January 15

Bloomsburg next stop. Again secrecy. But I watch the road signs and recall that both marshals live outside the city. Once inside the county jail, on inquiry from the sheriff as to when they'll come get me, one marshal replies, "Tomorrow, maybe. I'll call you." I begin to think that I'm as "sensitive secret" as the documents leaked out from under Kissinger's nose to Jack Anderson.

Having deprived me of all effects but a toothbrush and comb, my new jailers lock me into my customary second-floor cell and bath. And I begin to freeze as the temperature drops to zero and a gusty wind pummels my side of the building. It does no good to call for heat; my pointed suggestions are met with astonishment that the room is cold, or with evasions. When the heat is on, I read and think; when it is off, I flee to my blanket and try to sleep.

I reread most of Saint Paul's letters with relish and profit: "On the contrary, in all that we do we strive to present ourselves as ministers of God, acting wtih patient endurance amid trials, difficulties, distresses, beatings, imprisonments and riots; as men familiar with hard work, sleepless nights and fastings; conducting ourselves with innocence, knowledge and patience, in the Holy Spirit, in sincere love. . . . We are called imposters, yet are truthful; nobodies who in fact are well known; dead, but here we are alive; punished but not put to death; sorrowful, though we are always rejoicing; poor, yet we enrich many. We seem to have nothing, yet everything is ours!"

In light of the apostle's example and his Lord's before him— both political prisoners and enemies of the State—one can only recall with the Scripture, "We have not yet suffered to the point of blood." At worst, jail is tolerable; at best, it is church and university.

Sunday, January 16

No marshals yet. I suspect they will pluck me out at dawn, making a triumphal entry into Harrisburg before the eight o'clock traffic.

So alternately I freeze, read, pray, exercise. From the bowels of the building I hear the cries and shouts of a man in the Hole.

Even this squalid, insignificant little dump of a place has a Hole! Yesterday he gave the jailers an impassioned (though unimaginative) cussing-out. Waiting for transfer to a federal pen, he probably got a little claustrophobia over the twenty-four-hour-a-day lockup.

I drag a tiny table into the john, place my pillow on the hopper and write these reflections. Noise pollution wafts into my cell—though muted, thank God—from the omnivorous and omnipresent bastions of our culture, radio and TV. It is the great mind-blower, the stealthy substitute for consciousness. By fair means or foul, it gets its idiot message into heads and viscera even in dank cellars of the society, like this one. One is tempted to shriek at jailers and jailed alike, "Don't you know what they're doing to you? Turn that goddamned thing off!" It's gang rape in reverse—the few to the many, right off Madison Avenue.

I come across the old Grecian parable of Gyges' ring. By a curious accident a shepherd, Gyges, finds a ring of magic powers. He learns that he can make himself invisible by turning the bezel of the ring to the inside of his hand. But how will he use this formidable power? He flies to the palace, seduces the queen, kills the king and takes the crown.

Gyges lived justly before acquiring the ring, not because he loved justice but because he feared reprisal. Once the ring exempted him from consequences, he speedily gratified his lust and appetite for power.

Can a man live justly because he knows justice as the way of a man? Some men do; all men can. The chieftains of power, however, whose lofty privilege rests upon the backs of the manipulated, the betrayed and the exploited, answer the question negatively, both for themselves and for their slaves. Aloof from most limits of control themselves—they respect only counterpower—they hold men in systematized injustice, fearing nothing so much as the emergence of just men who will challenge them.

Dauphin County Jail
(Harrisburg, Pennsylvania)

JANUARY–MAY 1972

Monday, January 24

We begin trial today with selection of jury. A few motions for the judge to refuse in chambers—severance of Count No. 2, change of venue—and we should begin.

This is my fourth political trial. The only ones who share that distinction are Huey Newton and Bobby Seale, but unlike me, they are multiple winners. I don't know how I'd take a win. It would take some analyzing.

I sometimes ponder this ceaseless face-off with the State. Christ warned His followers that they would be hauled before kings and governors for His sake; He took His cracks at the Scribes, Pharisees and Herod; He tried to quietly teach Pilate something. But He ignored the State as such. He merely predicted that He would run afoul of the State, and that it would kill him. And He warned them, if they were true, the same thing would happen to them.

"The State is the organization of the evil instincts of man"— so says the American poet Kenneth Rexroth. And again, "War is the health of the State." Those are very tough assertions to deal with; Rexroth is left-handedly coming in on the frightful *raison d'état* of Machiavelli, Metternich, the Enlightenment, and especially of the Superstate. Men generally know they ought to be better, but generally, too, they find being better a fearsome and mysterious task, one that they reject. From their refuges of mediocrity and smallness they create government to protect themselves from interpersonal excess and from the ambition of other States. The State merely mirrors and collects the failures of its citizens; it lies as they lie, fears as they fear, hates as they hate, fights as they fight. It is no more than a concentrated collectivization of national values—or human worth.

When, however, a few disagree with corollaries flowing out of *raison d'état,* say love is the law of life, and man is more god than animal, a conflict readily and speedily develops. One becomes an enemy of the State.

Wednesday, January 26

Selection of jury drones on. The judge remains adamant about sequestration; obviously he has a lockup complex. His alleged motive in locking up jurymen for three-four-five months is his fear of publicity, which he assumes will be favorable to the defendants alone. Simple to imagine the resentment bred by three-four-five months of lockup separated from the communities they're supposed to represent, separated from families, friends, from cherished normalcy. We are to be the butt.

The judge now questions prospective jurors individually. Assumptions run, with the government, and to an extent with us, that neutrality really means neutrality. The fact is, the silence and passivity behind neutrality is pro-government, anti-people, anti-us. Such people—many of the "survivors" are of this quality—will sift evidence, including the evidence of our actions and lives, through their own fear, escapism, silence, and come up with kudos for the government, and conviction for us.

Wednesday, January 26

A delegation just came grinning into the jail— Ramsey, Liz, Jogues, Bill Cunningham—bearing the glad tidings. They could not talk, nor could I. We did not know what to make of it. I was rapt before the boob tube last night, watching and trying to interpret Nixon's "peace overture" speech, knowing with a dead heart that doublespeak was coming out too fast to analyze, and that once again the liberals would be thrown into confusion and quandary. And that the war would go on.

And now this—Dan's release, and an early one at that. The bad news comes automatically, but here is good news—a sane decision, given the circumstances. But I guess, in any sort of ultimate sense, that the Lord figured we needed this, and therefore gave it. He always gives us what we truly need—if I ever again doubt it. I just wrote Dan—a trifle incoherently for my joy. He has

DAUPHIN COUNTY JAIL, 1972

been restored to us. I see the divine sense in it all now; his struggle to stay with the living last spring, that look at Pluto's gates, the long, terribly hard fight back, against odds that I can only guess at despite my vantage point.

I can only think of Lazarus at this point, and the feelings of Mary and Martha.

Thursday, January 27

Jury selection still drones on. I am mostly reacting to Dan's parole release. Outside of acts of resistance, it is the first good news in several years. I received it last night in confusion and rapture—confusion because neither I nor anyone could explain it; rapture because of the hope, encouragement and help it will offer us all.

Why the government would release him in an election year and during the course of our trial is anyone's guess. Of course there is this factor as a counterbalance—the recent "peace overtures" of the President aimed at a public-relations image of benign leniency to resistance at home and abroad. I can imagine Nixon on television saying, "Every American has the right to disagree. It is the lifeblood of democracy." One gets the "howevers" and "buts" later on, in a different context.

That might be it. Nixon might want re-election more than he wants this sorry war. And "benign leniency" might be a better course than harshness. Obviously he badly wants to remove the war from the campaign as an issue; and he might have learned you don't defuse controversy by repressing one side.

One factor in Dan's parole is the pertinacity of our friends. They remind me of that little old pestering woman in the Lord's parable who wore down the unjust judge. He gave her what she demanded just to get rid of her.

Wearing down the oppressor is definitely not a formula for social change. But it does indicate what the times will demand of us in conviction, discipline, tenacity, stamina. At the foundation is conviction, which somebody called "the intelligence of the heart"; or which another saw as "belief coming from the hot core of one's being."

January 29

Whenever self-pity grips me—it is the huge temptation of the political prisoner—I think of Con Son or the Passion. The first is the contemporizing of the second, perhaps the most terrifying example in the world of man's hatred toward our species. The tiger cages at Con Son are death prolonged and defined (refined), and denied its release.

The United States is responsible for the tiger cages at Con Son. Without us they would not be open; without us more of them would not be built. Brazil has its torture chambers for political dissidents, Siberia its work camps, Spain its medieval cells. But none compare with the tiger cages, the horror of hell translated to concrete reality.

. . . One group by virtue of unique and ingenious circumstances observed certain areas of the prison known as the Tiger Cages in which are kept political prisoners who had the courage to express their belief in peace. . . .

The Tiger Cages are cells approximately five feet wide and ten feet long. Five persons are crowded into this space surrounded by cement walls and floors on which inmates sleep. About a foot off the floor is an iron rod to which the legs of the inmates are shackled. Lying in this position for years causes a paralysis of the legs.

Occupants are fed a small portion of rice and are fed dried fish, often molded, and always an inadequate amount of water which forces the prisoners through exhaustion to drink their own urine.

At the top of the cages are kept boxes of lime which is sprinkled into the cages to quiet any noise or disturbance. More often, however, those who protest against their treatment are beaten by trusties who thereby receive special privileges.

In opposition to prison officials, we used the walkway atop the cages to interview various prisoners. Among them several students, a Buddhist monk, and an elderly woman, sixty years of age, who was blinded from beatings. None we interviewed had criminal records but generally had been imprisoned, often without judicial trial, merely for participating in peace demonstrations.*

As for Christ, whose name we bear, the prophet and the Psalmist describe His awful Passion more graphically than the Gospel writers, deliberately laconic. Isaiah: "A man of suffering, accustomed to infirmity . . . pierced for our offenses, crushed for our sins . . . The Lord laid upon him the guilt of us all." The Psalmist: "But I am a worm and not a man; the scorn of men, despised by the people. All who see me scoff at me; they mock me with parted lips, they wag their heads; 'He relied on the Lord, let Him deliver him, let Him rescue him, if He loves him' . . . I am like water poured out; all my bones are racked. My heart has become like wax melting away within my bosom. My throat is dried up like baked clay, my tongue cleaves to my jaws; to the dust of death you have brought me down. Indeed, many dogs surround me, a pack of evildoers closes in upon me; they have pierced my hands and my feet; I can count all my bones. They look on me and gloat over me; they divide my garments among them, and for my vesture they cast lots." While Saint Paul says simply in Galatians: "Christ has delivered us from the power of the law's curse by Himself becoming a curse for us, as it is written: 'Accursed is anyone who is hanged on a tree.' "

The first Peacemaker, and the peacemakers since, often fall under human curse. But not I. Later perhaps, but not now. In contrast, I have a tiny six-by-nine cell, complete with miniature table, sink, toilet and bunk. The technocratic meritocracy, as somebody

* Congressman Augustus F. Hawkins, *Crimes of War,* Vintage Books, Random House 1971, pp. 258–259.

calls it, affords me this. I have my books, other prisoners (mostly black) to talk to, commissary privileges, loyal friends. And though every move occasions caravans of marshals and guns, every word occasions paranoia and official smothering, my spirit flies free, like a young bird recently from the nest.

Moreover, I can sleep nights, as many a liberal and prospective juror cannot—by their own testimony.

I want to tell my friends: The further one goes in resistance, with faith in God and dedication to nonviolence, the less reason one finds for self-pity.

Monday, February 14

I'm getting close even to the lawyers, who bust their balls for us. And Ramsey has become a dear and treasured friend. Boudin and O'Dwyer and Lenzner and Cunningham as well. We have learned to compassionate together, to suffer together.

Bill Kunstler came. The guy always unseats me—drive, drive, drive—a new case opening in Baltimore—retrial of Arthur Turco. And more and more, on into the horizon. Friends have worried about his pace, but when I suggest he oughta slow down and save something for Nixon II, he fends me off in classical fashion. Bill C., Jogues, Eqbal, Liz came out for a great Eucharist last night —Bill's birthday, and Frank Gallagher's passover, and fierce raids in Indochina—all family and friends remembered, all God's chillun. We put shoes on all chillun. We open Thursday or Friday. I can't go to Gallagher's funeral tomorrow. I will pray for him here.

February 21

We go to the threshing floor, already feeling like grain. The government's case opens with Mr. William Lynch, the government's head prosecutor. He modestly identifies me as leader (the others are followers!) of a widespread conspiracy to disrupt Selective Service, to bomb utility tunnels in Washington, to kidnap Mr. Kissinger. Mr. Lynch follows the indictment unwaveringly, with the relish of an author. He did, in fact, compose it.

It is ambitious, ranging from Philadelphia and the East Coast Conspiracy to Save Lives in February 1970 to December 1970, when Boyd Douglas had won release and was facing Liz's accusation that he was the informer. And everything in between, but with gaps and distortions.

Lynch in effect tells us that south is north, left is right, falsehood is truth, reality—world, national, personal—comes out of Washington, D.C. I am stunned by the arrogance of it, the colossal presumption—the disrupters branding us disrupters, the bombers calling us bombers, the kidnappers naming us as kidnappers. Lynch has enjoyed his complicity; the war criminals bought him with a sleazy government job and a fat salary—bought his silence and vote and acquiescence.

He tells us something we did not know. After they had shaken down my cell in June 1970 and confronted me with a letter to Liz, they confronted Douglas with the same letter. Lion-hearted patriot that he was, he admitted everything—giving it all up, as cons would say. He then brought Associate Warden Hendricks to Bucknell, showed him other letters of ours he had copied (stolen). Next, he sold himself to the FBI. From then on he was a spider luring us flies to an FBI web.

As a con man, he was good—I must admit. Why not? Confidence was his whole life. A psychologist once called him a "pathological liar," and his father doubted that he had ever told the truth.

More to the point, my poor friend was a sociopath, incapable of controlling on the one hand an obsessive desire for acceptance, and on the other a devouring self-interest. His conflicts and his crimes arose from trying to ingratiate himself with acquaintances, while abusing them unashamedly. He could not distinguish between offering a favor and returning a betrayal. He needed both kicks.

Yet his is not the greatest crime. The government caught him in a cheap little machination (nobody gets prosecuted for contraband mail), squeezed him, and he collapsed like dog stools in a rainstorm.

February 28

The Informer took the stand this afternoon. I sat to face him directly, but he would not meet my eye.

Douglas has gained some fifty pounds since I last saw him, and he ambles about like a pet bear who has been taught to rear up and beg. The analogy is not that unfitting.

The prosecution has had a year to coach him. Despite that, he is not a parrot, so he makes a poor imitation of one—slow in recall, fumbling, vague. And lies! There are not merely errors in memory, there are fiction, phantasm, editorializing. What becomes clear is that he decided on the plot he needed, the victims he needed to survive with Big Brother. Then he slowly enticed us into his enterprise, using as sweets our love for one another and our hatred of this war.

The question is, why? He testified yesterday to his patriotism— we were a "threat" to the United States. But that is false; his life doesn't show that he has a capacity for concern about people and country. So why?

The reasons, I gather, are as complicated as any case in psychopathology is. He had a compulsion to identify with so-called leaders, and especially with people of conscience—Professor Richard Drinnon, the defendants, me. So approaches were always his, accompanied by a powerful appeal for compassion. (1) I'm a con, carved up by their ghastly medical experiments; (2) I'm a victim with a measly $15,000 settlement; (3) I'm a student struggling to make it; (4) I'm a peacenik dedicated to life and resistance.

This was the guise behind which he hid. It was his cover. Behind it, there were his true needs: the acceptance and love needed by a profoundly insecure person; evidence of capability to dominate and master others, especially women; recognition of his intelligence, charm, conviction, courage.

The need for acceptance was accompanied by a frantic insistence that he get it. Hence the manipulation and treachery toward others—Drinnon, the women at Bucknell, the defendants, myself. It was as though we were not responding fast enough, or in a manner he desired, to his cries for help. And so he would brutalize us even if that meant sending us to jail.

Initially he might have hoped to blackmail us; he told another inmate of his conviction that the Catholic Left was loaded. But that hope vanished when they pinched him with a suspicion of contraband. Then the squeeze began, and he collapsed. Under threat of new charges and more time he had to switch his motivation, to guarantee a precarious survival. How to, therefore, (1) escape further punishment, and (2) secure a soft life, paid for by others.

The FBI bought him—poor brain, disordered affections, dreads, insecurities—and he tried to sell us with himself.

Sunday, March 5

Monday through Friday of this week was Introduction to Psych Warfare, or, the Imposition of Shame as Repression. Liz and I sat rooted for five days and just endured while the Informer wove his lies and fantasies about us and Mr. Lynch read our letters—*with proper emphasis*. We sat rooted while our hopes and affections and lives were stripped layer by layer—sat there impassively helpless, lest the jury and press interpret reactions as guilt. Privacy was shattered, nonviolence ridiculed, everything about us reduced to a caricature—a hideous, incompetent, frantic plot, worthy only of the irresponsible or the mad.

People conclude the following as probably true: Hoover forces the government to indict, which it duly does. The government in turn must then build a case, which it attempts, with limitless manpower and money. The plastic Goliaths in government can no more stomach defeat in Harrisburg than they can in Indochina.

What results is a very vicious but cohesive falsehood, tribute enough to their malicious diligence. The Informer spares none of us, showing the effects of eighteen months' indoctrination, while judge and prosecution prompt and protect him. By Friday he has me close to reaction, my patience and endurance shredded. He testifies about a conversation in which we plotted to kidnap Kissinger. Alarmed, he reminded me it could not be done without violence, without a gun. I shrugged this off, he says, as though admitting we needed a gun. At which he suggested a gun loaded with blanks. And so this gunman and con man, convicted of armed assault on an arresting FBI agent, blandly refers to my violence.

As the lies thump at one's head, one feels in a web, even struggling with the spider. How to break the web, or pacify the devouring spider? Pitting one's word against the Informer's is no answer; taking the stand is no solution for most of us, because of the danger of implicating friends. What we must prove is his life-long history of lying—to us, to the Bucknell University people, to the government. The last was the most monumental fabrication of all, but the government believed Douglas because it wanted and needed to believe him; it believed Ky and Thieu because it needed to believe them. It covers its blunders like an anxious bully, and immediately embarks on a new course of crimes.

Nonetheless we are far from finished. Friday night everyone was still grinning—the Scoblicks protesting their low count in the day's output of lies. Monday we cross-examine; we will see if our friend the Informer endures as well.

The worst is over—the rest is a cakewalk in comparison. Peace requires a drop of the soul's blood from time to time.

Saturday, March 11

On Monday afternoon we began cross-examination of the Informer. It ran all week through Friday—in fact, we haven't finished yet.

Ramsey Clark, Paul O'Dwyer, Terry Lenzner, Tom Menaker, Bill Cunningham, Leonard Boudin all punched away at him, until he reminded one of a rag doll among hyperactive children. They trapped him in lie after lie: he had deceived friends at Bucknell; he had deceived prison officials; he had deceived us; he had deceived FBI and Justice Department officials. He had taken everyone in, had everyone jerking on strings, hung up between malice and altruism.

"I can see it now. Douglas is complex, resourceful, creative—no wonder he duped you." Meant to state a fact rather than to soothe us, that remark by one of our lawyers came close to summing him up. (Most of us had long suspected that those who are serious about nonviolent resistance would experience infiltration, betrayal and indictment.) The Informer had escaped from stockade and prison several times; had impersonated officers and federal agents repeatedly; had passed bum checks in volume (one year $50,000 to $60,000); had worked the "split deposit" trick (depositing a huge check and then fleeing with a couple of thousand withdrawn); and had marked us as new challenges and victims. He was an imposter of the first quality, priding himself on wits and flexibility to secure an honest future with the FBI. He had even suggested indictment with us, envisioning no doubt conviction for all (light time for him, heavy time for us), followed by an honored career of betrayal in every Movement circle in the country. Luckily the Justice Department didn't share his inventiveness and nerve.

The judge protected the Informer shamelessly. Time and again he signaled the prosecution to object, inhibiting and harassing the cross-examination by our lawyers, and giving Douglas valuable time to recover. We now possess heavy cause for mistrial, if not for perjury charges against Douglas. But the judge waves this aside.

Perhaps it is just as well—the judge's disgusting alliance with the prosecution. Sooner or later we must expose the government's role in this shameful trial. The real culprit is obviously not Boyd F. Douglas; the culprits are Hoover, Mitchell and Nixon. On the one hand, the men of the "Justice" Department knew Douglas —they had his criminal and service records; they had his psychiatric history. On the other hand, they could have known us; I especially had a formidable dossier. Yet they went ahead with prosecution—index enough of stupidity, corruption, venality.

Slowly—this is my hope—our attack will shift from Douglas to the government. People must begin to understand that only archcriminals in exploitative structures would have the moral myopia and cowardice to indict those whose only interest is justice, whose only desire is peace. We must turn this trial around and do a little indicting of our own.

Tuesday, March 14

The price tag on this escapade has been highest for Liz. I have been insulated from public conjecture by jail. So in addition to all the other burdens, there has been this one, taken without a murmur or second-guessing or the slightest recrimination.

Cross-examination drags on; people not exactly sure that it should take this long. The insulation that the court drapes around our friend the Informer is shameful, and he responds by a combination of arrogance and/or amnesia. But we should end tomorrow, and we should witness a different phase of the government's case on Thursday.

Friday, March 17

St. Patrick's Day. I have a natural jaundice about the Irish thing, but today was good. Liz in her typically impudent way brought in green carnations for all the defendants and lawyers. And lo, in troops the jury also wearing them. It brought the house down.

Sunday, March 26

On Friday we rested our case, rejecting the traditional opportunity for defense.

The rationale behind resting had to do with the gossamer thinness of the government's case. In our judgment, and in that of trusted opinion, the prosecution has failed utterly to prove agreement beyond a reasonable doubt. Moreover, we had discredited the Informer, and had reduced to insipidity most witnesses following him, especially Special Agent Mayfield, Douglas' sponsor and tutor. For all its millions and its well-groomed snoopers, the mountain of government has brought forth a mouse of suspicion.

The rationale also was sensitive to the alleged dangers of taking the stand, especially for Liz and myself. Naturally our lawyers had a professional caution about this; they sense circumstances in which we might have to answer questions directly, might have to implicate ourselves and others, might have to flesh out the government's case. Why, they argued, should we hand it to them?

Finally, both lawyers and defendants were attracted by the "massive psychological put-down" (their term) implied by resting. It was, they maintained, a species of noncooperation summoned by the sordid record of Washington, beginning with Hoover's briefing of Republican leaders at the White House in September 1970, and ending with an informer-provocateur's testimony. Such a performance, they felt, deserved nothing better than a contemptuous silence.

While accepting the weight of conclusions like these, Liz, Eqbal and I disagreed vehemently. We rather preferred to respond to our obligations in the trial. The public, for example, to whom we owe the truth, had only a spotty knowledge of us; the judge's bias and rigidity had denied them anything better. What was our response to Cambodia and the enlarging air war in 1970? When did we realize that a citizen's arrest, of Kissinger or anyone else, was quite beyond our resources? Did Joe Wenderoth and I enter the tunnels; did that discussion go beyond discussion? What was behind the letters, and what was their meaning, in the context of the summer of 1970? What was our relationship, Liz's and mine?

How did we really treat Boyd Douglas, and why? The public nature of our Christian mission and of our politics required, it seemed to us, efforts to answer these questions.

Two or three days prior to a final decision, our lawyers reached agreement on resting the case. However, they made it clear that the decision was ours and that they would respond accordingly.

One day before a final and crucial meeting of defendants Dan appeared in Harrisburg. He and I and Liz met at Dauphin County Jail. We sought his opinion, and he gave it: the politics of the case required a defense, and people generally expected one. According to his reading, painful and unanswered questions existed about the charges, about our relationship with Douglas, about the letters themselves. I agreed, feeling we had an obligation of truth, not to the government or to the court but to the people.

At that time Liz remained undecided, though she had strenuously prepared herself to testify, and rebelled against the possibility of resting. I had done a lesser amount of work for the witness stand, but felt an overriding need to grasp the opportunity to extract from this trial political clarity about the government and about us.

During this period, though we made at least two attempts, we had ill success in arranging meetings of the defendants. Pressures on people were mounting, and exacting a heavy toll. Less and less did we talk together, pray together, plan together. This is not to say that we were alienated, bitter or hateful toward one another. It is to say something of the physical and psychological drain—several had approached the end of their resources and could not endure much more.

We agreed, under sheer necessity, to meet at Dauphin County Jail—the defendants, Dan, and Terry Lenzner. The atmosphere was terribly harried, worried, even emotional. Everyone was acutely conscious, I believe, that any decision could go against us, with heavy penalties attached. Everyone spoke his piece, and we listened to the opinions of Terry and Dan. The final vote hinged on realization that a defense would present the government with a case it had not proved, especially through the testimony of Elizabeth and myself. Reinforcing this view, we were conscious of the consistency of passive resistance, which began when we refused to plead to the superseding indictment. Resting the case at this juncture, some argued, would accord the government the contempt it deserves and amount to a huge psychological put-down.

With some, emotions ran uppermost. In fact, several felt threatened by the possibility of a showdown, and agreed to talk only reluctantly. Apparently the daily feeling of standing in that suffocating court like a clay image in a shooting gallery had had its price tag. Voices became emotional, strident, accusatory.

The performance was, as Liz put it, "sour," and as I would add, weak. Sour and weak enough so that one had to remind oneself that, given the general run, these were magnificent people. Not many had matched their resistance, not many had endured such reprisals.

In the end a majority prevailed, and Liz, Eqbal and I accepted this as gracefully as we could. More than the decision, I think the meeting left deep fissures among us. But even these became manageable; by Friday they were firmly under control.

I must say at this point something about the "mystery" of collective decisions. Indeed, they do constitute a mystery, requiring an absolute faith in community wisdom, or in a deeper sense, in the Spirit of God in a community of resistance.

It is the only effective curb on the inevitable psychological violence that sunders and divides people in agreement about resistance, but in disagreement about the means. Psychological violence arises from one's subjective view of means, a view inevitably complicated by a conviction that one's own view is objective and right. The process becomes force and counterforce, a minuscule version of Superstate "negotiation from power." Invariably it fractures resistance, makes the poor weep and the oppressor smile. True, a majority vote implies compromise, a hated word. However, the compromise is not with principle but with one's application of principle, and is made in recognition of one's personal limitations.

Perhaps a certain providence rules such community decisions as that one. Some of us were required to exercise an abasement— in my case, to compensate for recklessness—which plunged us to zero, and in the process freed a mysterious power. This power (a liberating grace, perhaps) allowed us to remain at peace with the decision, and exerted an unforeseen effect upon the jury. This I believe.

By 4 P.M. Friday we had our stage set and our jury present. As the judge called for the defense to open, Ramsey Clark stood to assert, with typical forcefulness, "Your Honor, the defendants proclaim their innocence and maintain that they will continue working for peace. The defense rests!" He sat down, and one by one, lawyers rose with each of us to state, for example, "The defense rests for Father Neil McLaughlin." When my turn came, so as to preserve motions for self-representation, I said, "Since I've discharged my attorneys, I rest my own case. Thank you."

Judge and prosecutor provided a study in dumbfoundment, alternately fumbling papers, grinning inanely, uttering incoherences of bewilderment and surprise. Obviously, resting the defense posed unmanageable questions. Hours later Mr. Lynch was not yet over his stupefaction, offering this weighty statement to the press: "You can't offer a defense when you don't have any."

So goes life in Harassburg. We will get summations on Monday, and then the jury will deliberate. And that ought to produce a verdict by the weekend.

Thursday, March 30

It is 6:30 P.M., the jury is deliberating, and I write this from back in the marshal's cage. (They must hold me here until 9 P.M., when the jury retires for the night.) A strange day. The judge opened with a charge for the jury; it went fairly well (for him) until the last fifteen minutes, when he launched into a review of the government's evidence, defendant by defendant. We had become *used* to his malice and incompetence, but it shook us nonetheless. Sort of one last putrid bone on a pile of putrid bones.

In any event, Paul O'Dwyer and the six went to a press conference, and laid him out. The charge was bad enough to be a strong point on appeal.

Everyone is holding up with verve and good humor. It has been an education. Nothing quite conveys the stench of death coming from the Beast's rectum like the stench from his courtrooms. Let's call them the upper colon, where all the bad enzymes are applied.

Leonard Boudin just left for Boston and replacement of his pacemaker. Nothing serious, he'll be laid up only a day or two. He kissed me twice and I was very touched. We cannot owe him enough—his creativity, humor and courage were certainly relieving aspects in the funeral parlor. He will head quickly for the Coast and the Ellsberg trial.* Such men as Leonard, Clark and the rest of our lawyers deserve vast credit. They are defending the law from the likes of Mitchell, Rehnquist and Nixon.

It will soon be Easter. One of the Psalms, the twenty-eighth I think, puts it well: "Even though an army encamp against me, I will fear not." If David, or somebody, could sing that without the empty tomb,† I guess all of us can take *any* verdict with dignity and equanimity.

Sunday, April 2

A strange week—hopeful, ominous, interminable. It was as though time had imposed on us a cage of its own, enclosing us all in waiting.

We discover that sum and substance have suddenly evaporated from this case—that our fears have had no basis. The trial itself, which once imparted the eerie feeling of being devoured and digested, now impresses one as having the consistency and value

---

* Daniel Ellsberg and Anthony Russo were on trial for stealing the Pentagon Papers. The case was ultimately dismissed because the government, in the opinion of the presiding judge, had tainted the entire case.
† The Resurrection.

and smell of gnat shit. These last months have been life at its drabbest and meanest, "sound and fury, signifying nothing."

Our bloated Goliath of a government has been hamstrung by building an imaginary case to appease Hoover's ego, by relying credulously on a confidence man who conned it into prosecuting, by a notoriously inept and malicious prosecution, and by our decision to rest the defense.

Last night the jury convicted me on Count No. 4—smuggling a letter from the penitentiary before our friend Douglas became the hired hand of the FBI. This is manufactured reality—a conviction on *that* while money, drugs, pornography, weapons and letters make their covert way into prison, while indeed guards, penal officials and inmates carry out of prison letters, written conspiracies, messages, food, machinery, spare parts, gasoline, oil, tires —anything valuable that public servants can strip from a prison.

A jury that gave certainty of deadlock on Saturday night gets no peace from the judge. He believes us guilty, so he cannot fathom why they cannot agree on guilt also. So through a series of measures, implications and hints to them he stresses that duty requires that they plod on to conviction. Already several jurors show extreme fatigue and nervousness. I watch one lady in the back row, her face haggard and sad, her mouth working almost spasmodically. Several others look drawn and iron-faced. These twelve rather ordinary middle-Americans must, under the judge's prompting, come to agreement on seven people charged with ten counts. Quite unlikely, given the whole package.

The press and spectators watch us with anxiety, their faces betraying sympathy and pity. As usual, they are too literal—another conviction for me, and for us all, possible conviction on Count No. 1, the conspiracy count, the most feared of all. I would like to ask them to transfer their loving apprehension to themselves and to the victims.

The jury deliberates for its sixth day. I pray for them as I pray for the marshals that guard me—that truth invade their neutrality.

Friday, April 7

The following simple little set of questions was asked me by a journalist the other day, now that it's all over and the only convictions out of the whole mess were the unauthorized letters Liz and I sent.*

1. With the trial's ending, how do you feel?

Excellent, if I may say so. I have a regimen for well-being that has carried me through thirty-one months in prison, solitary, long fasts, this indictment and trial. It includes an hour of meditation and prayer (one must remain vitally dependent upon grace); a great deal of reflection on relationships with those about; a lot of writing—letters and notes; and up to an hour of calisthenics, yoga and isometrics. As a result, I have never felt better, spiritually and physically, in my life.

It seems to me that one's experience, depending on its reality, tends to make one more useful, serviceable, more invaluable. That, plus the imperial character of our imperial social structure, suggests the long haul, the type of view the Vietnamese have had to embody for survival. At one level or another, with an increasing tempo of intensity, I have struggled in the human rights/peace scene for about ten years. Many more have struggled longer, a few at greater expense. Nonetheless, apart from any hint of arrogance or presumption, I think it reasonable to expect a long fight, and wise to be prepared. Hence, reliance upon the Spirit, discipline of mind and emotion, sensitivity to human need, respect for one's body.

2. I've often wondered what it meant to face indictment and trial while in prison. Did you ever lose hope, did you ever despair?

Odd you should ask that, since only recently I've had to analyze

---

* The trial ended with only two of the jurors convinced that any of those on trial were guilty of conspiracy to kidnap Kissinger or blow up heating tunnels. Philip Berrigan and Sister McAlister were found guilty of seven contraband counts. Eventually the government quietly filed for a dismissal of charges.

some of the apprehensions of the last fifteen months, just to understand myself better, just to get it together more.

Let's put it this way. The government's single-minded ruthlessness—from Hoover's November 1970 statement on—in blocking all escape (grand jury coercion, the seeming hostility of the judge, invasion of privacy, massive surveillance and investigation) had a cumulative effect on me. Contributing to this were my differences with other defendants about trial strategy and tactics. When the trial began and I saw myself as a warm, voiceless, passive body in a chair, forbidden to participate in my (and our) defense, forbidden to mention genocide, nonviolence, resistance or responsibility, I began to feel a dread quite foreign to me.

A political prisoner derives hope from two sources mainly: the prospect of freedom and greater service, and an ongoing movement. Neither sufficed during the trial; government vindictiveness had choked off the first, and as for the second, everything the Movement could muster was consumed in the defense of us, of Angela Davis and Daniel Ellsberg. It was quite a dark night of the soul, quite a reduction to zero.

I think it of some credit that, first, I did not communicate my fears to others, and second, I did not begin to hate. The courtroom impressed me as a morgue, or as a government whorehouse; the judge as a nondescript political hack, a nervous sponge out of the local patronage system; the prosecutors as drones, victims of federal surgery—emasculated and with circuit implants at the backs of their heads. But that was wrong; that was allowing my revulsion to color hopelessly both surroundings and people. No one can afford to do that.

Nonetheless I inwardly raged and feared, torn between a fierce desire for confrontation with the naked power around me and the need to retire, to remain anonymous and secure in my seat. I hated my feeling of powerlessness; I hated the cool rationality of our lawyers as they talked me out of my schemes; I hated the incomprehension and passivity of some other defendants. The slightest exchange with the court became a matter of anxious concern, of prolonged preparation, of nervous and angry brooding. Twice I went to the bench demanding self-representation;

twice a furious nausea made thoughts and voice barely controllable.

But out of that wretched misery came understanding. Out on the streets I could get a grip on the horrible war—I could speak and move about and organize and act. In prison, too, I could build resistance with friends, then move swiftly and resolutely. But not in that courtroom, not without endangering co-defendants; not without threatening months of legal work.

I was my first experience with personal helplessness, with a setting in which an unfamiliar and low-keyed resistance was the only kind practical. And I learned. I learned of my distrust of grace, and my lack of it; I learned that frustration can swell into insanity if unchecked; I learned that sometimes others must be allowed to defend one, simply because one is unable to do it oneself; I learned that fear is the primal passion, causing our first cry as we enter the world, causing our death rattle as we enter the unknown. It was fear that Christ finally conquered on the cross—"My God, why have you forsaken me?"—but the struggle against it was to the bitter and desolate end.

3. What do you think of the verdict? Whose victory was it?

A certain victory for us, a little ashamed face-saving for the government. When one considers that the government had our letters (very specific about resistance), a clever and indoctrinated informer to editorialize on them, ample evidence from Selective Service raids, and a machinery of unlimited wealth and investigative manpower, plus a very comprehensive body of conspiracy legislation to back them, their "victory" becomes a very paltry one indeed. The case was, moreover, argued before a middle-Pennsylvania jury—very cautious and thrifty and middle-of-the-road folk.

Expert and determined legal work saved us. It was a lawyer's day par excellence—a new and unexpected aspect of resistance. Not only did the lawyers work like slaves, they were friends and comrades to the defendants; their encouragement and advice pulled us through some bitter hours. It was a community effort of the highest quality, with lawyers heading the community.

If the government decides to retry us, some defendants will still attempt variations of defense. But in a conspiracy case of this weight and complexity, evidence alone suggests a central role for lawyers, as long as defendants cling to acquittal as a priority.

Aside from that, all of us will continue our confidence in collective decision-making, in community effort. Community has been our main strength in resistance; it did not cease being that during the trial, despite decisions that sometimes appeared politically unwise.

4. How do you feel about the verdict?

Overjoyed, to put it frankly. It far surpassed expectations. As a measure of prudence, we refused to jury-watch, to second-guess the jury, but nonetheless it was evident that their questions to the judge indicated he had worn them down to his definition of us. (They deliberated longer—seven days—than any jury in federal criminal history.) In fact, however, they did their best for acquittal, compromising finally in favor of two people convinced of conspiracy.

Elizabeth and I shared the same attitude toward a verdict. We tried to remain neutral, knowing the outcome was out of our hands. We tried to prepare ourselves for the worst. But the jury fooled us too. Jefferson would have been ashamed of our mistrust, our lack of confidence in the people. Their verdict argued powerfully for representative government instead of the aristocracy of affluence we now have.

As for meaning, this verdict offers a little face-saving for a government stupid and violent enough to prosecute us and to waste millions on such a prosecution. You will recall that we maintained our innocence from the beginning; everything we had done in resistance we had already admitted publicly. And so we refused to plead to the superseding indictment, and later refused to defend against it.

To us, and to the millions who believed in our innocence, the verdict offers valuable education and experience in continuing the struggle against elitist and militarist power. How we will capitalize on its lessons, however, remains to be seen.

5. I can't quite understand your satisfaction. Sister Elizabeth and you face more time from this conviction than a conviction from conspiracy—forty years for you, thirty years for her. Why the sense of victory?

Because on the best information we have, any sentence is untenable. Actually, *1791* is a medieval regulation, having an unconscionable penalty attached to it, mostly for the sake of bluster and threat against helpless prisoners. Federal prisoners don't respect it, because penal officials never enforce it in regard to contraband mail; inmates respect the common punishment (solitary) for serious contraband (drugs, money, weapons) far more than they respect the regulation. Penal officials don't respect *1791,* because they violate it by stealing all the time, and because prosecution of inmates for *1791* would swamp the courts. Because of these reasons and others the government has never prosecuted an inmate for contraband letters.

But it is somber indeed to consider that only after this verdict, or perhaps only after exhaustion of the legal process, will the government understand that a major conspiracy case based on contraband letters is legally flimsy and politically paranoid. It displays their impressive ignorance of those who resist them. When Nixon invaded Cambodia I might have *liked* to get an outside conspiracy going from inside Lewisburg Penitentiary. But to do so would have required convictions we did not have, plus genius and unimaginable luck.

6. Where does the Movement go after Harrisburg, or after the Davis and Ellsberg trials have ended?

I don't know where it will go. I do have a few ideas about where it should go.

7. What are those?

I can only speculate about them in the broadest terms, being in no position for practicalities.

In my view the essential weaknesses of the Movement lie with its defensive nature, with its ad hoc tendencies, with its elitist leadership. These characteristics stem from the fact that it is thoroughly American, secularist and pragmatic, quite separated from a living tradition of resistance beginning with the Jewish prophets, through Christ and early Christians, to Gandhi, King, and Dolci in our own day.

And so its main thrust has been resistance to military conscription; its main response periodic protest against official barbarisms that cannot be ignored (invasions of Cambodia or Laos, Kent State or the Harrisburg indictment); its main leadership male, invariably those with organizational and rhetorical talents. It is subject to fits and starts, to highs and lows and cycles; it cannot sustain itself, it cannot sustain continuity.

A Movement must be an offensive against evil, both personal and structural; it must resist domination, by itself or by the rich; it must exist for those most victimized, and so it must welcome women and the young.

These are very abstract, very tough and complex goals. Some will object to them on grounds of urgency: the Indochinese are dying, they need us now. Yet the fact is, the Indochinese have needed us since 1949, and we have not had the energy or stamina to respond. The fact is, our inability and reluctance to build a movement has cost them dearly. If we don't begin now, they will continue to pay.

Concretely, building a movement might mean a translation of Gandhian resistance into American resistance. He traveled millions of miles to instruct, to organize, to learn; he formed cadres of trained Satyagrahis; he established communes of nonviolent resistance; he broke the fear of jail, and led a march to prison himself. His example makes sense to me.

Since power is essentially moral, it lies with the people. If political power is essentially moral, people must learn that it lies within them. This challenges the illusion that it rests in Washington; we put it there mostly because we fear it ourselves. And paradoxically, there it remains as long as we agree that there it belongs.

Danbury Federal Correctional Institute
(Connecticut)

MAY–DECEMBER 1972

A Reflection, May 1972

For a long time now, perhaps since November 1970, when Mr. Hoover charged Dan and me with the plot to kidnap and bomb, I've felt like a lot of explaining is due.

I need to explain, because, like other men, I have a duty to truth, and because I possess no infallibility of thought or action, no special authority save my conscience, and an off-again, on-again dedication to the Gospel. What one does, after all, in private or public, must submit to the test of public opinion, public ethic, and even to the ambiguous standard of history.

Others deserve an explanation, I feel, simply because they wonder. They wonder about many things—civil disobedience, resisting in prison, fasting, doing time in solitary, friendship with Boyd Douglas, the meaning behind the letters, indictment and trial while in prison, priesthood, Christianity, nonviolent revolution, and much more. They wonder about the public horror, both domestic and foreign, and ask in what way and to what extent are our lives a response. They wonder about themselves, about the meaning of their lives, about responsibility to humanity and to this country. They wonder, fear, grow and regress—just like anyone else.

So I will try to explain, knowing that the explanation may never reach print, may never be read, may never cause others to ponder or evaluate our lives or theirs. For I'm a federal prisoner and part of that means that one cannot communicate with the public in any real sense, may never explore with others issues of life and death, war and peace, affluence and poverty, repression and freedom, mass murder and survival, bureaucratic lunacy and communal sanity. I have committed the unpardonable sin—questioned Caesar's lies and murder with my words and with my life—and so condemnation, ostracism and silence become my lot. So it has been, so it now seems.

To explain, I have to say something about prison, because that's where the Harrisburg indictment began. Because also, many resisters inevitably share my attitude toward prison and my resistance to it.

First of all, one goes to prison with a feeling of injustice, of great wrong, even of outrage. Willingness to stand for arrest, to endure a show trial, to take a heavy sentence, and to remain in the country rather than to run from the country—such willingness banishes the outrage not at all. If anything, acceptance of consequences exacerbates it to a deeper and more painful degree.

One who has gone to the people with his life, to point out official crimes and public excess, invariably knows the difference between right and wrong. Otherwise he would not be in trouble. Resisters therefore come to prison with certain unchallengeable conclusions regarding *the criminality of the government, the public innocence of resisters, and the necessity of further resistance.* What they encounter repeats and magnifies what they had learned already of government and its callousness toward human rights, and the cheap price it sets on human beings—as they experience lockups, head-counts, total regimentation, arbitrary brutality, "psych" games of bewildering ingenuity and deviousness, condescension and contempt. In brief, we are reduced to a common denominator of misery and impotence, encountering in prison the very factors of violence that make possible the tragedy in Vietnam. Only in prison these factors are turned against the prisoner.

I knew something of this from seven months of jail in 1968—now I saw it confirmed. I came to Lewisburg Penitentiary in May 1970, a captured fugitive, while my brother was underground making the vaunted FBI look ludicrous. Conflict became inevitable.

Other inmates knew me as "hot." Guards and the "rat" contingent viewed me with suspicion and apprehension, reporting contacts, companions and conversations, if they could overhear them—any variation from the prescribed behavior of other men. Wardens plied me with false affability and concern, giving orders meanwhile to watch my movements, shake down my cell and scrutinize (not merely censor) my mail.

I reacted and resisted. The name of their game was control—control of half the world, control of Indochina, control of anywhere and anyone turning a profit, control of me or anyone opposing them. I had other ideas, having come to jail for resistance to their control. I could not stop resisting; they could not stop

DANBURY FEDERAL CORRECTIONAL INSTITUTE, 1972

controlling. Out of this came the conflict—the immemorial conflict of master and slave.

Boyd Douglas approached me soon after arrival, and the plot thickened. People have questioned my gullibility in regard to Douglas. But let me offer a few explanations. Douglas was an inmate, guaranteed by other inmates—whom he listened to and counseled and ran errands for (including carrying contraband). Douglas had suffered from the government and had the scars of a medical experiment as proof. Of even greater moment, Douglas had discovered the Movement, had won the trust of decent and responsible antiwar people at Bucknell as well as my friends when they arrived at Lewisburg to meet and work with him.

Hindsight simplifies things. Though there were elements of rashness, I took normal precautions with Douglas, checked him out with older cons, listened to the resisters' opinion of him. Their views reinforced my own—he *was* reliable. However, let me tell you, either one trusts other people or nothing happens. Do you know what a real Movement is? It's revitalizing old relationships, or breaking them down to create new ones. And it's useless to talk about that without trust. But one can't trust and be concerned about one's skin—the skin game that is America's primary pursuit (and I'm not talking about pornography—rather, the nauseating self-interest that so frequently dominates Americans).

Nevertheless trust should include discernment and exclude stupidity and recklessness. I'm not sure that it did in my relationship with Douglas. Let me borrow one of Eqbal Ahmad's stories to show how I became more than slightly compulsive, and hence more than slightly vulnerable.

During the Algerian war revolutionary cadres were taught, "When our people go to jail, send them oranges!" Sound advice! Because jail for the revolutionary means: (1) complete divorce from the Movement and from the people—both objects of a prisoner's love; (2) helplessness to assist liberation except as a moral symbol; and (3) too much time to brood and fantasize. Out of these realities arises compulsion—compulsion to learn what is going on with resistance; compulsion to help resistance by reflection, advice and plans; compulsion to bring the Movement behind walls and bars—as though that were possible. And so, bring them oranges (or bananas, as the Indochinese might say) if you go to see prisoners. Tell them nothing, and forget immediately anything they tell you!

Experience taught both Algerians and Vietnamese that political prisoners become ready security risks because the Movement is life to them—an identity impossible to sever emotionally and psychologically, even by prison—and because prison allows the oppressor to surveil resisters closely, to set informers and provocateurs upon them, to entrap outsiders through them. Hence the extreme decision, born of tragic experience, to sever informational and organizational links with prisoners, for their protection and the protection of those outside. Despite the apparent callousness and certain heartbreak, "Send them oranges!"

I didn't get oranges—one could buy them in the commissary. I did get assurances of effort, solidarity and love from those outside, mostly through Elizabeth, filtered through the strange psyche of Boyd Douglas, who, we discovered, had compulsions of his own. As a consummate con man and pretender, he evolved a plot out of conversations with me and others: acceleration of draft-board raids in the East; destruction of utilities servicing federal buildings in Washington; and later a "citizen's arrest of someone like Henry Kissinger."

Most assuredly, I discussed such matters with Elizabeth and with Douglas, and indirectly with Joe Wenderoth. With Nixon shoving the war to fever point, it would have been shocking moral dereliction not to discuss them or something similar. The maturity of discussion, however, we owe to Boyd Douglas. As agent-informer he made discussion possible; as provocateur he encouraged the discussions; and as entrapper he gave substance to compulsions and fantasies (mine especially) by offering a dazzling array of skills and services. My compulsion was to maintain contact with the Movement and to assist it where I could; his compulsion was to save his skin (they frightened him into a confession of carrying contraband), and later to fashion a plot worthy of his talents and worthy of reward.

I must be still more frank about my compulsions at that time, compulsions that could have ended in tragic jail terms for seven people. The letters were their tangible expression, and behind the letters was my love for Elizabeth (a most extraordinary Christian and woman); my love for Movement people and for the work of nonviolent liberation they personified; and even my love for men like Douglas, for prisoners, and for a future of justice and peace that they could help to build.

Another question needs to be spoken to: How did I feel toward Boyd when the indictment came down, or when I faced him during the trial? Here was a man who was my friend, whom I helped and confided in, a man who had lied to me, read and copied my correspondence, deceived my friends, betrayed all of us, and attempted to send us all to prison indefinitely. My first reaction when we were indicted was incredulity. I could not believe this guy had turned us in. Then came a nauseating type of resentment —a nation of snoopers and informers brought home to us and laid at our feet—him Judas and us Judas goats. Following that, a profound sorrow and pity set in, not only for Douglas but for this drunk, unhappy country.

It struck me early after the indictment that the government was prepared to waste Boyd Douglas, to use him immorally and illegally as a pitiable weapon against critics and resisters. There is a frightful obscenity associated with that act, as frightful as the analogous use of antipersonnel weapons. One defendant put it this way, "Douglas *is* a human antipersonnel weapon." His entrapment and testimony, if successful, would rend lives as exploding guava bombs rend foreign flesh. The government would waste Boyd Douglas, even as it hoped to waste us, as thoroughly as the sterile, iron seed still sowing the peninsula of Indochina.

Of all people, informers possess the least future. It is one of the things they sell when they sell information: their identity becomes the government's, their lives the government's, and their futures as well. Every sale implicates them further, enlarging their dependency as it heightens their risk. They do nothing but go in deeper, in the fear that the government will terminate their subsidy and abandon their security. When will Big Brother abandon them to their victims?—this is the terrible living anxiety. No one that I can imagine is more expendable.

I watched Douglas testify for about two weeks under direct and cross-examination. I watched his bloated fragility—mannerisms, mechanical memory, petulance—characteristics I had never known in him. Later his patron appeared, Special Agent Mayfield—father figure, coach, prior ego—the same gestures, speech, self-righteousness, ambivalences. Both would display convenient loss of memory—"Not to my recollection"; both would grudgingly admit when truth became unavoidable—"That's possible!" Both were more clearly liars because they shared a skill at lying.

What will Mayfield, or the FBI, do with Douglas? That question tortured us. Shuck him off, most likely, his usefulness ended; discard him as one would old clothes. When that happens he will return to writing false checks and other larcenous adventures. He would have been better off staking a future in human rights, where poverty, public ingratitude and risk lends one a priceless honor and integrity.

Another question is raised: How did the trial look to me as the only defendant in prison for its duration?

It's a truism to say that everything seen from jail takes on a different perspective, yet it needs saying over and over. This applies especially to nonviolent resistance, and specifically to the trial we have just endured. One is in jail—jail is *the* penalty, and jail holds no special terrors. One has lived it, built community, seen the power of nonviolent resistance in jail, experienced both peace and dread, enlarged one and controlled the other. Most important, one has seen the dominators stripped of malevolence by determined, nonviolent effort. All this deepens one's understanding of a trial, and one's hopes for it.

Let me illustrate how imprisonment enriches understanding—of life, of resistance (the two are roughly synonymous today). I have done two stretches in solitary—once for two weeks, once for four —and two long fasts (for the same periods) because of political resistance (to the war, maltreatment of prisoners, etc.). A prolonged fast in solitary is a profoundly liberating experience; inevitably this question arises, "What more can they do to one?" And the answer is, "Nothing!" The current legal arsenal is empty, the ammunition exhausted, and Goliath, with his scabbard bare, looks bewildered and defenseless.

Such experiences helped me immeasurably when the government indicted us. Conviction to the first indictment carried a possible life sentence. The only real position one could take toward life imprisonment was to accept its possibility—it *could* happen! The government had our letters and they had Boyd Douglas. So I thought at that point, Well, if it comes to it, I'll take it day by day, just as I'm doing now. Millions have died in this war, and some have died to stop it. A life bit isn't too great a price!

I relate this to explain why Dan and Ted Glick and myself had a different view of resistance, including the trial, from that of the other defendants. (This had better be so; otherwise we would have to admit that jail had been no more than a plateau or a regression.) We tended far more than others to consider making a response worthy of the Indochinese struggle, as well as adequate to the vicious legal manipulation of the indictment. In our view, consequences (acquittal or conviction) were definitely secondary. We had seen formidable consequences, and found them less than fearsome. The only thing more the Powers could do was prolong indefinitely what we had seen.

This is not to criticize other defendants or other Movement people. They hardly need that or deserve it. It is to reflect on the variety of resistance experiences and to know that jail is climactic to all of them and that it must be borne, exploited and transcended.

Another question: How else did political differences inject themselves into defendant decisions?

We disagreed somewhat on the lawyers representing us, and afterward on their politics, strategy and contribution to trial preparation. We disagreed deeply over philosophy of defense. Should we conduct a political trial or a legal one? Should our goal be resistance in the courtroom or should it be acquittal? All felt the war should be a priority, since it brought us to the dock, but there was considerable ambivalence in applying that concretely. We disagreed on self-representation, co-counsel and noncooperation. Some defendants had no desire to allow others to represent them. Finally, we disagreed on offering a defense or resting it.

Despite the differences, people cling to certain basics; we loved and respected one another. As far as I can tell, no deep resentments will outlast the trial. One of the lawyers said following the verdict, "The real accomplishment of these months has been holding it together." A rather astonishing statement, but I think a true one.

Some object that our real accomplishment was the verdict, not our cohesion. But I'm afraid we didn't have a great deal to do with the verdict. Sure, everyone worked very hard preparing data for the lawyers; and everyone but me stumped on the road tirelessly. But top-grade legal work and the good sense of the jury had far more to do with the verdict than we did.

How, in fact, did we hold together, then? What were the main factors?

More than anything, I think, it was the way we made decisions. Very early in preparation we made a decision about decision-making, affirming that it had to be a majority exercise, a community assertion; this was an affirmation that the community was more than each of us individually. All but Eqbal had been prepared for this by both religious training and from the operation of our action communities—the Catonsville Nine, the Boston Eight, the East Coast Conspiracy to Save Lives, etc. However, this was no problem to Eqbal since he is a very intelligent and flexible man.

Now, I don't mean to suggest that such a mode of operation produces the best of possible worlds. It has severe weaknesses as well as impressive strengths. For example, in re weaknesses, it results in a moral and political common denominator, somewhat distant from resistance logic and over-all potential. Again, the question of experience enters the issue: six defendants had never experienced a trial, six had never been in jail beyond a few days. Those who had (Ted Glick and myself) disagreed constantly with the other defendants on the key decisions of the trial. (Dan, who helped immeasurably with trial preparation, joined in this minority.) What I'm trying to say is this: Our experience, moral and political sense, and hopes for the trial never found real expression in decisions. Acquiescence and submission were our general role in the end of discussion—only that. A very good thing, perhaps—to have proud and single-minded men back off time and time again, accepting the majority will of others. But that's another question entirely.

So much for the weaknesses. Regarding its strengths, the community decision, as we called it, possessed a genius of sorts. First, we agreed to agree on process, if agreeing on little else. But *that* unanimity was crucial. Second, we reduced personal animosities to a minimum, since (regarding decisions affecting all of us) no one was ignored, slighted, ridiculed, put down; little or no injustice was done. Third, we kept emotional and psychological attrition to a minimum. A deep awareness prevailed that we could not afford casualties—people ruined for resistance partially or wholly. Fourth, we presented a united front to the public, press, jury, courtroom. At no time, to the immense credit of six defendants, was there any reflection of irreconcilable differences, of pettiness or rancor. We acted like a loving community, and to a remarkable degree we were.

Were the government to try us again, I would fight with other defendants on substantially the same issues, in the hope that we would force openings in which we could speak of the war, and our lives in resistance. Nonetheless I would initially agree, as I did before, to majority vote, to community decision. It appears to result in a wisdom that we cannot fully comprehend at the time, or fully gauge. How does that simple saying go? "All of us are smarter than one of us."

One of the more painful quandaries we faced was that of self-defense. Ted Glick insisted on this for himself, as was his constitutional right and because he had experienced the power of *pro se* during his trial in Rochester. Our judge, who feared nothing more than antiwar defendants on their feet, quickly severed him before selection of jury. Following that, I tried to go *pro se* as the prosecutor's case opened, dismissing my lawyers and insisting on an opening statement. No way! The judge refused the motion. He would not allow my opening statement and commanded the lawyers to continue defending me. Later, as Boyd Douglas approached the stand, I made the same motion, intending to cross-examine him. Same result. Technically, if the right of self-representation under the Sixth Amendment means anything, I went the whole trial without legal representation, having fired my lawyers and not being permitted to speak for myself.

Regarding the strategy of defense, Ramsey Clark had tentatively outlined a short, spirited defense comprised of (1) Sister Jogues Egan and Dan testifying to the nature of the war, the resistance, the community of civil disobedience—whatever tolerated by the judge—but most notably about Liz and myself; (2) veterans (no more than three or four) of draft-board and corporate raids relating their involvement, stressing the emphasis put upon individual conscience and the autonomy of individual groups—a way of clarifying our notion of conspiracy vis-à-vis the government's notion; (3) discriminatory enforcement—the legal term for the government's sordid record in this indictment—from Hoover's testimony before the Senate subcommittee to the judge's repulsive collusion with Lynch and company, the prosecutors—as when the judge restated the government's case during his final charges to the jury. Discriminatory enforcement would also include the unprecedented act of prosecuting for contraband letters—in fact, basing a conspiracy indictment on contraband letters. And then (4) Elizabeth and I taking the stand, mostly to explain the letters, their alleged threatening nature (Counts 2 and 3), plus their references to bombing utilities serving government buildings in Washington, D.C.

Of course, as is known, none of that happened. All we experienced—endured, in fact—was the prosecution's case, with the scenery of judge and marshals.

Our judge! As I saw him, he was the product of three machines: institutional religion, the Republican oligarchy of central Pennsylvania, and the federal legal apparatus. If his actions during the trial meant anything, he believed that the Church should have nothing to do with social justice, and that wealth somehow conferred divine election on its possessors. I'm afraid that priests and nuns and a foreign scholar, and a bunch of smart-ass New York lawyers defending them, headed by the ex-Attorney General of the United States, all proved something of a blasphemy to him.

I had heard that he believed us guilty. Reportedly, he was overheard at a party one evening stating that. When some attempt was made to collect affidavits from the junior barons who heard him, these young gallants blanched and went resolutely silent. More significant than that, however, was his performance in the courtroom. We watched him coach, give aid and comfort to the chief government witness for two solid weeks, veritably charge the jury to find us guilty and give criminal weight to the most effervescent circumstances.

Perhaps we were presumptuously expecting that Judge Herman would suddenly, in the course of the trial, become a silk purse for us, after having been a sow's ear all his life. But how could this Calvinist Republican, machine believer, activist in veterans' organizations, hunter and fisherman understand the morality or politics of defendants impudent enough to break the law, and endure its consequences, for the sake of life? How could he understand our feverish discussions about even more serious activity on behalf of those who were otherwise scheduled to die? How could he understand, this champion of American affluence, the agony of Indochinese peasants, or be outraged by the American machinery that was shredding their bodies? How could he appreciate our position and accord it justice? No way; it didn't happen, because it couldn't.

Judge Herman presided with an owlish, tense self-consciousness, sipping water, exercising his facial muscles, and uttering nonsentences about nonrealities. Whether in chambers (with bullet-proof glass surrounding his desk) or on the bench (with a marshal at his side and an alarm button within reach), he symbolized the nation's leadership, boxed into an abominable "way of life" by truculence, suspicion, moral and political calcification —men old before their teens.

As far as I could discover, the prosecutors were all Catholics—an elephantine attempt to dispel suspicions that the government, in indicting us, was initiating a vendetta against the Catholic Church. Somewhere in the muddy thinking of the Justice Department arose the belief that fine Catholic prosecutors would better pursue a conviction of people like ourselves. Which struck us all as ludicrous, knowing that their Pius XII Catholicism could well guarantee them security and advancement in the Justice Department, but not prepare them to comprehend or to prosecute a group predominantly of Christian radicals.

They were nondescript, short on imagination, honor and energy. Heading them was William Lynch, whose competence as a lawyer was invariably augured by the color of his wattles. If they were red, one could count on Lynch being on his feet spouting *ad hominem* instead of law and generally making an ass of himself. If they were white, Lynch could be counted on to push his "plot," to the quiet satisfaction of Judge Herman.

Actually we overestimated Lynch, mainly because he had resurrected the first, untenable indictment, concocting a devilish new version, which tempered the legal consequences while increasing the possibility of conviction. It seemed clear he had a grandiose intent: (1) stopping or curtailing the Selective Service raids; (2) tying up the Movement with a long, expensive court action; and (3) immobilizing defendants in court or in jail for a very long time.

The outcome fell somewhat short of the mark. Nevertheless the indictment cost us a half million dollars, nearly eighteen months of our lives, an enormous amount of time and toil for lawyers and many others who made the defense their own, and it may prove to have had a chilling effect on the conscience and will of the defendants and others touched by this long, costly struggle.

In effect, Lynch's indictment had overtones of interest as an innovative conspiracy case. But much more, it stood out as a bold example of psychological warfare, as a type of head-game putdown employed when the government can't use naked force against its naysayers. Almost invariably the government scores with this kind of "heat-on-heads" process, mainly because peace people remain emphatically American, and therefore deprived of radical understanding and inner resources. Whether his success applies to us remains to be seen.

In the courtroom, however, Lynch wasn't that good. He and his team suffered in comparison to our lawyers—in appearance, presence and performance. His lackluster prosecution was marked especially by irritability, sarcasm, humorlessness and, it seemed to us, just poor preparation. Very early it became noticeable that Lynch and his satellites had but superficial convictions about what they were doing. True, they preserved the role of legal hatchetmen to the end, relaxing not at all in their fervid attempts to railroad us. But there was no stamina in their malice, no willingness to work hard at it. Only a smugness that became boring for lack of substance, and a vindictiveness that was profoundly ignorant.

One question intrigued me: If Lynch and satellites really believed us to be the threats they said we were, why didn't they work harder to convict us? Why were their witnesses so ill prepared, their defense against motions so blustering and shallow, their strategy and tactics so transparent and stereotyped? Did the mediocre performance of a so-called top government team indicate that nobody in government really works—except Kissinger, perhaps? Or did it imply patronage within the meritocracy, too ready access to the pork barrel? What the prosecution displayed was unlimited investigative, clerical and legal manpower, unlimited funds (estimates of two and three million dollars have been called conservative), and unlimited lack of substance—qualities that indelibly mark "programs" of the American colossus at home or abroad. Moral of the story: How to keep the vehicle of State waxed, shiny, chauffeured, and spinning its wheels!

Jury selection had eaten up four weeks in January and February, an enormously trying and depressing experience, simply because it illustrated so starkly the pervasive control of people by historical myth, bad religion, government propaganda and cultural stagnation. After observing it, one can better understand the common contention of sociologists and lawyers that our culture—dominated by commercial unrealities—exercises better social control than totalitarian measures employed by Hitler's Germany or today's Greece and Brazil.

Scores of middle-Pennsylvania citizens marched forward, only to disqualify themselves as prejudiced against us. Hoover had spoken, an indictment had come down—that was enough for them. Ironically enough, those most prejudiced against us had suffered most grievously from the nation's hot and cold warring in dead and wounded members of their families. How does the old, brutal adage go? "Beat a child (or a dog) often enough, and you'll make him grateful!" Such people seemed grateful for exploitation, making yet more pitiful their loyalty to official criminality.

Jury selection illustrated also that "selection" means two things: weeding out the unneutrals, and choosing the neutrals. That is to say, in a political case like our own, people best qualified to judge the case—the poor, blacks, resisters, students, academics, those who have known deprivation, those with experience, discernment, compassion—could never possibly sit. Automatically, those most capable of judging us, and judging the government, are excluded. (Here I speak more of the inadequacies of jury selection than of anything else. The jury turned out well as a result of tremendous work by lawyers, because of reaction to poor prosecution and because we might have won some sympathy.)

Apart from these factors, we underestimated the jury, just as we overestimated Lynch. Within the rationale decided upon by defendants and lawyers—which seriously weakened the political output while supposedly enhancing chances for acquittal—the jury became a target, rather like film critics gathered for a premiere, the object being to impress them and win them over.

To win them over—without a word about our lives, our resistance, our efforts to inject a note of sanity into the consciousness of a confused, violent and bloody-handed public. The ambivalence connected with this still torments me, still makes me writhe with shame. While understanding the concern surrounding Elizabeth and myself—the hope that she might be spared jail and that I might be saved from further time, and might be freed —such altruism does not connect with reality, does not engage the truth of the matter. The jury was not the truth of the matter— a criminal government was.

234

It is inexpensive, and somewhat idle, to speculate now about what might have been. Frankly, we played to the jury—calculatingly and unabashedly. Within the lines set down, the jury became our only hope. We learned to watch our decorum strictly, to curb our reactions to falsehood from government witnesses, to exude an air of confidence and cheerfulness. When Douglas testified that I suggested a gun for the "kidnapping" of Kissinger or that I shrugged off the death of a graduate student at the University of Wisconsin bombing, I contained my outrage, gulped, kept the peace and played the game.

It paid off—our behavior, our community with one another and with our lawyers, our well-scrubbed, rather middle-class social anguish, the suspicion we projected that such handsome, upright people could be nothing but victims of a legal guillotine. Our tactics allowed the jury to relate to us sympathetically, and to focus upon a shoddy and vindictive prosecution. The trial left us unscathed, but it also left us unexplained. And silence under duress when lives of moral and political moment are in the dock, when a criminal government is prosecutor rather than prosecuted—such silence is an incalculable loss to truth.

But within the outline, they surprised us, this middle-Pennsylvania jury. They didn't get all the truth, or even most of it. Nevertheless they heard enough to detect a graveyard smell of Mother State's vengefulness and spite, of might for right, of death for profit, of obsession to stand outside of law or to remake law to its ambition, of intent to conduct its wars in unhampered freedom. They might have gotten a whiff, instead of the burden of proof. And so they acquitted us.

The marshals: Every morning at 8 A.M. for nearly three months, two or three federal marshals appeared at the Control Center of the county jail to transport my cooperating flesh and resisting spirit to the courtroom. We greet one another affably, even warmly. They encircle me with a waist chain, handcuff me to the chain, pick up my legal papers and New Testament, and off we go. As we leave, everyone exchanges friendly goodbyes—we, the warden, underkeeper, clerks, guards. This chaining is, as they are prompt to tell me, nothing personal. Nothing personal in locking me up, nothing personal in delivering me like a trussed chicken. It's always that way—nothing personal, no hard feelings.

Outside, three more marshals wait in a car, in radio contact with Harrisburg Control back in the Federal Building. We start out, chatting easily about anything light and "noncontroversial"—weather, sports, airline travel, automobiles. They tell me about their families, haul out pictures, play music on the radio, tell about their parish priest back home ("He's really quite a fella"); they confide their pain at separation from their families ("This boy of mine's growin' long hair!").

They came from all over, these marshals—from the District, from the State of Washington, from Vermont, California, Michigan, Oklahoma, Texas and Massachusetts. A few were black. The whites—southern crackers, Irishmen from the Midwest, paisanos from New Jersey, even a Basque from the West, where his family had herded sheep. Most were Catholics, all were veterans, frequently "lifers"—as conscripts would call them today—who joined the marshals following retirement. Most drove big cars, helping to pay for them with liberal mileage allowances. Most were mechanically inclined, had families, went to church, consumed enthusiastically. And all possessed a reverent, almost vocationlike attitude toward their work: "Security is our job—we're trained for it."

They never let me out of their sight, never allowed a spectator to get near in the courtroom or in the halls, never relaxed the mobile cage of their bodies around me. The more I offered assurances—"You couldn't horsewhip me out of this building"—the tighter security got, always accompanied by a patient, courteous explanation. "You might not wanna run, but others might wanna grab you or hurt you. Lotta kooks around, you know." Which was essentially the same line as one from a warden at Lewisburg Penitentiary: "We gotta keep you here, but we gotta protect you too. Lotta these cons don't agree with you!"

After the trial began I made casual trips back and forth with casual marshals, sometimes even without cuffs; I worked at a table outside the marshal's cage, never in lockup; I walked from their offices to the courtroom unhandcuffed; I used the common john on the courtroom floor, exchanging pleasantries with newsmen and seminarians. As we rested our case and verdict time approached, security's noose tightened in proportion: chains and handcuffs; lockup in the cage until visitors arrived; searching of lawyers and defendants; a magic key produced for a solitary john; two-car escorts by six or more marshals; the manhandling of a student who one day tried to shake my hand.

There is nothing mysterious about parasitism—threaten the host and the ticks will fight. Marshals trained to a studied neutrality in the courtroom, a glazed-eyed, slack-jawed indifference to the pros and cons of death in a political trial, suddenly discard their neutrality as the verdict nears. Eyes get keen, speech becomes clipped, movements become purposeful, security becomes *serious.* Guilt needs a sanction, forthcoming from the jury, and when it comes, Moloch must have his victim. For Moloch is room and board, motels on the road, good meals and booze, college for the kids, a car for the wife, an easy and nodding friendship with *Power.* People like me threaten the marriage contract, bore holes in the boat, pray for wild weather. We even screw around with old Mother Church, and make her guilty about sleeping with Caesar, especially on those days when she straps on armor in the morning. A marshal confided this to me one morning, in a show of recklessness: "Don't you worry. As far as I'm concerned, you're still a priest!" But he was troubled and said it halfheartedly. I had broken the code of Church-State concordat—why wasn't I back in Baltimore nursing the flock?

So much for the judicial rituals. What of the meaning of Christian tradition for the future of the left? What contribution can it make? What helps us in a sense of where we come from? For our concern with these questions isn't incidental to the public consequences of our lives.

It's like some families (or peoples or cultures) who relive the lives of their ancestors and heroes; who digest their folklore, art, rituals, who cling to roots in a living tradition of which they are the fruit. Or it's like being a new leaf upon a great, gnarled old oak—below are trunk, bark, branches; around are air, moisture and other leaves. One has a history of meaning, and out of that an obligation to create meaning now. A past of meaning, a present of responsibility.

There are certain givens within this living tradition—light in struggle against darkness, good against evil, truth against false-hood, nonviolence against violence, conscience against the State, life against death. One sees them define life, knows their truth, connects them with similar manifestations in self and society, takes them into one's chemistry, lives them to liberate oneself and others.

Within this living tradition one knows that Amos, Hosea, Jonah and Christ have meaning today—indeed live in those who give them meaning. One says yes! to them: the same witness, the same stand-up, the same resistance is necessary today against personal and State evil.

Life has not changed, one discovers—only its accidents have. Christ's resistance against the hierarchy and empire of his day is essentially the same as resistance against a dominating tech-nocracy led by the rich, with an entourage of cheerful, generously endowed bishops in attendance, that we have today. Both systems are fundamentally totalitarian, both stink of lies and death. In face of such, what was required then is required now—truth, love, courage—all taking root in nonviolent resistance.

I don't see how the left will move and become a force for life unless it puts down some key taproots. For lack of them, it lacks continuity and stamina. It cannot connect with the present in a con-tinuous way because it has little continuity with the resistance of the past; and so it remains largely defensive in nature, ad hoc (crisis-oriented) and desultory, subject to fits and starts, people dropping in and dropping out. Finally, it remains emphatically elitist, partly because its leaders are the handful who possess continuity—and therefore permanence—in the struggle; and partly because leaders won't/can't engage the problem of tradi-tion.

We may be able to help with this. If we're true to ourselves and to our tradition, it may constitute our contribution. And it may be a signal one.

Perhaps this leads to some consideration of the meaning of priesthood and even of the traditional association of celibacy with priesthood in Roman Catholic inheritance. My love and admiration for Elizabeth McAlister has been thrown at me by wardens and others as if it was in some essential contradiction with my vocation as priest.

Back in the early fifties, when Dan and I were desperately trying to extract some meaning from seminary life, and to give some to the priesthood we faced, we devoured such French theologians as Suhard and Delubac and a couple of Dominicans whose names I now forget. Typically, like the vast majority of theologians, they wrote nothing that would help the Christian relate to the fierce power-grubbing that had turned the world into a fratricidal madhouse during World War II and in the Cold War years. But they were good scriptural and patristic scholars, and they did give substance to the Christian identity. From their work thoughtful readers could draw a few valid conclusions about the purpose of life and the forces of death, about nonviolence and violence, peace and war, freedom and State control. They helped us put the taproots deeper, helped to give us confidence and strength to make what Gandhi called "experiments with truth."

I remember especially a text by one of them about Christ as King, Prophet, Priest. It had a stunning relevance and meaning to me, and it stuck through the years, not because I was training for the priesthood but because I was a Christian and called to be one. *King:* one excelling in service, in doing the shitwork, even of the most hazardous and costly kind; one ruling not by domination but through extraordinary love; one who is the man (or woman) for others, to the point of danger, jail, death. *Prophet:* literally, one who tells the truth, and lives it; one who constantly juxtaposes God's sublime design for ourselves against our pitiful performance; one who calls contemporaries to conversion, to family bonds, to accountability for life; one who, finally, tells the rich about their crimes, who speaks truth to the powerful, and who resists with all life's resources. *Priest:* one who speaks for God to humanity, or for humanity to God, preaching the Gospel with his life, which is to say, living in the skins of the victimized

239

and abused as a means of living in one's own; who begs mercy from God for all, a mercy we experience in liberation, in wisdom, in compassion.

If Christ lives in us by nature and call, if we are members of His body, if we are sons and daughters and brothers and sisters as He was son and brother—then we share His inheritance. We are king as He was, prophet and priest as He was. The Pauline admonition "Become what you are" presents us with a preemptory challenge; we are invited to it and summoned, but also commanded.

All things become possible, one goes from "strength to strength," as the Psalmist would say: the peaceful tolerance of hardship, growing patience, nonviolence permeating one's existence, nonviolence toward persecutors and tyrants, acceptance of such penalties as danger, jail, death.

All this is why, from time to time, one becomes appalled at bishops, at clergy, at other Christians generally. The temptation to give up on the bishops especially is enormous, mainly because they cling to institutional management, which renders them largely uneducable. But priests, nuns, brothers, fellow Christians—all of whom can shuck off more of the false encumbrances of parish property and finance—why do they sell themselves so tragically short? Why so little awareness of themselves and humanity, not as they appear but as they are? Why such fear and dread of saying what they know to be right, of living what they know to be true? Why so little personal sacrifice?

But what of celibacy, that old trademark of the Roman priesthood?

Jesus is very specific: "Not everyone can accept this teaching [celibacy], only those to whom it is given to do so. Some men are incapable of sexual activity from birth; some have been deliberately made so; and some there are who have freely renounced sex for the sake of God's reign. Let him accept this teaching who can."

The whole issue of celibacy revolves around the rights of conscience. Christ did not demand or enforce celibacy as an essential for priesthood or religious life because He wouldn't. And He wouldn't because He couldn't—not without doing violence to conscience.

Christ would hardly trap Himself by such a question; He revered too much the primacy of conscience. Such cannot be said about His followers—mystics, philosophers, bishops—who consistently exaggerated celibacy as a moral panacea; causing it to become, in effect, an excuse to flee from the complexities of human love. "Let him accept this teaching who can." Some choose not to for perfectly valid and Christian reasons. Does that mean they live less for the reign of God than celibates? Hardly.

It is interesting, in fact critical, that Christ spent immeasurably more time warning against the abuses of wealth than the abuses of sex, which at best deserve only passing attention from Him. It is critical that His followers honored poverty far more than celibacy, many of them being married. Paul, on the other hand, was less patient, and less wise.

Could Christ have been teaching that voluntary rein upon human greed—which without discipline becomes a hydra of violence (domination, exploitation, war)—relates powerfully to an understanding of human sexuality and a reverence for it? Wasn't he stressing that our basic human problem was violence against the species, a problem to be addressed equally by both the married and the celibate?

Wednesday, June 21

One more monthly anniversary—thirty-three. Sometimes I think the months are trying to overtake the years— thirty-three in pursuit of forty-eight. Now, that's a sobering thought. If, however, they coincide one time or the next, I should not complain.

The second temptation of Christ, according to Matthew, says: "Then the Devil took Jesus to the Holy City, set Him on the highest point of the Temple and said to Him, 'If you are God's Son, throw yourself to the ground; for the Scripture says, "God will give orders to His angels about you; they will hold you up with their hands, so that you will not even hurt your feet on the stones." ' Jesus answered, 'But the Scripture also says, "You must not put the Lord your God to the test." ' "

What has been the "religious" response? Very simply, to succumb to the temptation. As shepherds organized the sheep, as religious foundations abounded, as treaties were negotiated with the State, as property and assets expanded, conscience was uninstructed, enfeebled, suspected; people were frozen in moral adolescence, and mystified by and in moral superiority; the Good News collapsed into ethical ideology; the bishops and clerics aped the barons and the burghers; the Church managed rather than inspired; until ethical confusion and public neutrality mark the Christian.

Christ did not throw Himself down. He refused to use influence, to coerce, to blackmail. He refused to do what His followers do all the time. The reign of God is not entered cheaply by deceit, by incantation or magic, by enlisting the spirit world. It is entered by the violent (determined), who seize it because God has first seized their lives. "The violent bear it away."

Religious power is the power of God moving gently into a person, dominating as it frees. It is not like human power, with its illusion-breeding violence, always aiming at control, always springing from desire. It permeates a person, paradoxically liberating as it masters, extricating her/him from intellectual myopia, emotional tyranny, volitional flabbiness. But every advance in liberation presupposes submission to the Spirit—to the desert as the soul's climate, to crucifixion of pride and fear, to leaps of faith into risk, into financial and physical helplessness, into imprisonment, and possibly into death.

One of Gandhi's secretaries once remarked that Gandhi's public energy and generosity arose from sublimated passion—sex, anger, ambition. "Gandhi," he said, "is under his own complete control. That generates tremendous energy and passion." He should have added greed to the list of vices disciplined. Gandhi rejected possessions, comfort, security. He craved two things, per-haps—to love God, and to love God's poor.

Neither Christ nor Gandhi leaped from the highest point of the temple in order to tempt men with the chains of dogma, property, or treaties with Caesar.

Wednesday, June 28

The sun has returned, and the earth awakens to its business following the drenching. So do spirits. I don't recall having experienced such a sustained downpour, even in England during the war, or in the Deep South—both areas notorious for overcast and rain.

The third temptation in **St.** Matthew: "Then the Devil took Jesus to a very high mountain and showed Him all the kingdoms of the world, in all their greatness. 'All this will I give you,' the Devil said, 'if you kneel down and worship me.' Then Jesus answered, 'Go away, Satan! The Scripture says, "Worship the Lord your God and serve only Him." ' "

Obviously Satan would not offer what was not his; he was too crafty and subtle for that. Luke makes the point even more emphatically: *governments* are his. "I will give you all this power and the glory of these kingdoms, for it has been committed to me, and I give it to anyone I choose. Worship me, then, and it shall be all yours."

Tourists marvel over the monuments of empire in Rome, Paris, London, New York. How many reflect on the horror of broken faith, economic extortion, legalized murder and human slavery required for their building? The "glory" of empire rests on the blandish-ments of Satan and man's deluded acquiescence; their "power" is corrupted by his violence. The official lie, the bureaucracy, the sword—these are the modern tools for dominating the weak, for gaining sovereignty over life and death, for satisfying naked ambition.

243

"Worship the Lord your God and serve only Him!" If man rejects an idolatry of self, property, ideology, and ends, embracing others, poverty, wisdom, and means, he frees within himself and others the only power deserving the name of political power— liberation from the tyranny of self and institution. "[The Lord] has sent me to bring good news to the poor, to proclaim liberty to captives, and to the blind new sight, to set the downtrodden free, to proclaim the Lord's year of favor."

Mao is right in calling for perpetual revolution; but he is wrong in his reasons and in his means. Man must accept personal and social revolution to become man, but the means of revolution must be loving, must be human. The signs of true revolution are much more profound and modest than anything historical or contemporary. For example, insuring that a few less children die.

Perhaps if Americans learned to build nonviolent communities of resistance, concentrating on the essential rather than the grandiose, they might in time learn to hold leaders accountable for peace, to throw open their prisons, to break down corporate monsters to manageable size, to dismantle their war machine. The power of God as well as true political power starts with tiny beginnings. The Reign of God begins like a mustard seed, true power in Christ's cleansing of the Temple, modern liberation in Gandhi's handful of salt.

Thursday, August 17

Just wrote Ramsey a welcome-home note. Six months ago he probably would not have gone to the North [Vietnam]. Another service.

Ironic. He is simply claiming that the destruction is what policy had said it should be at least four years ago [official air force policy]. Our experts asserted that anything living aboveground had to go, with contingency plans for tactical nuclear weapons. But when someone of Clark's establishment credentials says that we're doing just fine at implementing policy, the howl from the mandarins is "Foul!" and "Where's Queensberry?" Obviously policy and effort are one thing; what is told Americans is another.

"Happy are those who work for peace among men; God will call them His sons."

As I gather these notes, eleven young brothers sit in the prison hospital awaiting shipment to the (oh, familiar!) Federal Medical Center in Springfield, Missouri. Most are nauseated, pale, weak —they have taken only water since August 6, Hiroshima Day. One is black, ten are white: three resisters, eight assorted hustlers, addicts, bank robbers. Ex-, that is; now peaceniks for the duration. These men are fasting to the death against the docility of their countrymen, against the lethargy and timidity of the peace movement, against our mindless bombing and shelling of the Vietnamese.

Their fast, along with that of an allied group on the outside, has apparently struck the national consciousness with gentle ineffectuality. Americans are more fascinated than horrified by violence, so they have little stomach for the most heroic nonviolence.

At the press conference, Elizabeth confronts the press with their relish for prisoners' blood during jail uprisings and their apathy toward nonviolent prisoners' resistance. Abashed, some reporters agree and pass the buck to their editors. If approached, I suppose editors will pass the buck to their readers.

Thursday, August 24

Ten years ago, when the black poor were helping me become a human being, I recall the demands from lay Christians, black and white, for "leadership" from the clergy. Among liberal clergymen the same petition was voiced for "leadership" from bishops and politicians. Then, as one moved from the base of the pyramid to its midriff, the same need was sounded vis-à-vis the Congress and the Office of Economic Opportunity. Awareness and action, responsibility and resistance were supposed to arrive mysteriously from the next echelon of the pecking order—from those elements least likely to offer it.

When a handful of priests and young resisters (women and men) committed civil disobedience and went to jail, the calls for leadership from "militant" laymen grew strangely still. A new dimension of Christianity had opened up, as baffling and torturous as the cross. In private the initiators were judged more than slightly mad—driven to extremism by impatience and frustration.

On the other hand, the young resisters didn't give a damn about "leadership" from anyone; they knew it wasn't forthcoming, or that even if it came, it wasn't particularly desirable. What they looked for were people mature enough to give life to their opposition to war and war-makers, people who would put their lives where their mouths were—people who were ready to get burned. They realized that the essential question wasn't "Are you ready to act?" but rather "Are you ready to get burned?"

I am grinding this out—some spiritual constipation recently. My thoughts come out like rabbit turds, tough and round and poor. Sometimes I think that ninety percent of one's life and energies is spent explaining what one has done. Even when it is so painfully less than what one ought to do.

September 13

A week ago Tuesday, Judge Herman sentenced Liz and myself. Liz got a year, with three years' probation; I got two years, concurrent.

His decision to sentence was undoubtedly affected by demonstrations at the Federal Building in Harrisburg sparked by Dan, Jerry and Jim. They went there at calculated risk, knowing Herman's vindictiveness. Knowing also that until he sentenced me nothing would happen; there would be no dropping of charges by the Justice Department, no appeal, no parole, no end to the bitter limbo that began in November 1970, when Hoover branded us enemies of the State. Nothing—just more jail time.

I'll confess frankly that limbo has disturbed me more than the possibility of more jail. I've managed to keep profitably busy in jail praying, writing, building community. The inert and galling nature of the life has disciplined and toughened me. But limbo is another matter entirely—one has no hope of release; one doesn't even know how much more time is required. Two years of juggling these obscurities is quite enough.

Getting back to the sentence, it was politically devious and crafty, worthy of a Nixonian camp follower. Judge Herman, in the fashion of a small-town political toady, kept one shifty eye on November and the other on his own sweet skin. He hoped thereby to insure the Chief's re-election while avoiding reversal in a higher court. And keep me locked up in the meantime. So he planned headlines announcing two years for me, one for Liz—a face-saving gift to the government after its colossal blunder, as well as a vengeful dividend on the several million invested to put us away. A distracted and harried public would gulp the headlines and ignore the fine print.

Moreover, Herman championed Nixon's domestic repression through our sentence, mollified the law-and-order people, and issued in the process a not very veiled threat to peaceniks: Cool it.

Herman's sentence might have been a culmination for us, but it was a threat to others, especially to the Vietnam Vets indicted in Florida [at the Republican Convention].

The whole experience was an options-open shuffle, all options favoring our leaders. Herman knew that Terry Lenzner would push for a parole hearing following sentencing, so he gave me a concurrent sentence subject to immediate parole, thereby transferring my fate to the Parole Board. If they spring me before November, Nixon will look benign and merciful. If not until sometime later, that will make slight difference, since Nixon expects his "mandate" in November anyway.

Essentially the role of resistance is to deny control to the global henchmen, large and small, and then to try to accept somehow the consequent shit.

November 7

Returns trickle in. It appears that Nixon will sweep everything but the District and Massachusetts—a landslide and his total "mandate."

Nixon has the distinction of being history's greatest destroyer. Aside from his savage prolongation of the war, he has manipulated foreign relations, cowed Russians and Chinese, glorified the commercial plutocracy, neglected, deceived and insulted the public, and persecuted the poor. For this he receives universal gratitude and an overwhelming political "mandate."

The public is a pitiful orphan, its spirit broken, fawning and squirming its servility after a whipping. I feel sorry for us. We are reaping what we have sowed, and Nixon is part of the whirlwind.

November 8

"But now I tell you: anyone who looks at a woman and wants to possess her is guilty of committing adultery with her in his heart." That's Matthew again. Just as Christ went to the interior root of murder by exposing its beginning in anger, so He reminds us that the root of sexism is in the exploitative *idea* of dominating a woman sexually.

A society that deserves the adjective "human" must exist principally for those who are habitually exploited and abused. Recognizing this, those who champion women's rights point to war as a male enterprise, possible only because of the degradation of women.

As the thesis goes, the emancipation of women would give a deathblow to war—to male belligerence in both the institution and the economic necessity of war. And so women, formerly in the Movement, now attack war through their struggle to emancipate themselves and other women.

The trouble is that they see the exploitation of women more as a structural and less as an interior problem. It is surely the second before it is the first, and as such is shared by both sexes. Men seek out women as flesh objects, wanting sex without responsibility. Women in turn frequently accommodate and retaliate with wiles and entrapment, using their bodies as lures for material stakes.

Male supremism, enforced by men and tolerated by women, offends a basic spiritual axiom. "If there is no God," says one of Dostoevski's characters, "then I am God." When lovelessness reigns, it can only be because people are interiorly comatose and dying. Having rejected the God both personal and other—the Source of life and love—they have rejected each other. Materialism, unbelief, hypersexuality are all futile attempts to fill the void.

November 15

Today I start my thirty-ninth month in prison. Despite my best efforts, I live with one eye cocked on the fourteenth of each month. It's not that I'm deluded about the outside, or just that I long to enjoy some physical freedom again. It is rather that I have a family, and have work that obviously can't be done here.

"But now I tell you: love your enemies, and pray for those who mistreat you, so that you will become sons of your Father in heaven." The best proof of God's love for us is Christ's life and death, even while we were enemies, while we were doing violence to His will and to our nature.

The ultimate test of a person is love for enemies, i.e., those who do us wrong. The greater the wrong, the greater the test, and the greater the love required.

To our feeble and irascible temperaments, love of enemies is generally a disciplinary impossibility. But the fact is, God's love for humanity—intense, unvarying, absolutely comprehensive—often requires human agency. God wants to love the enemy through us. And so He makes this love available—if only we would use it.

November 16

"But when you help a needy person, do it in such a way that even your closest friend will not know about it" (Matthew 6:3). Here Christ has no intention to explore the labyrinths of human motivation. He advises simply, have the best possible reasons for anything you do.

Which sheds light on the lifelong fight to purify our interior life, to discipline mind and heart against our dervishes—devious, violent, ignoble.

Maximilian Kolbe did not, probably, grasp all the moral-political reasons for resistance to the Nazi murderers. But in the grisly unlife of Auschwitz he did grasp the Gospel truth that a man cannot express greater love than to offer his life for his friend. So with the unlikely courtesy of the commandant's permission, he took the place of the hostage slated for execution.

In Mississippi, in the fifties, I met another Polish priest who was a survivor of Auschwitz. His experience awed me, and so did his vitality, toughness, stamina. But he had nothing to say about the resistance to death-dealing, resistance to the colossal crunch of evil in those years. He had survived, but he did not resist.

Our reasons for living, for resisting the omnipresence of death around us, for casting out the demons of death within us must be as trenchant and wide as Christ's. One way to do that is to devour the Gospel, feeding it into blood and marrow, so that His life may shine through ours.

November 17

"Be careful not to perform your religious duties in public so that people will see what you do."

In terms of its root, the word "religion" means a rebinding, a re-tying. Rebinding what? Relationships—to God, to neighbor, to self.

People dismiss religion today with contempt as the claptrap, paraphernalia and sham of Judaeo-Christian institutionalism. A proper dislike of the sham generates prejudice against the real thing. And people indiscriminately condemn everyone and everything associated with religion, mostly to their own harm. For we need real religion. There is no substitute. People cannot dispense with God, any more than they can with their neighbor or themselves. People cannot deny that they *are* their relationships.

For a long time Christ's treatment of the two great commandments confused me; I wondered why He called love of God with one's whole heart, mind, being, the first and greatest commandment. He also stated that love of one's neighbor is like this but clearly He put it in second place. Therefore, service to neighbor depends more on adoration and obedience than the other way around.

I have always found humanism (liberalism is no more than a corollary of humanism) lacking in the test. It seldom takes the leap of faith, it seldom enters the fire; mostly it recognizes no mandate, obeys no command. Other people cannot command us to love one another to the ultimate cost. Only God can, and we will obey Him because He is what He is, and because He did for us what He commands us to do for each other. A mandate like that carries one mysteriously and painfully beyond reason.

"I always do the things that please Him"—even to the point of blood. But it must be understood that His love of the Father was the first relationship to Him, and that out of it arose His love for us. Indeed, that love of the Father, given an earthly, concrete translation, was His love for us. It was as well the source of His identity and sense of mission. He was the true religious person, rebinding what had been weakened and scattered.

November 18

Matthew wrote: "This is the way you should pray: Our Father in heaven: May your name be kept holy."

Notice the delicate tension between two worlds preserved by Christ's prayer—the two worlds in which the Christian must live—in one by calling, in the other by stewardship; one the Kingdom of Christ, the other the Kingdom of Satan.

A. J. Muste used to claim, "I stand straightest when I'm on my knees." A most astonishing phenomenon is occurring today. The near universality of death-huckstering, death-dealing and just plain old death is driving people once more to their knees.

More, the contemplation of the East is invading the practicality of the West; contemplatives are exploring activism, and activists are returning to prayer. An age-old truth is being rediscovered: the divine in people must be nourished or they become a social liability at best and, at worst, a social threat.

What of the "Our Father"? First, acknowledgment of God's sovereignty: He is the one Father. Next, the need we have of the Kingdom as the ideal human order. Finally, the three necessities: bread, forgiveness, the strength to forgive.

I have discovered two things about prayer since entering prison: first, that when I pray humbly and honestly I can hack this life even at its bitterest. When I don't pray, I cannot.

When I don't pray I begin to apply to life the only power I really know—violence. Inch by inch I begin to disintegrate, and so do my relationships with others. I begin to brood over the injustice of this experience, and the dark side of my soul assumes control.

But when I pray I accept my dependency on God and on friends. And a love not my own is lent me. And I can continue.

Thursday, November 23

This is my fourth Thanksgiving in prison. I remember the first in Baltimore County Jail with Tom Lewis in 1968.

A pretty violent and depressing experience—several in our cell block were quite torn up by being away from their families. Thank God, these years have not hurt me—quite the opposite, in fact. And I am as thankful that they haven't hurt others—or if they have, the hurt was unintentional.

Baltimore, Maryland

APRIL 1973

April 1973

Dear Alice,

You asked me to conclude the book with reflections on getting out, and my feeling on release. A few of these, then.

First of all, parole and a parole date of December 20, 1972, came with total unexpectedness. When I got an eighteen-month setoff in July 1971, after two years in prison, I anticipated a decision in January 1973, with no great hope attached to that. (I had been found guilty of sending contraband letters in April 1972, and sentenced to two years, concurrent, in September of the same year. Moreover, my prison resistance had hardly endeared me to the Powers.) I fully expected another setoff—perhaps into early 1974.

When the Board announced parole, therefore, to apply after slightly more than thirty-nine months, I was floored. But experience with the barons suggested that I restrain myself, and I struggled to do so. Since they concede little for the right reasons, I hastened to consider the wrong ones, but I could only conjecture. Perhaps the wide-scale support—as in the case of Jimmy Hoffa—had been the ticket. Perhaps I was a gesture to the leaders of North Vietnam, who are inordinately grateful to Dan and myself. Perhaps I was being used to quiet the political left, even as later Calley may be used to quiet the right. Or am I a saccharine token for Christmas? All of these, or none. In any event, I was paroled—released to minimum security—arrested to the limits of the State of Maryland.

To claim I had no apprehensions about getting out would be dishonest. I had my share. These arose mostly from the sheer isolation of thirty-nine months of prison (the last stretch added to seven months in 1968). I had been living a different life, a life of formidable restriction and separation, a life of enforced silence and circumscribed activity. Whatever the rhetoric about "jail in the cultural wasteland," life outside prison is a quite different matter.

There is a difference in pace; prison offers too much leisure. Often there was literally nothing worth doing unless men "made do"—unless they filled their hours with projects, unless they forced themselves to read, think and learn. An inestimable boredom arose from this structured wastefulness, a cruel punishment of empty days. Imperceptibly, in such a climate, one loses an edge in perception and work, despite naps, classes and resistance. One loses a sense of the preciousness of time, grows stagnant and dull.

By contrast, life outside verges on the frantic, even the insane, a reality intensified by the penchant of Movement people to use "names," creating gurus and leaders, showing a misguided and selfishly possessive gratitude.

Dan had experienced this up close. Released in February 1972, while I was still imprisoned and on trial in Harrisburg, his health still fragile, he had been seized upon like some fantastic new remedy to be devoured at will and for the general commonweal. Inundated by mail and phone calls from friends and enemies, he had taken survival measures. "If Nixon fails to finish you off, your friends will," a friend advised.

To prepare me, rather than trouble me, he warned me about this and predicted a similar reception. Our fond dream of a "better idea than Catonsville," wherein American resisters would take upon themselves a leadership of responsibility and service, had remained a dream. Hence, I encountered on release the same old leader syndrome in anti-war people—their tendency to enshrine fame ("people'll turn out for you") and to orchestrate for the media ("you'll get us some coverage"). Americans, anti-war people among them, seem immobilized without the security of leaders' status and convictions.

I had no intention of being anyone's leader except my own. Neither had Dan. I remember Gandhi's remark about the wholesomeness of the "leader" attempting to catch up with his people. Though I could never imagine that as likely here and now, I did in fact hope for "the better alternative," the purer act of resistance.

So much for hope. But I had no intention of allowing the Movement to define me as leader (any more than we had allowed the government to define us kidnappers and bombers at Harrisburg). I have an intense desire to be useful, but I will neither exhort others to reproduce my experiences or shoulder responsibilities that others can carry.

Since December 20, with the help of family and friends, I have broken through the bars into parole and minimum security: richer food, occasional liquor after a long abstinence, endless requests and well wishing, mountains of mail. I have tried to yield to the consideration of others, to patience and common sense.

I regret nothing that I have done, nor do I resent anything done to me. Government is what it is (we understood it well); government people are what they are (we knew many, and the stripes are similar); both had to do what they did to me, to Dan, and to other resisters. But the fact of *that* and our recognition does not remove the conflict; nor does it pacify or domesticate us. Our dialogue will continue—from without and within jail.

One last word to the patient reader. If answers were offered in this book, they were accidental. Indeed, unintentional. I have no answers but a search for God, for sisters and brothers, for love of the first so that I might love the second. And a search is essentially a question.

Such a search is rare enough to be perilous. But eminently and stunningly worthwhile. To the extent that it is, I dare to suggest it to my sisters and brothers—everywhere. As a question, not an answer.

Of such, I believe, is Christ's reign—His truth, peace and freedom. I wish you all these as I do people everywhere.

Phil

May 28, 1973

(From a statement by Elizabeth McAlister and Philip Berrigan, announcing their marriage.)

The Church has made celibacy the spirit of religious commitment, if not its heart. We had hoped that a time would come when religious communities would invite both celibate and married people to a situation of mutual support and service to the Gospel and to suffering people. But the present Church vision, policy, and leadership make that impossible. Nonetheless, we cannot but question and resist the priority of celibacy over mature conscience and the spirit of the Gospels. We have tried to live responsibly since our contract—in separation, in jail, in legal jeopardy, in official attempts to disgrace us. Separation from our religious communities has not been our choice for we believe that in our case, as with others, celibacy is not the issue. Responsible freedom is.

We see our marriage as a radical assertion of our faith. With God's grace and the help of our friends, we hope to continue to live the Gospels—in poverty, in community, and in nonviolent resistance, convinced of the contribution of religious resistance to human kind.

We realize that many friends will be disappointed and hurt by what we now reveal. We owe them an explanation as to why we have kept this truth from people for so long.

At first, we wanted our relationship to clarify itself without pressure. In the midst of that process, Philip went to prison (April 1970). At that point, public disclosure was impossible, since it would have put the total burden of explanation upon Elizabeth. Later in the year, we did speak to friends and family and their pain at our secrecy revealed that that had been an error in judgment on our part. As the Harrisburg trial approached, we contemplated disclosing our union but we felt that a free admission on our part would confuse both the substance of the trial and our relationship itself. Following the trial and up to the point of Philip's release in December, the separation of prison further prevented any public acknowledgment. Since that time, we have sought opportunities to publicize it and to share it with friends.

As we evolved our plans over the past five months, some friends encouraged us to announce this day (May 28) as the beginning of our marriage. Such a course would be easier on us and on the public. But we decided against this, feeling that it would not serve either the truth or others whose love is apt to be tested, as ours was, by separation, trial, and prison. Finally, we felt that such a decision would fail to serve the public, who all too infrequently hear the truth—without ambiguity and varnish—from any public person.

Today we celebrated our marriage with our families and with those defendants and lawyers who shared the events of the past three years: civil disobedience, the separation of 32 months of prison, and the Harrisburg trial. (On June 23, we will hold a general celebration for friends.)

The future still holds the possibility of a year's imprisonment for Elizabeth, followed by three years' probation. Philip remains on parole until September 1975. In the last few months, we have worked with a small group of friends growing toward nonviolent resistance. We are presently seeking a center out of which that work can continue.

We hope that our ministry will serve the Gospels and the victims of war. We also hope, with all our hearts, that at some future date, the Church will accept our marriage as well as our efforts for nonviolence and peace. And we continue to be profoundly grateful for the great gifts of that Church and of our respective religious communities.

ABOUT THE AUTHOR

Philip Berrigan was born in 1923 and was ordained a priest in 1955. He served 40 months in the U.S. Army during World War II as a sergeant and in the artillery and infantry in the European Theater. He served 39 months in federal and local prisons for resisting the war in Indochina. Father Berrigan is married to Elizabeth McAlister and is living and working in Baltimore, Maryland. His parole is up in September 1975.